PRESIDENTIAL TRANSITIONS

PART OF THE AMERICAN COUNCIL ON HIGHER EDUCATION SERIES IN HIGHER EDUCATION

Susan Slesinger, Executive Editor

Other selected titles in the series:

Other Duties as Assigned: Presidential Assistants in Higher Education
edited by Mark P. Curchack

Leaders in the Crossroads: Success and Failure in the College Presidency
by Stephen James Nelson

Leading America's Branch Campuses
edited by Samuel Schuman

Faculty Success through Mentoring: A Guide for Mentors, Mentees, and Leaders
by Carole J. Bland, Anne L. Taylor, S. Lynn Shollen, Anne Marie Weber-Main, Patricia A. Mulcahy

International Students: Strengthening a Critical Resource
edited by Maureen S. Andrade and Norman W. Evans

Community Colleges on the Horizon: Challenge, Choice, or Abundance
edited by Richard Alfred, Christopher Shults, Ozan Jaquette, and Shelley Strickland

Out in Front: The College President as the Face of the Institution
edited by Lawrence V. Weill

Beyond 2020: Envisioning the Future of Universities in America
by Mary Landon Darden

Minding the Dream: The Process and Practice of the American Community College
by Gail O. Mellow and Cynthia Heelan

Higher Education in the Internet Age: Libraries Creating a Strategic Edge
by Patricia Senn Breivik and E. Gordon Gee

American Places: In Search of the Twenty-First Century Campus
by M. Perry Chapman

New Game Plan for College Sport
Edited by Richard E. Lapchick

What's Happening to Public Higher Education?
Edited by Ronald G. Ehrenberg

Lessons from the Edge: For-Profit and Nontraditional Higher Education in America
by Gary A. Berg

Mission and Place: Strengthening Learning and Community through Campus Design
by Daniel R. Kenney, Ricardo Dumont, and Ginger S. Kenney

Portraits in Leadership: Six Extraordinary University Presidents
by Arthur Padilla

College Student Retention: Formula for Student Success
edited by Alan Seidman

Building the Academic Deanship: Strategies for Success
by Gary S. Krahenbuhl

Teacher Education Programs in the United States: A Guide
compiled by ACE/AACTE

The Entrepreneurial College President
by James L. Fisher and James V. Koch

PRESIDENTIAL TRANSITIONS

It's Not Just the Position, It's the Transition

Patrick H. Sanaghan
Larry Goldstein
Kathleen D. Gaval

Foreword by Stephen Joel Trachtenberg

Published in partnership with the

AMERICAN COUNCIL ON EDUCATION
® The Unifying Voice for Higher Education

Rowman & Littlefield Education
Lanham • New York • Toronto • Plymouth, UK

Published in partnership with the
American Council on Education

Published in the United States of America
by Rowman & Littlefield Education
A Division of Rowman & Littlefield Publishers, Inc.
A wholly owned subsidary of The Rowman & Littlefield Publishing Group, Inc.
4501 Forbes Boulevard, Suite 200, Lanham, Maryland 20706
www.rowmaneducation.com

Estover Road
Plymouth PL6 7PY
United Kingdom

British Library Cataloguing in Publication Information Available

Library of Congress Cataloging-in-Publication Data
The Praeger Publishers edition of this book was previously catalogued by the Library of Congress as
follows:

Presidential transitions : it's not just the position, it's the transition / Patrick H. Sanaghan, Larry
Goldstein, and Kathleen D. Gaval ; foreword by Stephen Joel Trachtenberg.
    p.   cm.—(ACE/Praeger series on higher education)
    Includes bibliographical references and index.
    1. College presidents—United States.   2. College presidents—Selection and
appointment—United States.   I. Sanaghan, Patrick.   II. Goldstein, Larry, 1950–
III. Gaval, Kathleen D.
LB2341.P6595   2008
378.1′11—dc22   2007030214

ISBN: 978-1-60709-569-9 (pbk. : alk. paper)
ISBN: 978-1-60709-570-5 (electronic)

Copyright Acknowledgments
The authors and publisher gratefully acknowledge permission for use of the following material:

An earlier (and more abbreviated) version of chapter 2 appeared in the Winter 2005 issue of *The
Presidency* under the title "Using a Transition Map to Navigate a New Presidency."

An earlier (and more abbreviated) version of chapter 5 appeared in the Fall 2005 issue of *The
Presidency* under the title "Presidential Transitions: Exit, Stage Right."

Manufactured in the United States of America.

CONTENTS

FOREWORD

t is good news that Patrick H. Sanaghan, Larry Goldstein, and Kathleen D. Gaval have written *Presidential Transitions*, yet it would have been better had it not been necessary. One would imagine, with all the brainpower routinely available on college and university campuses, that their helpful and thoughtful observations by now should have become part of the fabric of any institution of higher learning. Simply stated, we should all know this.

Obviously, we do not. It is a melancholy fact of university life in America today that the typical tenure of a president is merely about seven years. That is barely enough time, as Derek Bok of Harvard famously stated, to "get a handle on the madness." Bok speaks an important truth—specifically, that the arrival of a new president and the departure of the old one are not momentary points in time, but part of a durable process. Moreover, any transition, as the authors wisely note, is difficult, even when it is managed with grace and intelligence. To face repeated transitions every few years is not merely painful for the individuals involved, but leaves the institution itself rudderless or at least without a firm and known hand at the helm.

It is hard to believe, for example, that Harvard would enjoy the wealth and prestige it has if three presidents—James Bryant Conant, Nathan M. Pusey, and Bok—had not served for nearly 60 consecutive years for roughly equal terms. And one can only imagine, and mourn, the loss of morale at Trinity College in Hartford, a fine school, which had four presidents and one acting president between 2000 and 2006.

Why things go awry and how to prevent them from doing so are the subjects of this compact and highly informed book. The authors did their homework (or rather fieldwork), having interviewed dozens of men and women involved in university governance, including presidents, chancellors, trustees, and other senior academic bureaucrats. Thus, the book you have in hand is based on research among those who have succeeded and failed in managing presidential transitions. This is how organizational theory and of course practice ought to be developed.

Perhaps the most common pitfall in presidential transitions is that the candidate and those recruiting him or her simply do not know each other or understand each other adequately (complete knowledge and understanding being unlikely). Why this happens is obvious enough; while a presidential search may take a year or more, the actual time the final candidate and the recruiters actually spend together is often ridiculously brief. They don't have a full opportunity to get acquainted.

This book deals with the problem straightforwardly and practically by suggesting two techniques. The first is a strategic audit. This report should detail all the issues the new president will be facing, be they matters of finance, personnel, culture, admissions, student behavior, and so forth. Nothing is out of bounds.

Obviously, this tells candidates what they can expect and what will be expected of them. It also provides the institution with a more comprehensive report on the state of the college than would normally be undertaken by anyone. In this way, the candidate and the institution have equal or symmetrical information, a distribution that assures the fairest transactions (and an idea that won the Nobel Prize in Economics in 2001).

The companion piece, a report on future challenges, takes the gathering and, most critically, the sharing of information even further. It defines the various qualities and skills that the entire constituency of stakeholders—students, faculty, alumni, trustees, donors—believes the new president will have to possess in order to take on the looming issues and adapt to the particulars of his or her new institution's culture. It helps create a context for the criteria to be used when selecting the next president.

Both endeavors are clearly time-consuming and painstaking, but the time spent gathering, distilling, and applying the information will be returned when the transition to the new president goes smoothly and does not have to be repeated in a couple of years. And as for taking pains, it is more painful to have the wrong person in the job than to spend some long evenings reviewing reports and thinking about the institution's future.

This is more a book about process than results since process can be managed, but results only intended. The importance of process in this book is underscored by its subtitle: *It's Not Just the Position, It's the Transition*, and that, in all its many parts, is the subject the authors pursue with clarity and persuasive "personal observations." In August I will end a run of 30 years as a university president.

Thus the utility of *Presidential Transitions* will not apply to me. However, when I am newly a University Professor and President Emeritus, if someone asks me to serve on a search committee, I will be glad to know this book is here.

Stephen Joel Trachtenberg,
President and Professor of Public Administration,
The George Washington University
Washington, DC
May 2007

PREFACE

The impetus for this book was a discovery made by two of the authors during their annual effort facilitating a training program for 50 new chief business officers. During each program they conduct a horizon thinking activity referred to as the Future Timeline. During this activity the participants share their perspectives on the issues, events, and trends that are expected to impact higher education in the coming years. The outcome of the activity is a prioritized list of impacts that higher education is likely to experience over the coming ten-year period.

After conducting the program for several years with fairly predictable results such as facilities renewal, rising fringe benefit costs, and increasing demands for technological upgrades, there was a dramatic change at the top of the list. Leadership transitions had never been mentioned before; yet, when the topic surfaced four years ago, it was the top concern of the vast majority of participants. The issue remained in the number one spot in the subsequent year and has not fallen from the top of the list yet. Transitions are taking place in huge numbers each year and we know that some are not going well. "Ample evidence suggests that many presidential transitions are poorly managed, personally dissatisfying, and in some cases even demeaning for the primary players—the presidents themselves."[1]

The results from the Future Timeline intrigued the authors because of their past experiences with transitions. One of the authors had prior experience facilitating transitions for incoming presidents, as well as assisting one president when he transitioned out after many years of service on one campus. Although the consultant was well prepared for these engagements, he relied mostly on his general organizational development experience and knowledge of the principles involved. It wasn't until later that he began studying higher education transitions as a separate topic.

The other consultant previously served on four college campuses. During his 20-year career, he experienced four presidential transitions on three of the campuses. It didn't strike him at the time but, looking back, it is interesting to consider what had worked well and what had been problematic for those presidents —both those departing and those starting a new position.

In recent years he has consulted with several new presidents to help with aspects of their transitions. As an objective third party, he has visited their campuses to conduct operational assessments focused primarily on administrative areas. These engagements were designed to generate the information that would be helpful to the president as he established initial priorities for action.

There was an interesting convergence for the two consultants. As they were learning about the impact of leadership transitions among the participants in their training program, they were experiencing firsthand the impact of transition difficulties. The first consultant was shocked as he watched a highly successful president fail miserably when he was recruited to a new institution. How could someone who, by all accounts, had been a rising star, find himself in a position in which he was anything but successful? What type of cultural mismatch could account for such a shocking outcome? Similarly, what were the factors that resulted in another long-serving president reaching the conclusion that he had better step down quickly because he had lost his enthusiasm for the position.

The situation for the other consultant was related more to the number of presidents calling on him for assistance because the situations they inherited were considerably different from what had been described during the search process. The situations he uncovered include, among others, a structural deficit requiring significant budget cuts to bring it under control; underperforming senior managers and/or incompetent executives who should have been removed years before; and dysfunctional relationships between major operational units. In each case, these were major issues that consumed a considerable amount of the new president's time and energy. Clearly these situations had to be known to many participants in the search process. Yet no one shared them with the candidates.

The third author has a somewhat different background. After spending more than 20 years at the same institution, she has experienced transitions from a completely different perspective—that of an insider with direct involvement in the process. She served as the transition manager with responsibility for overseeing the process to help the incumbent president make a graceful exit, and followed this by assisting the new president and the institution with a smooth transition into the position. Through these processes she successfully followed many of the practices recommended in this book.

Our differing perspectives are supplemented by the dozens of interviews we conducted with presidents, board members, and other higher education leaders as well as the extensive research we undertook. Our goal in this book is to share practical advice that has been proven to work for both presidents and their institutions. Beyond advice about positive steps to be undertaken, we also caution about the factors that have led presidents to be unsuccessful in their attempts to take over the reins at a new institution and survive once they had done so.

The authors wish to express their appreciation to the many colleagues who contributed to this effort through their willingness to participate in interviews on the higher education presidency and especially transitions. Those individuals are listed in appendix C. Several of these individuals also reviewed early versions of some of the book's chapters. Special gratitude is expressed to the individuals who invested their time and effort to write first-person accounts to amplify some of the issues addressed in the book. These can be found at the ends of most chapters.

ACKNOWLEDGMENTS

Kathleen D. Gaval particularly wishes to thank and acknowledge Nicholas S. Rashford, S.J., and Timothy R. Lannon, S.J., the former and current president of Saint Joseph's University, respectively. Both gentlemen have contributed significantly to her development as a higher education professional. Their transitions set a standard for communication and were the basis for her interest in researching the topic of leadership transition.

Larry Goldstein wishes to acknowledge two higher education leaders who have influenced him in a variety of ways. Donald C. Swain, president emeritus of the University of Louisville, exhibited outstanding leadership and business skills as a president and modeled a graceful and productive transition to retirement. John V. Lombardi, chancellor of the University of Massachusetts, Amherst, has been a wonderful resource on numerous matters related to higher education and particularly the presidency.

Patrick H. Sanaghan is especially grateful to Michael DiBerardinis, secretary of the Pennsylvania Department of Conservation and Natural Resources, and James "Torch" Lytle, practice professor of education at the University of Pennsylvania Graduate School of Education. These individuals have shared invaluable insights on leadership issues and contributed to his understanding of transitions and their implications for individuals and organizations.

Larry Goldstein and Patrick H. Sanaghan wish to express appreciation to Susan Jurow, senior vice president for professional development and communications at the National Association of College and University Business Officers, and Nicholas S. Rashford, S.J. These individuals were co-authors of articles that subsequently grew into two of the chapters in this book—chapter 2 and chapter 5.

The authors express their appreciation to the following individuals who contributed significantly to this book in various ways. Susan Slesinger, executive editor for education at Praeger Publishers, provided excellent guidance throughout the process of developing the manuscript and helped steer the book to completion. Haylee Schwenk, project manager at BeaconPMG, applied her superior editing skills and provided excellent advice on style and presentation format. Bridget M. Austiguy-Preschel, senior project manager at Greenwood Publishing Group, provided timely input on key issues that arose during the final stages. A special thank you goes to Maryann Terrana, a valued colleague, who reviewed the manuscript and offered wonderful insights and suggestions. Finally, Rachel Dadusc of Dadusc Indexing saved the authors a tremendous amount of effort by creating the index for the book.

NOTE

1. Moore, John W., and Joanne M. Burrows. *Presidential Succession and Transition: Beginning, Ending and Beginning Again.* Washington: American Association of State Colleges and Universities, 2001.

CHAPTER 1

The Journey Begins

Approximately one-fourth of all institutions "in any year are preparing for a presidential change, are in the midst of one, or have just selected a new president."[1]

In the life cycle of every college and university there are changes in leadership. Some institutions have time to prepare; others have it thrust upon them suddenly. Many presidents carefully plan their departure while other presidents decide quickly (or boards of trustees decide for them). The individual circumstances of their transitions may vary, but the steps that institutions take to identify a new leader, adapt to a new leadership style, and continue the forward momentum of the institution have similar challenges.

As of 2005, the latest year for which data are available, there were 4,216 degree-granting institutions in the United States.[2] Each of these institutions is led by a chief executive officer. Depending on the type of institution, this individual's title might be president, chancellor, or something slightly different. Each of these individuals experienced a transition when he or she first took office and, barring unforeseen circumstances, will experience another when each leaves the position.

Based on a recent survey by the American Council on Education, the average presidential tenure in 2006 was 8.5 years, significantly longer than five years before, when the average was 6.6 years. Presidents of private institutions tend to have longer average tenures (9.1 years) than presidents of public institutions (8.1 years).[3] Based on these numbers, it is clear that there are a significant number of transitions occurring in any given year. The individuals directly affected by these transitions number in the tens of thousands while those indirectly affected reach into the hundreds of thousands.

There are significant implications from these data alone. However, we combined these data with information from various media sources about the number of presidents who leave their positions involuntarily, or at least under a dark cloud. What accounts for the fact that, in almost every weekly issue of *The Chronicle of Higher Education*, there is a report of another president who is

under fire? Recent examples include several presidents operating under votes of
no confidence by their faculty, others fired because of financial mismanagement,
some removed because of sexual impropriety, and still others who have left with
little or no notice due to philosophical differences with their boards. One of the
more unusual situations in recent months was a faculty vote of no-confidence in
a *candidate* for a presidency. This individual had not even been hired and the
faculty already were organizing against him. The situations we encountered
have affected both great higher education institutions, including some Ivy
Leaguers, and those of less renown. These obviously are very serious situations.
We believe that many of them are completely avoidable. And, even when they
are unavoidable, there are steps that can be taken to soften the impact on the
campus.

Any leadership transition has the potential to be disruptive and derail the
institution's forward progress. Even when managed well, transitions at the top
create uncertainty for those working in the institution, as well as those served
by the institution. The greatest impact, however, is on the person experiencing
the transition firsthand. This book is intended to serve the needs of everyone
involved in a transition. It provides guidance to those affected most dramatically—the departing and incoming presidents—and others who must ensure
that the institution continues to operate smoothly despite the change in leadership. There are several groups in the latter category, starting with the boards of
the institutions experiencing the change. Much of this responsibility falls on
their shoulders and it must be handled well. Next is the senior leadership team,
which will both assist the departing president with winding down her tenure and
help the new president get her feet wet, most likely starting even before her first
official day on the job. And then there are the many other individuals who must
play key roles in managing the transition process so that momentum is not lost
and it is as minimally disruptive as possible.

We start in chapter 2 with the many issues to be considered when a president
is about to take office at a new institution or moves up within his current institution. This chapter addresses all the details—both large and small—that must
be managed if the president is going to hit the ground running—but not so
fast that he misses some important checkpoints. It covers issues that should
be attended to before the president even arrives, such as gathering information
about the institution, establishing learning and support networks, and connecting with the senior management team. It also provides suggestions about the
specific issues that every new president should address. Things such as engaging
with people, listening well, investing effort to build trust, and seeking feedback
from multiple sources all contribute to the likelihood of a successful transition.

Chapter 3 builds on the foundation established in chapter 2 by focusing on
the critical relationships that must be maintained by a new president. As with
elements in the second chapter, the relationship-building process does not wait
for the president's arrival on campus. There are four groups in particular
whose relationships with the president will determine whether he is going to

be successful. We start with the board, even as early as during the interview process. From then on it must remain a top priority for the president. The relationship with the board is the most important of all because disconnects at the top will derail the presidency, no matter how smart or charismatic he may be.

Second only to the board is the faculty. At the end of the day, the institution's faculty is its most valuable resource. The president must establish a genuine connection with faculty members early on and continue to nurture it to keep the institution moving forward. He must demonstrate his care for this critical constituency by consulting faculty on important matters, bringing them into the conversation when strategic plans are being developed, and paying attention to their concerns.

The next critical relationship is with the senior management team. No president can do it all alone. She must be supported by a team of colleagues who are pushing in the same direction while at the same time protecting the president from ambushes. The team members must support one other and the president. She must have authentic relationships with each member of her cabinet and have effective mechanisms for interacting with them. The president must develop appropriate processes for working with the team members and leverage their strengths both individually and collectively.

The fourth critical relationship is with the president's immediate staff. These people have the ability to polish his image to a high gloss, or cause it to appear to be tarnished. Their attention to details relating to calendar, communication, entertainment arrangements, and other similar themes will influence how the institutional community views the president. The impact of the presidential staff extends to others as well, such as local officials, alumni, and community leaders. The president must form a partnership with his staff, relying on them for guidance and advice, and respecting them for their contributions.

In the next chapter, chapter 4, we deal with the unpleasant reality that all too many presidents are unable to serve out their terms and leave on a high note. The data are somewhat ambiguous in this regard. Some suggest that as few as 15 percent of presidents leave their positions involuntarily. Our research indicates that the number is considerably higher—certainly no less than one-third, but possibly as high as one out of every two presidents.

Clearly this number of presidents are not being fired. We realize that. But we also know that many presidents' departures are strongly negotiated behind the scenes. In other words, the change is made before the president is ready to leave. The departure may be announced as a resignation or retirement, but it is commonly understood that it was not completely voluntary. What are the factors that cause that to happen and what can be done to prevent it? Suggestions for avoiding this fate are provided, along with some warning signs to be monitored.

Even if the statistics referenced above are as high as we believe they may be, there still are a large number of presidents who wrap up a successful tenure and approach their departure in a planful manner. The emphasis in chapter 5 is on these outward transitions. Advice is offered for reaching the difficult decision that it is time to move on, making the announcement, and managing all of the farewell activities that attend to the end of an administration. Additionally, we describe actions that a president should take to help her successor be as effective as possible. This includes tasks such as preparing strategic audit and future challenges reports and engaging in relationship mapping. We also provide a number of suggestions for boards as they deal with these complex issues. The chapter concludes with a discussion of the unique issues that arise with a sudden and/or unexpected departure of a president. Such transitions occur when there is a serious transgression, a situation that forces a president to abandon her position due to a family crisis, or something as traumatic as the death of an incumbent president. There are special considerations related to these events and care must be taken to address them.

Chapter 6 addresses an issue that receives very little attention, yet is fairly common—interim presidencies. Numerous institutions are faced with the need to engage someone on a temporary basis while they search for a permanent president. Interims come from within and outside the institution. And it makes a difference which approach is used. Internal interims have a leg up on the externals because they know the institution, how it works, who the key players are, and the issues currently being addressed. On the other hand, internal interims also are known to the institution. And it is possible that they have made some enemies along the way. This chapter addresses the multitude of factors that an interim must deal with, and provides advice for the board that seeks to hire or promote an interim. It also tackles the dicey issue of the interim as a candidate for the permanent position.

In chapter 7, we highlight the lessons we have learned during our journey through the transition landscape. It includes key messages and summarizes the things that we feel are most important to remember. It cautions about the pitfalls and potholes to be avoided. It also highlights the many positive actions that a president and the board can take to enhance the likelihood of a successful experience for all parties involved. It closes with thoughts about areas of further investigation and research. We learned a great deal throughout our journey. We have addressed much of it here, but we realize there is much more to be explored.

There is one other thought readers should keep in mind as they explore the complex world of higher education transitions. Numerous anecdotes, examples, and suggestions are presented. Although some may seem extreme, they are actual situations that have been reported in the media or represent situations in which the authors were involved or have learned about directly from the participants. In addition, numerous first-person stories, provided by presidents, board members, or others are included to illustrate some of the key concepts in the chapters.

NOTES

1. Keller, George. "Foreword." In *Presidential Transition in Higher Education: Managing Leadership Change*. Edited by James Martin, James E. Samels & Associates. Baltimore: Johns Hopkins University Press, 2004.

2. National Center for Education Statistics, "Degree-granting institutions, by control and type of institution: Selected years, 1949–50 through 2004–05." http://nces.ed.gov/programs/digest/d05/tables/dt05_243.asp (accessed April 2, 2007).

3. American Council on Education. *The American College President*. Washington: American Council on Education, 2007.

CHAPTER

Creating a Transition Map

A carefully planned and executed entry becomes the new president's first act of leadership.[1]

Hundreds of presidential transitions take place every year in higher education. Too often, these transitions are not managed very well. Unfortunately, with an incoming president there is no second chance. It must be done right the first time or the president and the institution will suffer. The negative impact of a poorly chosen leader or a failed transition into a campus can have a devastating impact on a campus for years.

We have found that there is a "mindfield" that needs to be deeply understood and navigated if presidents are to be successfully transitioned into their new roles. We use the term mindfield to convey a sense of strategy, complexity, and challenge, versus a minefield that should be avoided or feared. Trustees, faculty, and administrators need to embrace the mindfield, openly discuss its elements, and fully understand its complexity *before* they make critical decisions about their institutions' presidential transitions.

Success leaves clues and in the following pages we will detail the thinking, strategies, and steps both a new president and institutional leadership should understand so that their transitions are successful.

Effectively designing and managing a presidential transition is a complex and difficult task. There are many challenges facing a new president: the power of institutional culture, the "shadow" of the previous president, the hidden problems, connecting on a personal level with diverse stakeholders, managing the learning curve, whom to trust. The list goes on and on.

New presidents must be strategic and proactive in creating a "transition map" that will enable them to navigate the potholes and the opportunities that await them. Having a planful, thoughtful, yet flexible approach—both before and during the transition process—is critical to success.

It is important to note that the transition journey is both an intellectual and an emotional voyage. Too often presidents focus solely on the intellectual elements (e.g., self-studies, audit and financial reports, historical records, board minutes) and downplay the emotional elements of their transition journey. They do so at their peril.

Over and over again in our interviews, current and past presidents told us that the personal journey was as important as the intellectual one. Too often, they did not pay enough attention to maintaining balance in their lives, their families suffered, they tried to take on too much too fast, and they did not read the signals from people around them.

One cannot think her way into a presidency no matter how brilliant she is. John Moore and Joanne Burrows suggest that a new college or university president has about a year and a half to assert her leadership.[2] If a new leader takes too long to get on board, she will lose credibility. If she begins to act too quickly or tries to change too much too soon, she will meet resistance and raise deep concerns about her thoughtfulness as a leader.

The ideas and strategies we suggest deal with both the intellectual and emotional aspects of the transition process. It is essential to pay attention to both. It will be quite a challenge to operationalize all the ideas we present. It is important for the new president to choose those that fit his needs, personality, and circumstances. The new president should choose wisely because there is only one shot at a successful presidential transition and everyone is watching very closely.

PRE-WORK

In the following pages we suggest a number of activities to be undertaken by a new president before he actually begins the job. A wonderful window of opportunity is created when a new job is accepted and utilizing that opportunity well will enhance the likelihood of a successful start to the presidency.

It takes time to properly prepare for any presidency, but especially one's first presidency. There is tremendous temptation to jump into the new position right away. It is exciting to think about the new opportunities and challenges and there is a tendency to want to start tackling them immediately. In many cases there is pressure from the institution to come on board quickly to help fill the void created by the previous president's departure. Doing so, however, can lead to problems. As explained below, there is much to learn about oneself and about the institution. It takes time to do this effectively—several months at a minimum. New presidents should have four to six months to wrap up their responsibilities to the current position and prepare for the new role.[3]

Conduct a Self-audit

As the president transitions out of one institution and into another, he is presented with a wonderful opportunity to assess his current leadership style. The more insight the president has about himself as a leader, the more effective he can be in the new position.

The following suggestions have proven to be highly effective processes for many presidents. They will take both discipline and a little courage.

Assess Strengths and Weaknesses

The new president should take time to write down, on a sheet of paper, what he believes are his most positive skills and qualities. This is not a time to be humble. It is very important that he acknowledge his strengths and put them on paper.

On a separate sheet of paper—limited to one sheet—he should write down his areas of needed development. What gets in the way? What messages have been heard consistently over the years about weaknesses? This should be as specific as possible (e.g., I am not detail oriented, I rush my decision-making process, I avoid conflict at all costs).

Spending time to capture both strengths and weaknesses can create a learning experience that can provide insightful and strategic information.[4] Self-awareness is a critical leadership quality.[4] This single exercise can develop self-knowledge and help prepare the president for his new position.

Some strategic questions that presidents we interviewed have asked themselves after their self-audit include:

- Is this an opportunity for me to do things differently?

- Can I build on a strength and make a real contribution to the new campus?

- Can I eliminate the effect of a weakness and become even more effective?

- Do I overuse any of my strengths to the point that they become a weakness?

- What really motivates me?

- What do I aspire to accomplish?

Answering these kinds of reflective questions can enhance a person's self-awareness and contribute to that person's effectiveness as a leader.

Meet with Friends

Our close friends know us well—our gifts as well as our flaws. New presidents should use what they have learned through a self-audit in a meaningful discussion with a few close friends. They should test their self-audits for accuracy. Did they miss any strengths? Overstate a weakness? Understate one? The new president should share her findings and see what reactions it generates. The primary purpose is to obtain a reality check from people who are trusted. Understanding how others see us is an important perspective to possess. It will better prepare the president for the new position.

Engage in a 360° Feedback Process

This process has been around for more than 20 years and there are many quality articles and books that describe it in great detail. Simply put, a 360° feedback process involves leaders actively soliciting *anonymous* feedback from people who interact with them in the workplace, and know them well. This could be faculty members, peers (e.g., deans, vice presidents), subordinates, alumni, trustees, or community members.

A simple survey is created with a few strategic questions that will provide the subject with invaluable information about how she is seen and experienced as a leader. Typical questions might include the following:

- In my current role, what strengths do I exhibit as a leader?

- What are some areas of needed development for me as a leader?

- What are two or three pieces of advice that you would like to give me that would enhance my effectiveness as a leader?

- What blind spots do I have?

- Is there anything that people might be afraid to tell me?

- How do you experience me as a communicator?

After this handful of relevant questions has been developed, they should be incorporated in a one-page survey, which is then distributed to 20 to 30 diverse stakeholders. It is important that these individuals know the person well in her current leadership role. Both friends and allies should be chosen, as well as a few critics. These people should be advised that their specific responses will not be shared with the subject. The subject will see only a confidential report summarizing the data. No identifying information should be included on the survey form in order to preserve respondents' anonymity. This is a critical element in the process. With anonymity, there is a greater likelihood of more honest information, which is exactly what is needed.

All survey responses should be submitted to a trusted colleague within the institution or an experienced external consultant. That individual should create a report summarizing the answers to the key questions.

A trusted advisor or colleague should review the report with the president to provide insight, an external perspective, and emotional support if needed. The president will need to take the time to internalize and distill the most important lessons from this process. This can be a very powerful learning experience, even a humbling one. It will provide a reality check on the president's intention versus her impact as a leader. Knowing this information can create real choice points for determining which strengths need to be leveraged and which weaknesses need attention.

Obviously, this process takes courage and a real openness to feedback. If the process is undertaken, it is important for the president to read about it in some detail so that it is done correctly and she receives the most benefit from it.

Do the Homework

Utilize Existing Networks

Although higher education is a vast and complex arena, it is like a small town in many ways. Just about everybody knows somebody they can contact to obtain information about a specific individual. There are few secrets because people talk to each other. Every senior leader has a highly developed network of colleagues and friends who can provide strategic information about a particular campus. New presidents need to know what the institution's reputation is; its organizational culture; its strengths and challenges; its history and, hopefully, its "ghosts" (the things never discussed openly but that represent real problems).

A new president should use this network vigorously and get to know the institution in a deep way. This will only make him smarter about the institution as he transitions into the new campus. Additionally, internal stakeholders will quickly sense that he has done his homework. This conveys both political savvy and respect for the institution.

Two of the authors are consultants who facilitate strategic planning in higher education. We would never say yes to a project without using our network to find out the "real deal" about an institution before we accept an engagement.

We know of one brilliant, but personally flawed, academic who wanted to become a provost rather badly. He sought this position in at least six institutions, always ending up as a runner-up. His academic credentials were stellar, his personal ones much less so. He finally figured out that faculty talk with each other across the country and that they had shared information about him. When he became one of the final three or four candidates, his reputation preceded him and faculty rejected him each time. It is the same for presidents, who must recognize that their reputations are well established and known to others.

Make Anonymous Visits to the Campus before Beginning the Presidency

New presidents should walk around the campus, talk with people, go to a game, visit the student center, cafeteria, and library. Observe a class if possible. It also is important to walk through the community and neighborhoods surrounding the campus. Get a feel for the place. Are people welcoming? Hurried? Unfriendly? Pleasant? (This also is an effective strategy for presidential candidates in a search process.)

Some presidential candidates have visited a campus with their son or daughter or other relative who is interested in going there. How do they treat parents?

What does the prospective student think about her treatment? Try to participate in a student-led tour of the campus and ask questions. We realize that, in some instances, this might be a challenge because of the location of the campus or the fact that the candidate might be recognizable, but strive to do it when possible. It will be invaluable.

New presidents should make more than one visit so they can talk with more people and contrast their initial impressions with later visits. It is a good idea to use a journal to capture impressions and review these notes with a trusted colleague, spouse, or significant other. This is a one-time opportunity because once on campus, the new president will be caught in a whirlwind of meetings, interviews, dinners, and visits with trustees that can take one's breath away. These visits help new presidents pace their learning. They should be used wisely.

Obtain as Much Information as Possible about the New Institution

This includes reading strategic plans, self-studies, and briefing books. As the new president reads, she should maintain a journal, capturing impressions and learnings as well as surprises and discoveries.

As the new president reviews the strategic plan, she should be asking questions such as How good is it? Is it ambitious? Realistic? Well-informed? She should try to find out if they actually accomplish what they set out to do. This is crucial information for a president to have.

We have as a client one institution that completed 85 percent of their ambitious and thoughtful 5-year strategic plan by the end of the third year! That information indicates volumes about the campus's spirit, leadership accountability, commitment, decision making, and resource allocation.

A similar assessment should be made of the institution's self-studies. Are they well-written? Informative? Critical? Candid? Do they highlight the strategic issues as well as other important considerations? Do they tell a story about the institution? It is important to pay attention to which names appear in the strategic planning and self-study committees as well as other task forces. Do some people's names appear in multiple places? These might be useful people with whom to build relationships, especially the chairs of these important institutional groups.

Google them! There is a tremendous amount of information out there. Pay special attention to local newspapers and what they say about the institution. Is the press coverage favorable? Nonexistent? Informative? If they are considered a good neighbor and have positive town-gown relations, there will be significant amounts of coverage indicating this. Conversely, if the relationship with the community is not good, there will be plenty of coverage detailing the reasons and their implications. If there is little to no coverage, what does that say about their standing and presence in the community?

It is also a good idea for new presidents to Google themselves. They likely will discover things that they did not know about themselves. They can be assured that folks at the new institution will be Googling them. The new presidents should be aware of what their new (or potential) colleagues are discovering.

The institution's Web page also should be visited. It is the institution's primary communication vehicle to the outside world. What impressions are created as the links are visited and information is read? These impressions should be captured in writing. Is there a coherent message or story, or is it simply bells and whistles? What are they trying to communicate to the outsider? What are they highlighting to students and parents? Is the focus on athletics, academics, faculty quality, student life, or something completely different? This research, including the documentation of it, is worth a substantial investment of time and effort. Are there areas that should be investigated further? The information gained through this process will be invaluable once the new president arrives on campus.

Request the Creation of a "Learning Network"

Once selected as a new president, before coming to campus, the president should request that senior leadership (e.g., provost, chief business officer, vice presidents, deans) develop a "learning network." The purpose of this group is to help the new president quickly learn about and understand institutional history, complexities, and challenges. This network should provide access to every stakeholder group the new president will deal with in the future. Trustees can suggest a few names but the bulk of the names should come from the current senior leadership because they are closest to the institution's community members.

The senior leadership should be asked to select 15 to 20 key individuals who are known for their institutional wisdom, integrity, and openness. The goal is to have a wide variety of perspectives and not hear just from the "usual suspects." Of greatest importance is that individuals are not selected solely by virtue of their title or position. The learning network may include some individuals who occupy an important campus position or have a lofty title, but that should not be a factor in their selection. What is needed are those individuals who are able and willing to contribute to the new president's knowledge of the institution.

The initial meetings with these key individuals should be conducted individually. It is important that the new president have an opportunity to make real and personal connections with these institutional thought leaders and influencers. After meeting with the new president, these individuals often will convey their initial impressions to their personal networks. This communication process becomes a crucial factor in shaping and molding early opinion and perception of the new president.

During the initial interviews with these individuals, the new president should take the opportunity to ask for the names of others with whom she should meet. This will enable her to develop the learning network by expanding the range of people with whom she communicates.

Most importantly, it will convey to stakeholders throughout campus that the new president is open to the ideas of others, respectful of institutional culture, and that she is proceeding in a thoughtful and deliberate manner. These are important messages to convey.

New presidents should pay close attention to the quality of the individuals chosen to be in the learning network. This is the first delegated assignment to the new leadership team. How well did they organize this group? Who owned the process? Did they select the right individuals? A careful analysis will tell the new president a great deal about the ability and capacity of the senior team. This analysis is directed at how they function together, as well as individually.

It is helpful, after several months on the job, for the new president to have breakfast meetings with specific campus groups (e.g., faculty senate, administrative council, staff organization). During these breakfasts he can share what he has learned so far. He can note the institutional strengths that have been identified and surface some of the issues that need improvement. Most importantly, after the new president has shared his insights, he should provide opportunities for feedback. The following questions will stimulate this type of feedback. Am I on track? Does this resonate with you? What have I missed? Where else can I learn about the institution?

Establish a "Support Network"

All new presidents can benefit from a small group of trusted advisors who can act as a support group during the first year or so of the transition process. Dan Ciampa and Michael Watkins describe this support group as "a personal advice network, composed of a judicious mix of internal and external advisors."[5] Avoiding hasty judgments, a new leader should identify, as quickly as possible, those within the organization who can be trusted to act in this capacity.

The "support network" differs from the learning network in two ways. First, the primary purpose of the support network is to provide the new leader with *emotional* support. Leadership is a difficult and daunting journey. As a new president begins to understand the institutional challenges and to calibrate her strengths and limitations in the face of these challenges, there is a need for a safe outlet to share thoughts, feelings, and even fears. A group of trusted advisors provides a safety zone for a leader and promotes personal growth.

Second, unlike the learning network—which consists of insiders—the support network should consist of both insiders and outsiders. The insiders, some of whom may be members of the learning network, provide a measure of the campus "pulse" and offer advice from the perspective of active participants. The outsiders, who bear no partisan view of norms and culture, provide a more objective perspective. Having both perspectives gives the new president a more balanced and holistic picture of the work in which she is engaged.

If a president has a mentor or coach with whom she worked in the past, that individual should automatically be included in the support network.

Their familiarity with the president and the relationship that has been established will help considerably as the support network begins its efforts.

Several presidents we talked with suggested finding another veteran president with whom to connect and interact regularly. Developing a relationship with someone who has had presidential experience can be most helpful. These individuals can provide an objective view and sage advice.

Other new presidents supplemented this with a colleague also experiencing his first presidency. There are several professional development programs focused on helping new presidents transition into the role. The Council of Independent Colleges, the Association of American State Colleges and Universities, the Harvard Graduate School of Education, and other organizations offer programs in which new presidents can gain valuable knowledge and insights as they prepare for this new role. A number of individuals indicated that they met a colleague at one of these sessions with whom they have remained connected throughout their transition period, and even beyond.

Creating a support network is critical for first-time presidents. No matter how accomplished one has been in other positions (e.g., provost, chief business officer), the presidency is a whole new ball game. We have found that when people are asked to be part of a support process for the new president, they most readily agree and perform this task very well.

Master the Institutional Culture as Quickly as Possible

It has been our experience that one of the most important elements in a presidential transition is organizational culture. Culture must be navigated strategically for the new leader to be successfully integrated into the organization and for the institution to accept, learn, and grow with the new leadership.

Because it is built over many years, each campus has a unique, complicated, strong, and pervasive institutional culture. While internal stakeholders understand the culture at a deep level, it is rarely articulated or written about. Everyone understands "the way things are done around here" and what behaviors are rewarded and punished. Culture drives daily behavior, organizational thinking, and decision making. It is often steeped in institutional history so it is important to understand and respect that history. New presidents should listen carefully to the stories people tell about their institution because powerful themes are usually embedded in them. Do the stories talk about campus pride? Athletic achievements? Courageous leadership? Tragedies? Faculty excellence? Stories last for decades and weave a cultural tapestry. New presidents should pay close attention to what people say within the institution and how they say it.

A new president must understand the elements of the campus culture, both to leverage it and, when necessary, seek to change it. He must be able to recognize when and how it can be challenged and be able to explain it to others, especially outsiders.

We know of one institution that has had four presidents in seven years! Can all of these individuals have been poor choices? Were these people not smart enough? Were they not motivated enough to be successful? We believe there was a "cultural mismatch." The new presidents just never were accepted by campus stakeholders, especially faculty. When this mismatch occurs, it is devastating to campus life and has a lasting impact.

New presidents should become students of the culture of their campuses. It will convey that they respect current norms and values, and that they are learners. It also will enable them to have more influence over time. Culture is powerful. Learn about it. The following actions will contribute to the new president's learning process as it relates to culture:

- New presidents should talk to members of the learning network about the culture. Ask them to describe it. Ask for stories or incidents that will help reveal the culture of the institution.

- It is important to pay close attention to how decisions typically are made in leadership groups. Are they collaborative? Majority rule? Is there confusion about how decisions are made? Who makes the really important decisions? Does consensus rule everything?

- Effort should be invested in gaining an understanding of the governance system. Who are the players? Is the process fast, slow, or *very* slow?

- The members of the search committee also can be queried about campus culture. Are they evasive? Unsure? Very clear about their institution's culture? Ask for examples. This important group often can convey volumes about culture.

- Find out how the campus celebrates successes. Do they celebrate at all? What's honored on campus? Academics only? Athletics? Men and women's accomplishments equally?

- Find out what events shaped how things are done today. The following questions will provide insights about the past. Was there ever a union strike? Did a senior leader leave unexpectedly? Was there a crisis at some point and, if so, how was it handled? Was there a president or board chair that made a positive or negative impact on how the campus was run? We know of one institution that experienced student protests in the early 1970s. It still influences how administrators interact with students today.

- Identify the legends that are praised and why they are remembered. Do people talk fondly about a former president, a faculty member, a coach?

ONCE THE NEW PRESIDENT ARRIVES
Build Trust

Trust is one of the most fragile and yet enduring elements in organizational life. Without a high level of trust on a campus, it is very difficult to accomplish meaningful things. Trust enables a leader to accomplish things through the efforts of others. A new leader must be able to build trust in her leadership as quickly and authentically as possible. In many cases, we have seen that a new president has to build and/or repair trust within an institution and between stakeholder groups. This can be a daunting task. Several specific actions can be taken to enhance the likelihood of a positive trust climate enveloping a new president.

Be a Good Listener

"The two personal qualities that most people often note in new colleagues are their ability to listen, and the speed with which they learn."[6] This sounds simple. It is not. To be a good listener means that you have to put your interests, internal debates, brilliant answers, and quick retorts aside and pay attention to what others are thinking and feeling.

When people feel listened to by leadership, they feel valued and respected. When this happens *authentically*, people will share their stories and aspirations. This will provide a new president with a rich source of information that is both human and strategic.

We have witnessed several presidents who are multitaskers, seemingly able to do two or three things equally effectively at the same time. Even if this is true, the impact on others in meetings and conversations is one of impatience and lack of connectedness. This is not good.

New presidents must be brutally honest with themselves during their self-audits. Am I a good listener? If not, this skill must be developed because it will be one of the most valuable abilities possessed by a new president.

Ronald Heifetz tells us that "Most leaders die with their mouths open."[7] This is especially true with very smart, assertive, and ambitious individuals who have grown up in higher education. Winning the debate, arguing well, finding the flaws in the ideas of others is often rewarded in our institutions. Unfortunately, this rarely builds trust.

A new president should periodically seek feedback from those close to him about his listening skills. By paying attention to this he will build a connection with others, increase his credibility, and communicate that others have valuable things to share.

We have witnessed several "listening tours" in which the new president visits stakeholders throughout the campus and listens to their ideas. They may prompt the discussion with a few effective questions, even give a short speech up-front, and then solicit feedback. These tours can be very effective in teaching the new president about the institution and also convey to stakeholders genuine respect for their ideas and the institution itself.

We strongly suggest that, as well as listening, the new president reflect back what he is learning. This is critical because listening is not enough. People need to know he is actually *learning* something about the institution they care about.

We know of one president who conducted a year-long listening tour. As time went on, people started wondering what she was learning. It seemed like a really long time to listen and, over time, she began to lose credibility by not sharing information. The groups that met with her toward the end of the tour felt as if they were wasting their time because no feedback had been forthcoming. New presidents need to remember that, if they are going to conduct a listening tour, they need to reflect back what they are learning. They also need to check with people to confirm that they are correctly interpreting what they are being told.

Meet with People

A senior leadership transition is a major change in organizational life and often causes stress for the institution's stakeholders. Personal interaction becomes critical when transitions occur. This is not a time to rely on e-mail pronouncements. People need to *see* their leader.

The new president should utilize strategic visibility as he transitions into campus. He should make his presence known to as many campus stakeholders as possible. Although he cannot be everywhere, there is a psychological demand and expectation for this. He should be smart about how he is seen and should avoid being trapped in his office. It is obviously important to attend athletic events, major academic forums, student performances, and other important events on campus. The president needs to be sure to make visits to the smaller functions as well. A debate competition, student government open house, or community service events, though less well attended, demonstrate the president's interest in the full range of campus activities and constituencies.

"Walk the waterfront," one president told us during one of our interviews. It is important to do such things as meet with new faculty, greet parents, visit classes and the student center, and eat lunch with faculty. The president should always do this with different tour partners so she is seen with different faculty members and staff and not simply her executive assistant or chief of staff.

We have seen several new senior leaders organize "chews and chats" with people throughout the institution. These are informal meetings, usually involving food (e.g., breakfast, lunch, afternoon tea) at which the new leader meets with approximately six to 12 individuals to ask and answer questions. Many of the questions people ask new leaders are about their personal history, career path, personal values, and professional interests. This is not a performance. It is a casual gathering of new friends. It is a wonderful opportunity for a new leader to connect with people and become known to them. People do not trust people they do not know. Become known.

Members of the learning network can be helpful in orchestrating chews and chats. It is also helpful for some of them to be present to provide emotional support and to offer feedback following the meetings.

It is critical that a new president develop authentic relationships with as many people as he can, especially the high influencers and faculty. Some groups are more important than others and warrant special attention. Obviously the board of trustees, the faculty leadership, and senior staff fall into this category. (See chapter 3 for a more complete discussion of this issue.) There is another important group that may not be prevalent on every campus—unions. Some institutions have unions representing various categories of employees. The new president should make it a point to spend time developing positive relationships with the leadership of each of the unions. Demonstrating respect for these important influencers can contribute significantly to the positive image a new president seeks to establish.

We believe that, without meaningful relationships, the new president will fail or at best accomplish very little. If he has real relationships with his leadership group, the trustees, the faculty, unions, and other influential groups on campus, he can build what is popularly called social capital. This relational capital allows him to lead because people trust him as a person and as a leader. They are willing to follow his directions and aspirations for the institution.

Developing authentic relationships cannot be faked, practiced, or rehearsed. It has little to do with charisma and much to do with the quality of the individual. That is why self-knowledge is so important. A new president has to know who she is, what values and principles guide her behavior, and what she wants, both her appetites and aspirations.

That is why completing a self-audit is so important. With 360° feedback, a list of strengths and weaknesses and feedback from family and friends, the new president enters the presidency fully aware of who she is and what she wants to convey to people. This is a valuable asset to have.

New presidents should judiciously talk about themselves. People on campus have a natural curiosity about the new president. Telling personal stories about one's family growing up, places one has lived, personal interests, and hobbies is very helpful. This does not mean the new president has to bare his soul to others or go into details about a messy divorce. On the other hand, a little self-disclosure goes a long way. Disclosure helps people connect with the new president on a personal level. This is essential if he is going to effectively lead his institution.

On the other hand, the new president should use care when discussing his predecessor, previous position, and former institution. He should ensure that discussions focus on himself as an individual and not on something that likely will draw comparisons (1) to the previous president or (2) between the present and former institutions. Unless it is clear that the president is praising the previous president or emphatically praising the present institution, it is likely that the listeners will view such comparisons negatively.

Talk with Students Whenever Possible

Students may be the richest source of information and perspective a new president will encounter on a campus. They can provide an ongoing temperature of the campus because they are usually open and willing to share their ideas. Listening to students also conveys a sense of respect for them which is a wonderful presidential message to communicate.

New presidents should utilize the student government, fraternities and sororities, and other established student organizations like Phi Beta Kappa and student clubs to connect with students. In addition, they should seek out students who might function outside these organized groups. These usually are the voices that are not heard. There are some obvious questions to use to get students sharing information. What are their concerns? What do they like about the campus, classes, extracurricular activities, student life? What would they like to see changed and why? How do they enjoy what they are learning? One president with whom we spoke told us that simply asking a student to talk about himself was a wonderful icebreaker. Getting them to share their personal background, why they're at this institution, what they're studying, provided a point of connection between the students and the president.

The purpose is to start a conversation that will inform the president and the student. This does not need to be a well-orchestrated, formal process. Informality is fine. Meet them where they hang out, not in the president's office. Try to reach a broad and diverse group of students. It is important that this not be a one-time activity. It is not about public relations. It is about connecting to students and seeking relevant information while demonstrating a caring attitude. A president should regularly meet with students formally (e.g., student government) and informally throughout the year.

One president of a small institution employed the weekly practice of taking four students out to dinner at a local (relatively inexpensive) restaurant. She did this by asking students she met during her campus walks if they would like to have dinner with her. Whenever they said yes, she asked that they bring three student friends with them. They would meet at a designated location and she would drive them to the restaurant.

Conversation would flow, questions were always asked, and opinions solicited. The president really enjoyed these dinners because she connected with students, their needs, and hopes. There never was a shortage of students who wanted to have a free dinner with the president. Many times she got a call from a parent asking if their son or daughter really had dinner with her! She followed this practice for more than five years and found it to be a great investment of her time and money.

Stay at Home as Much as Possible during the First Year

New presidents should limit their off-campus travel during the early portion of their tenure. This will be difficult to do because of the false sense of urgency created by trustees, alumni, development staff, community stakeholders, and others to meet and greet as many external constituents as possible. We realize that these meetings need to take place but new presidents should be very disciplined about it. They should talk to trustees very early in the transition about their needs to have the new president on the road versus her need to connect to the campus. It is an essential issue to discuss and the president must be proactive about it.

Once again, there is no second chance to connect with the campus stakeholders. If the new president is frequently absent during her first year, it will be hard to make up for the lost opportunity when she decides to come home and pay attention to the locals. This opportunity should not be lost. We recognize the importance of connecting with alumni, state officials, and other key external constituents, but we believe that events should be scheduled to occur on campus so the president is not required to be away an extensive amount of time.

We had one president whose vice president for development gleefully reported that she had scheduled more than 75 off-campus visits during the first year of the new president's tenure. We told her that this was far too many and needed to be cut in half. She was not happy about doing so and lobbied very hard for her way. Fortunately, the president listened and reduced his schedule so he could be present on campus during his important first year.

There can be exceptions to the general guidance to stay close to home during the first year. We are aware of one president who made the decision to devote the better part of a month early in his tenure to visiting his trustees. (See "Going on the Road to Connect with Trustees" following this chapter.) This was a calculated risk that paid dividends for him. The lost opportunities created by so much time away early in his tenure were offset by the excellent relationships that were established with the trustees.

Seek Feedback

One of the most powerful and effective ways a new president can achieve credibility and build trust in his leadership is to be open to the feedback of others. If he has the courage to communicate to his staff and key individuals that he will regularly solicit *anonymous* feedback on his performance, he will build trust and gain their respect.

This is not a task for the lighthearted. It is an unusual act for a leader, with risks attached. He might receive information that he is not ready for or that will surprise him. It should be done anyway. We have met some arrogant leaders who laugh at this suggestion. They often reply, "My people can tell me anything." We have found that rarely to be the case.

We suggest that new presidents solicit this feedback after the first 90 days of the transition period. This gives people a chance to provide meaningful feedback and allows the new leader to "rightsize" his behavior. After the initial 90-day feedback, it is a good idea to solicit feedback again in six months, and thereafter on a yearly schedule.

This does not have to be an elaborate or complicated process. A simple survey can be sent to 20 key stakeholders (the immediate staff, key constituents, and others who interact with the new president) asking several insightful questions. Some useful questions for an early feedback effort are listed below:

- What have been some positive actions or behaviors you have experienced in your interactions with me?

- What are some things I need to work on to improve?

- What advice can you give me that will be helpful in my current role?

- What might be something I am unaware of that I should know about?

- How would you rate my performance so far? Excellent / very good / good / fair / poor. Please explain your answer.

The key to the effectiveness of this kind of feedback process is to ensure the *anonymity* of people who participate in it. This type of survey can be organized through the board, senior leadership team, chief of staff, or an external consultant. They should *never* come directly to the president.

The president can share the final summary with his support network to obtain their reactions and advice. It also is a good idea to share this information, in general terms, with his immediate staff. This will take courage and discipline but it is well worth the effort. When a president shows that he is open to the feedback of others, willing to learn, and, most importantly, willing to change, it sends a very powerful message to followers. When done well, it can build trust and credibility and impact the institutional culture in a very positive way.

It also communicates a powerful leadership message. The president *wants* feedback and honesty from stakeholders. The positive implications of this are enormous. It sets a presidential tone that listening to others, respecting ideas, and incorporating feedback into future actions will be part of the way the president works.

It also speaks directly to what we call the "president's disease" or, as some people call it, the seduction of the leader. This happens when powerful individuals in important positions do not have access to the information they need to grow, change, and learn, because people simply will not tell them, even when asked.

One of the most important findings we discovered in our discussions with presidents is that few people speak the truth to power. It takes real courage to tell a president that she may be wrong, or that a decision she is making is too hasty, or that her judgment needs more wise counsel. It is a difficult thing to do, especially when the president has a big ego, is charismatic, or is deeply respected.

An entire book could be written about this important complexity. The president represents more than his leadership role; he represents the institution with all its power, textures, history, and tradition. In our interviews, we directly asked many of the presidents on whom they rely to tell them what they need to hear. Many replied honestly that there are too few people willing to do so and acknowledged that this is a challenge that needs to be addressed.

We talked with a relatively new board member of a major public university. He told us of an intense, off-line conversation, he had had with his long-serving president. This board member, who is the top leader in his own organization, is used to very direct and honest communication in his work life. He assumed that this approach was appropriate in this situation. He was wrong.

During a private conversation with the president, the board member raised a sensitive university issue. He shared his belief that a particular issue was not receiving the attention it deserved during board meetings. In addition, he expressed concern that, when it was discussed, strong political opinions were influencing the dialogue as opposed to factual information. He proposed that a task force be convened to gather the facts about this issue so that a fair and balanced discussion could occur.

What surprised the board member most was the president's reaction. Rather than discuss the merits of his proposal, the president appeared appalled, bewildered, and angry. The board member soon realized that the president never had people talk to him in this manner. What was normal for the board member (i.e., direct, even blunt conversation about an issue), was not the way things were done at this university or with this president. After a few uncomfortable moments, the president excused himself and left the room. Further conversation never occurred, and the board member believes that this conversation has damaged his relationship with the president.

Only the president can truly encourage honest communication, information flow, and feedback. The new president needs to do more than talk about it. She needs to be proactive about soliciting feedback from others. She should openly test her ideas in one-on-one conversations, small group meetings, and, especially, with her learning network and cabinet. People will watch her reactions when different ideas, opinions, and perspectives are shared. These reactions canot be faked. She really must demonstrate that others can influence and inform her thinking. It is essential to remember that, for the most part, it will be counter-intuitive—even uncomfortable—for people to test and push back on the ideas of the president. It is her responsibility to create the culture of openness.

If the president cannot remember the last time someone respectfully challenged his thinking, it should be a strong signal that he needs to seek out the ideas of others. His position as president does not guarantee he will be right on everything. If it seems as if people are consistently agreeing with his ideas, he should take pause and reflect on this. This is a good opportunity for a president to use his journal to summarize important conversations over time and note when his ideas were tested. Paying attention to this disciplined process can serve as a reminder that he needs to be proactive in seeking the feedback of others.

We fully realize that on many campuses there are people, especially faculty, who have no trouble whatsoever testing, challenging, and complaining about any ideas offered up by the president. In fact, on some campuses, every idea generates a negative reaction. We are suggesting something more thoughtful and routine than the sniping that occurs on those campuses. We believe the president must be intentional and vigilant about creating a culture of respectful openness throughout the campus. This is a weighty responsibility, but one that will enhance the quality of information available to the president.

Search for Hidden Problems/Challenges

It is important to be proactive about discovering potential problems and potholes. Moore and Burrows unearthed that 80 percent of the new presidents they interviewed discovered big, complex problems *after* they came on board![8]

Candidates would be wise to actively solicit information about potential challenges during the interview process. Obviously, this needs to be done respectfully, courteously, and tactfully, but candidates should not hesitate to be assertive in this area. For example, it would be appropriate to ask interviewers to identify the difficulties or problems that tend to persist at the institution, and then focus in on why they continue to persist. Or she might ask what makes them, as stakeholders, nervous about the institution? A particularly interesting approach is to ask, if the local newspaper were to do an exposé about the campus, what might they find that would be embarrassing for the institution?

By being appropriately assertive the candidate conveys several messages: She wants honesty in her relationships with people. It is okay to surface difficult or sensitive problems because she wants to deal with them as soon and effectively as possible. She is proactive and not reactive in her leadership style. She expects a give and take in her interactions with people on campus.

If people are not forthcoming, or there is a confusing mixture of messages about potential problems, the candidate must pay attention to these signals. How people react to a candidate's questions will be a clear diagnostic of how they respond to difficult questions and what can be talked about and what cannot.

GETTING DOWN TO WORK

Manage Expectations, Both the New President's and Others'

In a study of second-time presidents, Estella Bensimon reported that experienced presidents were more likely than first time presidents to get to know the institution before making any pronouncements.[9] Judith McLaughlin also found that they approached learning about their institutions more systematically.[10]

"My research suggests that new presidents are at a greater risk of moving too rapidly than of proceeding too cautiously."[11] There is often a strong tendency for a new president, even an experienced one, to *do something* to assert his leadership and make his mark. New presidents should resist this urge if possible because it is fraught with danger. They should not try to move too fast or seek to accomplish too much in their first year. Intelligent change takes time. Many of the most important issues and challenges that are discovered have been around for a long time. These issues have their own complex roots, histories, cultural norms, and relationships deeply embedded within them. Understanding all this takes time, effort, and patience. Rarely do the issues demand immediate action; attention perhaps, but not action.

This does not mean that the new president does not act on an important issue like a looming deficit. If the institution has severe budgetary problems, he should not charter a three-year study. He should put together a top-notch task force to develop a plan to address it as soon as possible. The same is true for other immediate crises. The president must be able to recognize the difference between a true crisis—something that requires an immediate response—and a long-standing problem that may take months or even years to resolve. Such issues as organizational culture, faculty workload, endowment challenges, governance issues, and trustee quality need thoughtful consideration followed by agreed-upon action.

This is one of the most difficult and complex elements in the transition map. When a new president comes to campus, expectations are usually very high. History is being made. Possibilities and opportunities are heightened. The urge to do dramatic things is strong. Nevertheless, it is important to be thoughtful and planful throughout a presidency, but especially during the first year when so many eyes are on the president. She should not make fast decisions on complex issues. She should take the time to understand the complexity of a challenge or problem before acting.

We realize that a new president often has to deal with an immediate problem after arriving on campus. She should do her homework, solicit the ideas of others, and share her thinking so people can provide feedback before the matter is addressed.

Do Not Attempt to Develop a Vision Too Quickly

We have found that new presidents often believe that they must create a new vision for the institution as soon as possible. The board is often the culprit here, urging the president to craft an exciting and ennobling future. The pressure from the board creates a false sense of urgency because few institutions need a new vision right away.

One president told us, "I don't yet understand this place, its culture, problems, history, politics, and hopes. How am I supposed to tell people where they should go?"

A new president should communicate to the board and the campus that her arrival creates a wonderful and natural opportunity to assess institutional progress and priorities. She should let them know that, after she has been on board for a year, she will commission an inclusive and engaging strategic planning process that will create a vision worthy of everyone's commitment.

The following is some advice for self-styled visionary presidents. There are quite a few presidents who are either seen as, or think they are, visionary leaders. This is a very mixed blessing. Having vision is all well and good and, in some cases, desperately needed. We have found that it cannot be solely the president's vision if it is to be successfully achieved. If stakeholders throughout the campus cannot see it, feel it, touch it, and believe in it, all the vision in the world will not help the institution.

Every president needs to help craft an inclusive strategic planning process that engages the passions, ideas, and perspectives of everyone on campus. It is important for people to share the pictures, aspirations, and hopes they have for the future. If a president can help facilitate and champion this kind of process, a shared vision will be created. Unlike unilateral visions, shared visions will be implemented.

New Presidents Should Share Their Priorities with the Campus

At the convocation, the president should communicate the *handful* of priorities on which he will focus his attention and efforts (e.g., fund-raising, completing a new building, student or faculty recruitment efforts, academic renewal). Stakeholders should know what his agenda is so they can support it. The president should let people know what the board expects from him. Every president is hired to do certain things. The president should communicate these things so people clearly understand them.

Keep in mind that, in situations in which the previous president left involuntarily, the board has made a statement through the selection of the individual now serving as president. Even if the previous president's departure was not publicly contentious, it is likely that they went outside the institution to select the successor. This fact alone is an indication that the board is looking for something different from what it had previously. It is important for the president to consider this when establishing and articulating the priorities.

Write Draft Memos for Feedback and Reflection

Several new presidents shared this process with us because they found it very helpful. When they are thinking about changing something on campus, they draft memos or informal thinking papers that explain their rationale and provide the facts related to the matter. They put these out to the campus in draft form (using established channels such as the faculty senate, administrative council, alumni network) and encourage feedback on their ideas. These memos generate extensive discussion throughout the campus.

Feedback mechanisms are established utilizing small focus groups, e-mail, Web forums, or other methods, so stakeholders can participate in the discussion and refinement of ideas. This moves the ball forward slowly and intelligently. It also helps the president make more informed and wise decisions regarding the particular issues.

THE SENIOR TEAM

Develop the Senior Team

A new president needs to dedicate herself to building an effective team with the senior leaders (e.g., provost, chief financial officer, vice presidents) she has inherited. The pace and complexity of the first few months can make this difficult but it is an important and strategic thing to do.

The team at the top will enable the new president to accomplish what is most important for the institution. The senior team members understand how the campus works, its history, problems, and promise. Most importantly, they already have effective relationships with stakeholders throughout the institution. In short, she needs them and their cooperation.

Everyone will be watching how well this new team operates and works together. Their effectiveness or lack thereof will be highly visible. There will be no place to hide and everyone on campus will know how well they are doing because there are no secrets in higher education. People talk to each other all the time, every day.

Two of the authors recently facilitated a strategic planning conference for a very large and complex institution. During the discussions, a respected faculty member asked the new president how the senior management team was doing. The room fell silent.

The president carefully and honestly responded that he believed that he has talented people on the team, but they still have a way to go before they will become a high-functioning team. He communicated that some hard work lay ahead, but that he is optimistic about the future of the senior team.

We could tell that everyone in the planning meeting of 60 people greatly appreciated both his candor and authenticity. The faculty member voiced what was on a lot of people's minds and the president's response confirmed what they suspected. It was a very powerful moment for the president, the participants, and the institution. The president's transparency and honesty spoke volumes.

People realized that, if the senior management team is not high-functioning and working on the same page, the planning process is doomed to fail. This does not mean that others do not share responsibility for planning and implementation, but an effective senior management team is essential for success.

There will be situations when members of the senior team need to be dismissed in the first year of the president's tenure. This is usually done for one of two reasons, either incompetence or incompatibility. In the former case, the person simply is not up to performing the tasks at hand. They cannot be retained because it will impede the institution's progress and adversely impact the new president's transition. Moreover, incompetence cannot be hidden. The community will be watching to see how the new president handles the matter. Irrespective of the circumstances, the president must do what is necessary in a professional and respectful manner. This will set the tone for the entire organization and send a signal that people are valued—even if they must be removed from the environment.

Assuming the incompatibility does not result in incompetence, the response must be different. The typical situation is one involving a personality conflict between the president and an otherwise acceptable member of the senior team member. Whenever there is a situation like this, the president ultimately wins. The institution simply cannot afford a protracted battle between senior leaders. In contrast with the incompetent, the president may need to take more time to address the matter. If the individual has successfully performed his job, but does not get along with the president, the person must be allowed more latitude to find another position. Otherwise the president's reputation will be damaged.

Under optimal circumstances, the new president should not have to address issues related to senior team incompetence. Given that these usually are already known, the board should address the situations *before* the new president comes on board. The last thing an institution needs is for the new president to inherit a long-standing problem team member and have to dismiss the person as soon as the president arrives. This will make people nervous and create an unnecessary shadow over the president's first year. The board must take courageous action with this situation and clean house as judiciously and effectively as possible. And, when they do, they should focus on filling the vacancy with an interim appointment, leaving the permanent selection for the new president.

Another important consideration for a new president is the possibility of vacancies to be filled within the senior leadership team. It is not uncommon for cabinet members to opt to pursue jobs with other institutions when a president announces her resignation or retirement. Despite well-intentioned attempts to retain everyone on the senior management team, it is likely that there will be one or more individuals who elect to pursue new opportunities. This usually results in some positions being filled by interim appointments. This is preferable to the situation of having permanent hires made shortly before the new president arrives. It is much more desirable for the new president to oversee the search for any vacancies within the cabinet.

Obviously this represents a significant opportunity for the new president, because he has the chance to select the new staff member—either directly or by overseeing the search process. Great care must be taken because each new person added to the senior leadership team increases the complexity of the new president's transition, and introduces another transition to the institution.

There is another factor to consider. There is a tendency on the part of new presidents to fill positions with colleagues from previous institutions at which the president previously worked. This has significant appeal because the president naturally is more comfortable with someone he already knows well. Many times, the familiar person is the best person for the position and the president knows this. Nevertheless, a carefully conducted search process should occur. This is for the benefit of both the person hired and the president. When a formal search process is not conducted, the person selected starts the job with a cloud over his head. Grumblings will surface even if there are no qualified internal candidates. Many will assume that the individual would not have been selected had a competitive process been used. Even when a search is conducted, there is a tendency on the part of some to be jealous of the relationship that exists between the new president and the person hired. The president should move carefully in this situation to avoid introducing unnecessary complexity within the senior leadership team.

It is important that the new president invest the time and energy to build and maintain a cohesive, well-functioning team. This will not happen by itself. Therefore, a thoughtful and careful plan needs to be created.

Help Facilitate Sensitive Conversations

Any time a president enters a new organization, there is apprehension, excitement, hope, worry, and many questions. The goal of a leader is to be proactive and create the opportunity for people to voice their hopes and concerns. This can be done in several ways.

If possible, the president should meet with her senior team members and get to know them *before* she actually arrives on campus to stay. The president can ask the team members to create (anonymously) a set of questions that will enable them to get to know her better and surface the tough questions that are seldom asked. For instance, senior leaders generally worry about their futures. It is safe to anticipate a question about whether she expects to bring in her own team members once she is settled, as well as one about her track record managing or leading a senior team.

These questions could be solicited by a trusted faculty member or an external consultant. The goal is to create safety so individuals can ask the questions they truly want answered. The quality of the questions will be a powerful diagnostic about what is on people's minds.

After the questions are solicited and organized, the president should review them and craft responses. The answers need to be as thoughtful and careful as possible because others will be watching and listening very carefully.

The new president should meet with her new team and have a conversation focused on the questions. We recommend about a half-day meeting, hopefully including a meal. Ideally, this meeting should be facilitated by someone from outside the team so everyone involved can fully participate. It is desirable for the new president to be open to follow-up questions while she works through answering some of the pre-arranged questions. This is a good sign that the team members feel open and safe enough to clarify and probe.

On one campus, a new president utilized an interesting and proactive approach to surfacing sensitive conversations. The president had her new senior team members meet with a consultant who had worked closely with her for more than a decade. She trusted the consultant's character and knew he would be very honest in conveying his impressions of her to the team.

During the early days of her transition, she had the consultant meet for a half-day with her new senior team. The primary purpose of the discussion was to create an opportunity for the senior team members to ask any questions that would enable them to deeply understand the new president. Obviously, the consultant could not betray any confidences, but he was able to speak to how the president utilized her power, dealt with conflict, made decisions, etc. The discussion was lively and engaging. The team members reported that they learned a great deal from the conversation and greatly appreciated the opportunity to ask tough questions. They also realized that the new president was willing to take a risk with them and was seeking to be as transparent as possible. This earned her their respect and trust.

Define the Decision-making Process

For a president, making important and difficult decisions comes with the territory. It is essential that the president clarify and define his decision-making process. In the initial stages of a new president's term, there will be many decisions to be made. It will take great discipline to avoid the avalanche of decisions that people have been holding back waiting for his arrival.

Often, there is confusion regarding who makes which decisions. Do I need the new president's approval before I move forward? Whom should I involve in making this decision? What level of authority do I have? What issues do I need to bring to the president's attention? Do I share everything, or can I be selective? This is just a sampling of the range of issues that will cause individuals anxiety about the decision-making process.

Early in the transition (ideally through an off-site retreat), the president needs to clarify how he makes decisions. The following model has been helpful for senior leaders in articulating their decision-making process for important decisions. It should be adapted to meet the institutional culture and personal decision-making style.

Level A decisions: These decisions are made solely by the president. These are decisions that he believes he has the content expertise and experience to make. A note of caution is in order. There should be a small handful of these or the president will not be utilizing the talents of his staff.

Level B decisions: These decisions involve others. The leader solicits ideas, listens carefully, but still makes the final decision unilaterally. This is when significant conflict can be created. When people provide their input and contribute ideas, they often expect to be involved in the final decision. The leader must be clear up-front and clarify that the decision is his to make, even though he wants to hear what people have to say *before* he decides.

Level C decisions: With these decisions, the leader becomes a peer of the realm. He is a member of the senior group and only has one vote. These decisions usually involve a great deal of discussion, dialogue, and debate. Each person contributes his or her ideas, and everyone is an equal. It is important to clarify how the final decision will be made *before* the discussion begins. Is the group trying to reach consensus? Will the decision be made by the "85/15 rule" in which, if 85 percent of the group says yes, the decision is a go? Will it be simply majority? Remember to clarify first, then decide.

Level D decisions: In these situations, the president gives the members of the group the authority to make selected decisions. He should clarify the purposes and intended outcomes of the decision and discuss any givens. Following that, the group members do what is necessary to make wise decisions. This is a delegated decision and is often a sign of a high-performing senior team.

Schedule a Retreat if Possible

We have found that an effective staff retreat during the first 30 days of the new president's transition process—or even before the new president officially arrives—is an excellent way to get to know new staff, organize an agenda for the future, surface issues, and build relationships. This initial retreat should be one to two days in length and be very well organized and facilitated.

It is not a good idea for the new president to facilitate this type of retreat, even if she is an excellent facilitator. She needs to focus on her full participation and not be worrying about things running smoothly, process issues, or logistics. The president should rely on an outside facilitator who is trusted and brings excellent facilitation skills. This could be a respected faculty member with experience facilitating retreats or an external consultant. The most important consideration regarding the facilitator is that he or she be highly competent, credible, and trustworthy.

We suggest the facilitator interview each person who will be attending the retreat prior to the event. He needs to establish some kind of connection with each participant and solicit input about the retreat goals. This takes time but it helps ensure a positive outcome. The last thing needed for a retreat of this importance is to have an assertive facilitator who pushes his own agenda, does not connect with participants, or lacks an understanding of the complexity of higher education. Obviously, this kind of retreat can be risky but, if well organized and properly facilitated, is well worth that risk.

A six-month follow-up retreat is suggested to check on progress, realign efforts, discuss lessons learned, and continue to build relationships. A yearly retreat can be institutionalized thereafter.

Conduct Informal Supervisory Meetings

Effective supervision is a key element in any successful president's management process. Unfortunately, we have found that meaningful supervision is rarely practiced in higher education institutions. It sounds like a good idea but people find it difficult to make the time to do it right. And, when they do, too many managers are reluctant to provide honest feedback—especially feedback that might be critical. Feedback is an essential element of effective supervision. Too often it is assumed that when motivated, smart, competent people are hired they will do what is necessary to be successful. This is rarely the case and even less so with problem performers.

A new president has a wonderful opportunity to establish expectations, performance goals, and support guidelines for his immediate staff early in his transition process. We suggest that he conduct an *informal* supervisory meeting with each of his staff during the first 30 days on the job. This meeting should be one to two hours in length and have some modest structure. It is helpful to have these initial meetings in a relaxed, neutral setting whenever possible. Later, a more formal setting may be appropriate.

The primary goal for this meeting is for the new leader to get to know his subordinates and discover their interests, contributions, aspirations, and concerns. Some questions presidents have found helpful in this initial meeting are listed below:

- When you look back over the last one to two years, what are some things you accomplished about which you feel the most proud?

- What have been some of the important lessons learned in your current role?

- What causes you frustration or concern in carrying out your current responsibilities?

- What are some beginning goals that you have been thinking about that you would like to accomplish over the next year?

- What courses or learning experiences do you believe would be helpful to your professional development?

- What do you need to know about me that would be helpful in understanding my views about leadership, organizations, higher education, or how I view life in general?

- How might I be helpful in making you even more successful in your current role?

The president needs to make this a two-way discussion in which both participants get to know each other. The subordinate should know in advance that this is an *informal* meeting that will be followed up later with a more structured meeting. The subordinates should be given the proposed questions before their meetings so that they have time to think about crafting their responses. The tone of these meetings should be collegial and focused on building constructive relationships.

MANAGE THE LEGACY OF THE PREVIOUS LEADER

When a new president enters an institution, the reputation and legacy of the previous leader can be a heavy presence. Thomas North Gilmore refers to this as the shadow of the previous leader.[12] Many people recognize that it is a difficult journey to follow in the footsteps of a failed president. We have found that following in the footsteps of a legend or star can be equally daunting. Those of us who have followed a legend know what it is like to hear, "Dr. Johnson established that program a decade ago. Why would you think about changing it?" Or, "That's not the way President Smith did that."

A new leader might want to consider the following suggestions for these situations. Establishing a relationship with the legend before she departs is very helpful. Most often, she will be very open to this. The legend can be a source of wisdom and wise counsel as well as a source of political goodwill. The new president will demonstrate his respect for the outgoing leader by building a relationship bridge to her. Others will notice this.

It is helpful if the new president makes it easy for the legend to say yes to his overtures. Whatever he can do to make his interactions and discussions convenient for the legend will help make the connection. Going to visit her at her office works well. Establishing some type of regular communication process (e.g., e-mail, telephone meetings, lunch meetings) with her also is recommended.

As the new leader gets to know the institution through self-studies, board materials, strategic audits, and other resources, he can clarify issues and seek understanding through discussions with the outgoing leader. This can flatten the new president's learning curve and build institutional knowledge that will prove invaluable. Whenever the new leader can let others know that his predecessor is being especially helpful with his transition, this should be done. Bottom line: The new president should build a relationship with the previous president whenever he can.

Comparisons with the former leader are inevitable, especially if she was well liked and respected. The new president will have to get used to these comparisons, especially in his first year on campus. This will take a diplomat's skill and a layer of thick skin. The last thing people want to hear is, "I'm not President

Smith and I will do things my way." Or, "I am a very different leader than the former president. You just will have to get used to me." These remarks will not build goodwill.

New presidents must be proactive in connecting with people, being visible, and making themselves known. If he gets trapped in his office, or finds himself out of town raising money, attending conferences, or serving on external boards, the shadow of the previous leader will overtake him.

A new president should *never* criticize the previous president, even if there's much to criticize. It may be tempting and people will attempt to create opportunities for such criticism to occur. It is common for some people to solicit the new president's reactions, but he will gain nothing by being critical. Even if the previous leader was a poor one, she is part of the fabric and history of the institution. Keeping his opinions to himself will show respect for the institution and demonstrate his leadership maturity. It also is important that he not let others criticize the former president in his presence. If this occurs, he should politely stop the conversation in its tracks and shift it to a more constructive dialogue.

Whenever possible, the new president should meet with the board chair and the outgoing president. He should be proactive and suggest that the three individuals meet as soon as he has been hired to discuss the following issues:

- Transition process
- Creation of a learning network
- Need for a strategic audit and future challenges report (See chapter 5 for additional information.)
- Expectations for each other
- How communication will take place with each other during the transition
- Identification of any large or complex challenges facing the outgoing president
- Procedures and protocols to be followed during the transition
- The outgoing president's culminating agenda.

This meeting should be informal and is best held off-campus at a neutral setting. This does not mean this meeting and subsequent ones are secret. It just is helpful to be away from prying eyes and ears for this conversation.

FOR THE LONG HAUL
New Presidents Should Seek Personal Balance

"Transitions place extreme physical and emotional demands on new leaders. You will need to find ways to conserve your energy and preserve your emotional balance and perspective to stay on the rested edge."[13]

The first 90 days of a new president's transition go by quickly. The traditional tour involves meeting with hundreds, if not thousands, of people. It can become overwhelming and difficult to make sense of things.

We have observed that a number of new presidents, especially first-timers, allow the job to consume them almost entirely. Unless the president has real discipline around seeking balance, her job easily can become a 24/7/365 endeavor. There always will be people to meet, conversations to have, strategies to craft, and problems to be solved. They will always be there waiting; that's the nature of the job.

A presidency is more like a marathon than an endless stream of sprints. But care should be taken to maintain an even keel, especially at the beginning of the first year. Early patterns of work will be established at this time and will be hard to change in the future.

We know of one president who has one important principle for balancing her work day. There are no meetings before 9:00 a.m. She rises early, does her physical exercise routine, eats a healthy breakfast, and meditates. This way she starts her day refreshed, renewed, and steady.

One president we talked with told us that he has a close group of friends outside the campus that he tries to have dinner with on a biweekly basis. None of these good friends are connected to the campus in any way so the president can relax, tell stories, joke, and enjoy their company. His dinner companions never ask him about work. He finds these dinners to be invaluable and strives mightily to make them as often as he can.

It is important for a president to be disciplined about personal balance and to have a plan on how he will maintain his spiritual, physical, emotional, and intellectual selves—before he arrives on campus. If he does not manage his calendar and schedule, others will take it over. A new president should make sure he takes the time for his family and friends, hobbies, and interests. The institution will benefit from a balanced president, not one who is consumed by the job.

Maintain a Journal

Within the first three to six months the new president will have hundreds of conversations with internal and external stakeholders. This experience can be overwhelming. Maintaining a daily or weekly journal, while requiring discipline, can be an extraordinary resource for capturing impressions and insights about these diverse discussions. A story will emerge from the journal which can provide a wealth of useful information.

Some presidents have found the following focus questions to be helpful in creating structure for their journal:

- What conversations have resonated for you? Which ones stand out?

- Whose names are consistently mentioned? Why?

- What questions persist and what does this tell you?

- Who do you think are your allies? Any beginning enemies?

- What are you learning about organizational culture?

- What issues are beginning to emerge? With whom do you need to discuss these issues?

- What decisions need to be made? What decisions would you like to make?

- What are you learning about this institution? What surprises or discoveries have you encountered?

It is most helpful for a president to review her journal discoveries with members of her support network to explore the emerging themes and obtain their reactions and feedback about what she is seeing and learning. Obviously, she would not share confidences or dig into too much detail. The purpose is to explore the themes that emerge.

We know of one president who kept this type of journal over a decade. He found it invaluable and it became a living history lesson for him. He was able to reflect on conversations held long ago and distill their lessons. He believes that his knowledge of the historical journey created a strong contextual foundation for his leadership.

Watch for Emotional Dips

A presidential transition can be an emotional roller coaster ride. Some of the presidents we talked with mentioned the pattern of emotional dips that they experienced early on in their transition. The first occurs after a month or so when the complexity and enormity of the challenges become clearer. At this stage, the president knows just enough to be overwhelmed. Sharing his doubts and concerns with his support network will be very helpful at this time.

After six months or so, another dip takes place. At this juncture, he has gained some real clarity about the institution, built some relational bridges, has a good understanding about what and how much needs to change, and has a preliminary understanding of how difficult the changes will be. Even in smooth-running, stellar institutions, the expectations of continued excellence are ever present. No campus is static, no matter how accomplished it is or how many resources it has. The president is expected to take the institution forward and upward toward an ever brighter future. It is at this time that the doubt can set in and presidents may question their ability to manage or meet expectations, implement changes, and handle the complexity. Once again, wise counsel from trusted advisors will be invaluable.

At the end of the first year or so, another dip might take place. The learning curve has flattened a great deal, stakeholder expectations become clearer, and trustees want to see some real action. The preseason is over and the game has begun. If the president has done his homework; learned a great deal about the institution; developed authentic relationships with faculty and other stakeholders; and has a plan to deal with the institutional issues, challenges, and aspirations; he can be successful. If this has not happened, complexity will be overwhelming and inertia may set in.

Trustees must keep an open dialogue with the new president to ensure that this does not happen. The dips are natural occurrences, rather than signs of weakness, lack of intelligence, or the absence of motivation. Trustee support is essential at these times. Utilizing the support network, talking with former and current presidents, and consulting a mentor or coach are all helpful processes and strategies that can be employed.

Manage the Spotlight

A new president will be under enormous scrutiny throughout her first year. The spotlight does not go away after that, although it usually dims somewhat. Everyone is watching the new president as she learns how to lead the institution. Actions take on great meaning and are often interpreted in creative, unexpected, and even strange ways.

Diane Downey, Tom March, and Adena Berkman describe this phenomenon. "The pressure of firsts weighs heavily on new leaders' initial actions. First actions, first decisions, first encounters significantly define how others will view the leader for years to come."[14]

The president has to be fully conscious of the impact of initial impressions and the pressure of firsts. Understanding this, the president must be disciplined in aligning what she intends to convey with the impact it produces. Questions to ask include the following: What message do I want to convey to people? How do I want to be seen? How do I want to come across? And, most importantly, how can I be genuine and be myself with others? It is important for a president to be intentional about her communication and leadership. Authenticity is essential. Faking it will fail.

It might be helpful for a new president to work with members of her support network and rehearse her speeches, especially convocations and commencements. Political leaders often conduct mock press conferences during which trusted advisors pepper them with questions. This might be a very helpful practice for a new president to follow. A little rehearsing up-front will improve presentation in the real world—especially for those with limited public speaking experience.

For example, practice questions that might be asked in formal and informal settings might resemble these examples. "What are you going to do about increasing faculty salaries? We're long overdue for a big raise." "Why don't we give our adjunct faculty health benefits?" "How come the gay and lesbian student groups don't have an office on campus?" "When is the science building going to be overhauled? We've been waiting too long for this to happen." Developing responses to these potentially difficult and controversial questions will help prepare the new president for those situations in which she is likely to be confronted by an irate audience. A new president should enlist assistance to create a dozen or so potentially hot issue questions and review her answers with her support group.

People who speak professionally for a living review and rehearse their speeches in front of a mirror many, many times before they deliver them in public. High-profile business leaders are often coached by professionals on how to tell a story, respond to a question, and deliver a key point. It is helpful to invest in these kinds of professional services, especially when the new president has only limited experience in this area.

It is important to remember that the president is always "on." This may not seem fair, but it is true.

Be Careful with Key Decisions

When dealing with decisions about complex issues that will begin to surface in the first 90 days, it is important for the new president to remember that it probably took a long time for these issues to arrive on his desk. He should resist the urge to act fast and demonstrate his brilliance. Instead he should conduct data gathering, ask lots of questions, obtain cabinet input, and involve trustees if appropriate. He should gather different perspectives before moving forward. This may seem like common sense but the urge to look decisive can be overwhelming. He should slow down and move carefully.

This does not mean avoiding sticky or volatile issues. It means that he does not have to solve every problem by the next morning. He should create time and space, obtain information, and then decide.

Before making an important decision, a new president should ask his advisors and cabinet two questions. First, what will be the reactions and responses from different stakeholders? The president should seek specific examples so he can begin to get a picture of potential responses. Once again, this does not mean that he avoids strong reactions; it means that he clearly understands the possible responses and is intellectually prepared to deal with them.

The second question is, What are the long-term implications or impacts of this decision? The goal with this question is to identify the unintended consequences that might develop next year, or even several years from now. With the responses to this question, the president can ensure that he avoids the obvious pitfalls.

***

It is clear that there is much to consider when a president transitions into a new institution (or is promoted within an institution). There are many potential challenges and details that require attention. With a carefully crafted transition map, the new president has the best chance for a successful start to his new role.

Following the steps presented here will make it much easier for the president to meet and overcome these initial challenges. Moreover, successfully navigating the transition will make for a smooth initial period, thereby increasing the likelihood of a long and rewarding tenure in the presidency.

With the arrival of the new president on campus, he now represents the institution with all its majesty and mayhem. In many ways he is no longer seen as an individual. Instead he becomes *the* representative of the institution. To both inside and outside stakeholders he *becomes* the institution. He should make his impressions count, strive for authentic and positive interactions, and make decisions judiciously while attending to the many issues discussed in this chapter.

MY TRANSITION TO A PRESIDENCY
MOHAMMAD (MO) H. QAYOUMI, PRESIDENT,
CALIFORNIA STATE UNIVERSITY EAST BAY

The transition from a candidate to president-select is a very pivotal moment with long-term implications. First, after being selected, it was important for me to make the mental shift internalizing that I no longer had to convince key stakeholders and important decision-makers that I was the best person for the job. My focus shifted to actions that would encourage them to remain happy and satisfied with the decision they had made. I realized that a successful transition would certainly go a long way in this area.

I didn't wait to be selected as president to begin thinking about what my first steps as a new president would be. As my candidacy progressed, I explored different issues along with options for addressing them. I developed some rough idea about a transition plan and the individuals who would need to work with me to implement the plan. By the time I was selected, I had identified a few signature themes that would create a general framework to prepare for more serious dialogues with key campus constituencies. The signature themes were based on what I was able to learn about the campus during my preparation for interviews and supplemented by what surfaced during my interactions with the campus constituencies. Everyone seemed interested in knowing what was my vision for the university. However, I had made the decision early in the process that it would be more important to communicate the process for creating a shared vision than to offer my own. Even though I had some preliminary thoughts about the vision, I recognized that I didn't know enough yet to have a fully formed vision for the university.

Visiting the campus soon after the announcement of my selection was important to me. I visited the campus the first day after my appointment. There was a jovial mood on campus and I was pleased to have been a part of the celebrations. It was apparent that everyone on campus was interested in getting to know me and also was very curious about the depth and breadth of changes I was envisioning for the institution. For this reason I felt it was desirable to contact my predecessor to solicit an invitation to the campus. I sought the identification of a staff member from the president's office to work with me to develop the itinerary for my initial visit. I made sure that I talked with the public relations staff and received a briefing on the local media and the issues that would be of greatest interest to them. I also reminded myself that I was merely the "president-select" and that I needed to be mindful and respectful of the fact that there still was an incumbent person at the helm of presidency. I recognized the need to ensure that I did not interfere with her final months in office.

When I arrived on campus for my initial post-selection visit, I first met with the incumbent. My goal was to establish a rapport and a set of ground rules that would facilitate the transition. One of the important ground rules that I set for myself was not to make any judgments or public statements about prior decisions made on the campus. As a new president my goal was to forge the university's future rather than attempt to deal with the past. I wasn't there during the previous period and I didn't know what factors influenced the decisions that were made. As such, it would have been inappropriate for me to offer opinions on them.

The initial meeting with my predecessor was held off campus and away from the eyes of the media. In addition to meeting with my predecessor, I used the initial campus visit to meet with the academic senate leadership, members of the president's cabinet, student government representatives, union leadership, and a few other key campus groups. In these first meetings I sought to give people assurance that there would be an orderly transition. I also used this opportunity to share my general collaborative philosophy.

As one would expect, I was faced with a variety of questions. I tried to ensure that they were answered consistently with each group. I knew that the campus newspaper and local media would be anxious to meet with me. I asked the public relations office to arrange for visits with them. I also ensured that my schedule was flexible enough to allow time for walking around the campus and dropping in at the student union and a few other campus buildings just to meet and greet people.

Once my schedule was set for visits to the campus, I asked for a temporary office in which I could meet with people and begin to conduct business focused on the future. I thought it best to have an office away from the administration building. As suggested above, I didn't want to interfere with my predecessor's efforts. Conducting my meetings away from her office helped with this. One of my goals was to have my office in a more public building—one in which I was likely to encounter faculty, staff, and students in a more informal way. An ideal building for this was the university library. I believe there was symbolic value from this decision that built positive capital for me at the earliest possible stage.

There was an extensive amount of preparation needed to make my campus visits successful. It was critical to plan the trips and meetings with clearly focused predefined objectives. The planning for the visits was well worth the investment of effort because it allowed me to gain the maximum benefit from them.

One of the key considerations for me was the fact that I was involved in two transitions, one at my new institution and another at my previous campus. As soon as my appointment was formally announced, I became a lame duck at the former institution. I began discussions there about the transition from my previous role and we established a timetable for handing many of my day-to-day activities to key subordinates and the individual who was stepping into my former position on an interim basis. I was glad to have laid the groundwork for this because it enabled me to concentrate more of my efforts on the upcoming challenges.

In an ideal situation I would have liked to have inherited a transition team at my new institution. It would have helped me prepare more effectively before I assumed the presidency. Instead we identified one individual to serve as the coordinator of my transition. This individual coordinated the key briefings that were needed prior to my official start date.

Prior to each visit I asked for data on pertinent issues so that I could be prepared for meetings once I was on campus. I also identified key questions that needed answers prior to my visits to help the staff prepare for the initial meetings. Examples of the issues that I focused on included enrollment, budgets, labor negotiations, and pending legal issues. These meetings and campus visits helped me develop a working agenda for my first hundred days and, hopefully, laid the foundation for a great start to my presidency. With this preparation I believe I have assembled the basic ingredients to elevate the institution to new heights.

Hayward, California
May 2007

HOW LONG CAN I LAST?
JOHN V. LOMBARDI, CHANCELLOR, UNIVERSITY OF MASSACHUSETTS

Every new university president or chancellor asks this question. For some the answer does not matter much because they are on a career track that anticipates three or four years of activity before the next move up the administrative ladder. For others, however, a particular institution may have great personal attraction and the new leader may harbor the hope of lasting forever (or at least until retirement looms). With some few exceptions, this is not a reasonable assumption. Rare special circumstances can indeed make a college or university leader immortal, but usually these involve very large amounts of new revenue, no crises, no significant changes in the trustees, and almost always, a private institution. If none of these conditions prevail, the new academic executive is in a more or less normal set of circumstances, and the real time frame will usually run somewhere between five and ten years.

This time frame responds to the peculiar characteristics of the academic environment where no one (well almost no one) ever leaves. A university president arrives to an audience of faculty (by far the most important constituency) who think of a career as 30 to 40 years. Most of the faculty have been around for 20 and expect to be around for another 20, give or take a decade here or there. They are not in a hurry, they have time, they have already outlasted several presidents, and the most significant of them cannot be fired. Consequently, new presidents, who receive a short honeymoon, must always be mindful of their own shorter administrative time frame.

Upon hiring, the new president is given what we can think of as a bucket of goodwill coins. Beginning the next day, the president begins to spend these coins. One is spent for turning down a budget request from a powerful dean; another for failing to appoint the favorite candidate of a trustee for department chair; a third because the football team found itself with a significant corruption scandal; a fourth coin when a donor's favorite cousin has a total SAT of 800 and a high school GPA of 1.7, and the president refuses to overrule the admissions office denial; and multiple coins because the state budget came in with no faculty salary raises. On occasion, the president can earn a goodwill coin back with a basketball championship or a very successful fund raising year. By and large, however, a president's life is consumed in spending the goodwill coins by making choices among multiple very good alternatives. Rarely do presidents worry about making choices between the good and the bad, because the bad choices are easy to reject. Instead, most choices are between very good alternatives for which the institution has only sufficient revenue for one.

Additionally, many decisions involve personnel, and some faculty members almost always care about every personnel decision. As a result, any negative personnel decision produces unhappy faculty. Unhappy faculty stay unhappy. They do not leave or find alternative employment and the president cannot fire them. In addition, although in theory the new president has the opportunity to clean house and start out with fresh campus leadership by replacing the provost and deans, usually those replaced retreat to the faculty where they form a nucleus of discontent. Each dismissed academic administrator or unpopular decision about faculty or other personnel costs the president a number of goodwill coins which can rarely be recovered, even if the replacements are better.

After a time, the president will reach into the bucket to spend another goodwill coin and touch the bottom. That is the moment to think about returning to the faculty, retiring, or seeking another administrative position.

How can a president extend the time purchased by the bucket of goodwill coins? One tactic is to do as little as possible, as charmingly as possible. This is the presiding posture in which the president says all the right things, delegates any unavoidable issues to others, and moves from place to place, on and off campus, continually articulating a persuasive and buzz-word loaded vision. The skill of appearing-without-doing is a finely honed administrative talent, and those who have it, will extend the life of their initial allotment of goodwill coins well beyond the normal.

Similarly, the president who drives change, seeks a challenge, never shrinks from a potential conflict, suffers fools poorly, or speaks clearly will spend the coins quickly, finding the bottom of that bucket within a few dramatic years. Change is especially expensive, for while universities are change agents for the societies that support them, they are highly resistant to changing themselves. Nothing spends goodwill coins faster than intense, driven internal university change.

Understanding the function of the goodwill coin bucket offers a frame of reference for new presidents and chancellors to measure their time and plan their exit. One always wants to leave while a few goodwill coins remain in the bucket.

Amherst, Massachusetts
April 2007

THE BSU BUDGET SURPRISE
MICKEY L. BURNIM, PRESIDENT, BOWIE STATE UNIVERSITY

After day-long campus interviews, I stayed overnight to meet with the system chancellor. He was quite affable and confirmed my impression that Bowie State University (BSU) is a fine institution lacking only the appropriate leadership for the challenges that it faces. He proudly pointed out that, during the last session, the Maryland General Assembly had added a 40 percent increase—$8.84 million—in the university's state appropriation. This was seen as a result of growing legislative support for BSU, political influence by BSU supporters in the state legislature, and some impact of the desegregation agreement between the Maryland Higher Education Commission and the U.S. Office of Civil Rights.

A few days later, I accepted an invitation to return to interview with the board of regents, the University System of Maryland's (USM) governing board. This session reinforced my impression that the board's greatest concern was for strong focused leadership and that the major challenge facing the university was serious internal conflict over the faculty role in the governance process. Variations of this conflict theme appear frequently on college campuses across the nation, but it had taken on a particularly protracted life and acerbic tone at BSU. The board pledged its strong support for the next president in dealing with the governance issue. I felt good about the interview and started to feel real excitement about the possibility of my selection.

One week after my campus interviews, I was faxed a written offer from the chancellor to become the next president of Bowie State University. I was quite pleased for I believed that I had the opportunity to lead an institution with tremendous potential for growth in enrollment, degree program expansion, and external constituency support. Furthermore, the university system was attractive because it was organized similarly to the one in which I was then working. This, in addition to the apparently strong support of the state legislature as evidenced by the previous year's increased appropriation, led me to conclude that this was a tremendous opportunity to lead a larger and more complex university, one which was positioned to thrive under just my kind of leadership. Even though it had been a very fast moving process, I gleefully accepted the offer. I did so without reviewing the university's financial statements and recent audit reports, against generally accepted protocol, because I knew BSU to be part of a well regarded system that was enjoying increasing support from the state legislature.

Two weeks before officially beginning my presidency, I visited the BSU campus to participate in the semester-opening faculty-staff convocation. It was important to me to greet the faculty and staff as the president-elect and to let them know of my excitement and eagerness to work with them in pursuit of the BSU mission. After the convocation, as the three of us walked together, the interim president broached BSU's budget problem with the chancellor. The chancellor's budget staff was pressuring her to reduce the tuition revenue budget from $29 million to $24 million. This was a very serious problem for BSU because the interim president had calculated that more revenue was needed to operate the university than had been available the previous year. The major concerns were operating budgets for the academic departments and money to hire sufficient numbers of adjunct faculty. The chancellor promised to confer with his vice chancellor for administration and finance and talk to the interim president and me in a telephone conference call a few days later.

The conference call involved four participants: the chancellor, his vice chancellor for administration and finance, the interim president, and me.

During the call, the vice chancellor emphasized that BSU's tuition revenue budget was based on enrollment growth numbers that significantly exceeded the university's recent trend and that budget analysts in his office thought it very unlikely that BSU could achieve those numbers. He further pointed out that if BSU built its budget on these very optimistic enrollment numbers, we would run a very real risk of creating an operational deficit for the year. I urged the interim president to reduce the tuition revenue budget to $24 million and she acceded. Part of her rationale for doing so was that a mid-year budget amendment could be made if the tuition revenue came in significantly above what was budgeted.

During my first month on the job, I was visited by the chair of the board of regents' audit committee who was accompanied by the head of the system's internal audit division and the system's comptroller. The message they delivered was that BSU was in very poor financial health. Its financial reserve position was near the very bottom for the USM and BSU had incurred operating deficits for the last three years. This was the first time that the financial position of BSU had been described to me in this way and I then realized that I had begun the job with an incomplete picture. Having fully understood the institution's financial situation would not have caused me to decline the offer because I saw this as a problem which could be managed and overcome in fairly short order. The conversation with the regents, however, would have been different had I known the full story at that point. This meant, in all likelihood, that our desired growth and expansion would be delayed and more difficult than I had thought.

The fall semester's enrollment came in below the budgeted numbers and I was forced to work with my cabinet to consider how to cut an additional $1.5 million from our operating budget. This was a very painful process to undertake since the university's needs and the expectations for growth and progress were so great. Nevertheless, we tackled it head-on, being careful to keep our key internal campus constituencies fully apprised of the situation and our approach to a solution.

As this is written, we are probably still in the honeymoon period. The governance issue has been dormant and we are overcoming the budget surprise. We will finish this fiscal year in the black and will add at least one percent of the budget to reserves. Budgeting and forecasting procedures are being re-examined and revised with the requested assistance of the chancellor's office. Finally, we are being deliberate in keeping the regents, the chancellor's office, and the campus constituencies informed about the university's needs and financial position.

In conclusion, if I ever consider another presidency, I will certainly be more diligent in researching the financial position of the institution under consideration. At a minimum, I will ask direct questions about the institution's finances during the interview process and review the two most recent financial audit reports. This approach would have given me a much more complete picture of the institution that I was considering and would have enabled me to make the decision about the presidency with fuller awareness of the challenges that I would face immediately.

Bowie, Maryland
May 2007

NOTES

1. McLaughlin, Judith Block, ed. *Leadership Transitions: The New College President*. San Francisco: Jossey-Bass, 1996.

2. Moore, John W., and Joanne M. Burrows. *Presidential Succession and Transition: Beginning, Ending and Beginning Again*. Washington: American Association of State Colleges and Universities, 2001.

3. Gross, Karen. "My First Year as President." *Inside Higher Ed*. http://www.insidehighered.com/views/2007/07/13/gross (accessed July 20, 2007).

4. Goleman, Daniel. *Working with Emotional Intelligence*. New York: Bantam Books, 1998.

5. Ciampa, Dan, and Michael Watkins. *Right From the Start*. Boston: Harvard Business School Press, 1999.

6. Dowdall, Jean. "Interim and Internal." *The Chronicle of Higher Education*. http://chronicle.com/weekly/v51/i15/15c00101.htm (accessed June 3, 2007).

7. Heifetz, Ronald. *Leadership Without Easy Answers*. Cambridge: Belknap/Harvard Press, 1994.

8. Moore and Burrows. *Presidential Succession and Transition*.

9. Bensimon, Estella. *On Assuming a College or University Presidency*. Washington: American Association of Higher Education, 1989.

10. McLaughlin. *Leadership Transitions*.

11. McLaughlin. *Leadership Transitions*.

12. Gilmore, Thomas North. *Making a Leadership Change*. San Francisco: Jossey-Bass, 1988.

13. Ciampa and Watkins. *Right From the Start*.

14. Downey, Diane, Tom March, and Adena Berkman. *Assimilating New Leaders: The Key to Executive Retention*. New York: AMACOM/American Management Association, 2001.

CHAPTER 3

New Presidents Will Go Only as Far as Their Relationships Take Them

In higher education, relationships are the coin of the realm.[1]

hroughout the book we highlight the interpersonal side of being a
president. We believe that this is critically important in any leadership
position, but even more so for those at the top of the organization. We
heard repeatedly from presidents and others that it is the individual and stakeholder relationships that a president develops and maintains that will most
dramatically influence his success in the role. Failure to attend to these important
matters puts him in the unenviable position of traveling uphill regardless of which
direction he takes in a given situation. The job is challenging enough—he should
not make it more so by failing to devote attention to its nontechnical aspects.

The good news is that relationship management is not complex or particularly
difficult. It requires attention, common sense, and—on some level—application
of the Golden Rule (i.e., do unto others as you would have them do unto you).
So much of any relationship is just being attentive and sensitive to the needs of
others. If this is all the president does in terms of relationships, he will enhance
the likelihood of his presidency being a success. But he can go a little further by
demonstrating a genuine interest in others, paying attention to the little things
that are happening around him, and allowing himself to be engaged by others.
All of these actions, coupled with successfully addressing the challenges of the
position, will create the potential for him to establish a legacy that will survive
long after he has retired or moved to another institution. The remainder of this
chapter examines the relationships that are most critical to a president's success.

MANAGE THE RELATIONSHIP WITH
THE BOARD OF TRUSTEES

The relationship between the president and the board of trustees sets a tone
that certainly carries over to the leadership team, and, in many ways, permeates

the institution. This is one time when, if things are not good at the top, it is difficult to get anything accomplished throughout the institution. In order to be successful in completing any major initiative—from curriculum reform, to policy development, capital projects, or development of the overall budget—there is a need for a solid working relationships between the president and the board.

The Presidential Search Process

In many ways the working relationship begins to develop prior to the actual transition, going back to the search process itself. Ideally the leader of the search committee, who serves as its chair, is the trustee who will also chair the board when the new president takes office. This often is not the sitting chair as he may be nearing the end of his term as the outgoing president concludes her time in office. The qualities required of a search committee chair include a strong commitment of time and energy to courting candidates, a low tolerance for breaches of confidentiality, and the persuasive talent to build consensus among divergent stakeholders in the process. A poker face helps too. Eventually, all stakeholders share their dreams and biases toward the position of president and it is important to listen and learn as this plays out. In the end, the value lies in development of the list of diverse qualities that are necessary for a president who will lead a specific institution at a particular time in its history.

Identifying a representative, diverse group of members from the institutional community to serve on the search committee is more than a symbolic gesture. In this way many viewpoints test the candidates and multiple aspects of the institution's progress and its challenges are exposed. In addition to trustees, a search committee ideally is comprised of respected faculty leaders from the colleges and schools, members of the senior leadership team, staff, students, and alumni association.

The search committee in private institutions needs to have significant numbers of faculty. A balance of members from all schools, as well as gender, race, length of service, involvement in institution-wide issues and balanced viewpoints are all important considerations. Trustees' strong leadership and final role in the selection of the new president will be self-evident. Choosing search committee members—including business people who will partner with the president in fund-raising, as well as academics who will focus on the mission— is critical. Student members are valuable for their direct evaluation of a candidate's fit with the sense of place. Rounding out the committee with a few members of the senior leadership team also ensures that work style and leadership questions are asked and that all divisions are covered.

The search committee can become large; 12 to 15 or more members is not atypical for private institutions. The search committee can be even larger, running to 20 or more in large public institutions. Although the size can make the committees cumbersome to manage, the chair and search consultant—if one is engaged—can manage the process so that it works to their advantage.

For example, the committee can rely on a subgroup to screen résumés, and interviews can be conducted in small-group settings, through which more information can be obtained from candidates.

The decision of whether to choose a search consultant and, if so, how to choose one needs to be addressed early in the process. Research indicates that about one-half of institutions utilize search firms in presidential searches.[2] The identification of the right firm usually involves several interviews. It is essential to meet with the actual consultant(s) who will work on the institutional search and not merely a senior company representative. Sometimes the senior representative may represent the company well, but this does not ensure that their assigned consultant will represent your institution well. The most critical match, however, is between the individual search consultant (and staff) that will work on the particular search and the institution and board chair.

A board should seek a firm with a solid reputation, good success record in filling higher education presidential positions, and one that is well-regarded throughout higher education. Institutions occasionally choose to rely on local search firms specializing in general executive searches. This is fine unless the institution seeks to recruit from a national pool of candidates. In these situations, the institution is better served by relying on one of the several national search firms that specialize in higher education executive searches. They have a better sense of the subtleties of higher education institutions and they are much more likely to have access to qualified candidates who may be less visible.

A healthy relationship between the committee—especially the chair—and the search consultant is a necessity. Identifying a professional who understands the mission, goals, needs, and aspirations of the institution, who integrates well personally with the search committee, and who has an exacting sense of process provides a credible framework for the search. The match is made when a search consultant clearly appreciates and can communicate the institution's mission and goals, has the network of contacts to attract strong candidates, and has a style that meshes well with the search committee chair. The selection of the correct consultant and firm not only engenders confidence, but provides the resources of an objective third-party. A good consultant often is the one to frame the difficult questions and provide process options to guide the search committee through complex or sticky situations.

A good search firm brings more than just a process. In fact, professional executive search firms provide invaluable expertise, not only in developing a strong pool of candidates (the importance of which cannot be overstated), but in initiating positive relationships with applicants. They also are adept at obtaining in-depth reference information and conducting background checks. It is impossible to overstate the importance of this key step in the search process. It is no longer safe for an institution to assume that what appears on a candidate's curriculum vita or résumé represents his actual accomplishments and credentials. Another strength that an executive search consultant brings is the ability to assist the committee with the development of focused interview questions. They also can synthesize the feedback from those who participate in the interviews to assist with the evaluation of what is learned about each candidate.

One search committee developed a survey that was sent to several hundred faculty, staff, students, and alumni, asking them to identify the top characteristics needed by the next president. Three qualities stood out among the responses: one who understands the business side of higher education, a good communicator, and someone with an entrepreneurial spirit. This was quite a different set of skills from the previous, successful president, but it reflected strong input regarding what was viewed as the skill set for the time and institutional challenges ahead. The information was shared with the community and became a part of the advertising used to attract the new president.

Engaging the candidates and being able to interact formally and informally with them provides a backdrop for understanding the interpersonal traits that each one brings. In this way the chair-president relationship starts to develop early and the lines of communication are formed and strengthened through the entire search process. The search committee is a witness to the building of this relationship, which bodes well for the transition process.

The Relationship between the President and the Board Chair

Once the search is completed and the new president and board chair are engaged in leading the institution, it is vital that they work to establish mutual trust and a confident and effective way of working together. It is the chair's role to set the tone for the board and it is the president's role to promote the long-term vision. Ideally, the vision is developed collaboratively through an inclusive and participatory process allowing significant input from members of the institution's community. Once the vision is developed, the president becomes its owner and the overall driver of institutional efforts directed toward achieving it.

The unique relationship between president and chair is one that requires ongoing and open communication. This high level of communication requires a substantial investment of time by both parties. The investment is rewarded with a mutual understanding of the issues and challenges faced by the institution, as well as the support needed by the president to move the agenda effectively into the board process. Many presidents and board chairs communicate by telephone weekly, often supplementing this with e-mail exchanges between the calls. This pattern of regular communication often leads to strong friendships. Friendship is not an essential element of success, but a close partnership or mentoring relationship frequently develops and can be beneficial both to the president and the institution.

It is not uncommon for hidden preexisting issues to surface for new presidents. We believe that about half of these relate to finances and the other half to personnel matters. Early clear communication and an agreement on the long-term goals are critical. The clear guidance regarding communication offered by presidents and board chairs alike is, share the good and the bad. Avoid surprises at all cost. This mantra applies to working with the full board as well.

Effective Board Processes

Presidents with whom we spoke described the value of setting expectations and taking the early opportunity to establish strong board processes and solid relationships. This is the recipe for a well-functioning board. One way to do this is to assess the current board processes. As a new president takes office there is a natural opportunity to examine areas of board process and assess the overall effectiveness of board meetings. The chair and president can consult with trustees and identify processes that they would like to maintain or change. Processes that might be addressed include the amount of information in board packets, the timing for receipt of information, the structure of meetings, the regular cycle and schedule for meetings, or time allocated within each meeting's agenda.

Another critical starting point is for the board to understand and support the president's efforts to achieve the institution's vision. Some presidents begin each board meeting with a review of the vision statement, along with the current major goals directed toward achieving that vision, to set the stage for the discussions that follow. Others include the mission and vision statements prominently in board materials. Either way, there is value in regularly reconnecting trustees—who come to campus only periodically—with that long-term view for the institution.

Assisting the board in understanding how the institution functions and how the president operates provides them with the clarity necessary to participate effectively in discussions and decisions. Each of the vice presidential areas contributes substantial information to board discussions. A working knowledge of how the area functions, and what the major responsibilities are, provides confidence for trustees and valuable input for the leadership team.

As with the president and chair relationship, there should be no secrets, surprises, or hidden agendas when dealing with the full board. The president and senior leadership team organize the information and provide trustees with what they need to be effective in their role. One president described her philosophy, indicating that she does not manage the board; on the contrary, she views it as her responsibility to assist them in fulfilling their fiduciary responsibilities. That entails being honest about challenges and opportunities while allowing and encouraging trustees to ask the tough questions. Communicating early, clearly stating the many facets of an issue, providing enough information, and detailing the president's intended course of action allow trustees to have meaningful and timely input.

Another aspect of strong board process is relationship-building. Well-functioning boards tend to have presidents who work on developing connections with individual trustees. They take the time to learn each trustee's personal interests and how they can help the board and the institution. This is important when a president is new, as well as when new trustees are added to the board. One president told us that his office staff tracks his ongoing interaction with board members monthly on a spreadsheet to ensure that he does not neglect to make contact with any individual.

Another president shared a story about his discovery that the board members at his institution did not really know each other. The board met briefly three times per year for very structured meetings. Most of the board's work historically was conducted by an executive committee of the board.

After observing the board members' lack of familiarity with each other, he proposed to the board chair that the board engage in an off-site retreat to build the board's capacity by focusing on their own education. In addition to the educational component, the retreat was planned to include significant social interaction. Invitations were extended to board members' spouses and the senior leadership team members were encouraged to have their spouses accompany them as well. The event was a rousing success and became a standard annual practice.

The new president of a public institution traveled throughout the state to develop a one-on-one relationship with each board member. This institution has a system-level board (and no local board). Immediately after she was hired, the president established the practice of visiting regents in their hometown to educate them about the uniqueness of her institution. It took a considerable amount of her time during her first year on the job, but it has paid huge dividends. As far as she knows, she's the first and only president to make this kind of investment of time and effort. She continues the practice with each new round of regent appointments. She also makes it a practice to attend each board meeting, even when there are no agenda items specifically relevant to her institution. She believes the familiarity with the regents has been helpful when issues related to her institution have come before the board. The only cautionary note about this is to be open and inform the system office that it is happening.

The above example hints at the complexity for the president of a public institution which is part of a system. We have stressed the importance for new presidents to develop and maintain effective relationships with their board chairs. The likelihood of this happening in a system environment is pretty low, especially if the system is comprised of a large number of institutions.

Rather than merely accepting this as a reality that cannot be overcome, a new president should take the time to develop solid working relationships with the leadership and staff in the system office. He should take time to connect personally with the president or chancellor of the system, and also get to know the senior staff.

Too often the new president relies on the fact that his leadership team already knows their counterparts at the system, and gives only cursory attention to meeting the system officials. On the one hand, this is a good gesture because it demonstrates respect for the leadership team and suggests that the president will not micromanage. On the other hand, given the significant amount of influence the system officials have over the institution, it is a mistake for a new president not to invest some time and effort to connect on a personal level.

Even in cases in which the president's team members operate effectively within the campus, it is possible that they do not have effective working relationships with their system counterparts. Rather than find this out when a desired approval is not received, the president can discover this through one-on-one meetings with the system staff. Armed with this knowledge, he can either help the relevant member of his staff develop a strategy to overcome the relationship challenge or seek to find another campus representative to interact with the system counterpart. And, if the problem genuinely rests with the system staff member, the president can explore ways in which to remedy the situation at that end. Either way, it is not a good idea for a president to ignore these critical relationships. They can be just as important, if not more so, than the relationships between a president and the local board.

There is one other challenge that is unique to public institution presidents. For a variety of reasons, many public institutions have created independent foundations to handle some of the activities that routinely occur within a private institution. These foundations are charged with myriad tasks such as fund-raising, overseeing the institution's endowment, overseeing the operation of the athletics or research activities, managing various for-profit investments held by the institution. In each case, the foundations are governed by a board whose focus is much more narrow than that of the institution's governing board. And unfortunately, in some instances, these board members forget that the foundation is a support organization for the institution, not the other way around.

One of the authors has experience working for a public institution that relies on four separate support organizations to assist the university. One of the organizations focuses on fund-raising and management of the university's endowment. Another is responsible for overseeing the university's athletics programs. The third is charged with providing guidance for the university's research enterprise. The final organization is a very focused entity which exists to oversee the distribution of state resources appropriated to finance health care provided to the region's indigent population.

The board for the university and the research foundation have complete overlap. Each member of one board is a member of the other's board. This is not the case, however, for the fund-raising foundation, athletics association, or the entity involved in overseeing the indigent care appropriation. As such, the university's president is responsible for maintaining relationships with an incredibly large number of individuals—each of whom justifiably believes that he or she is performing an invaluable task for the institution.

Although the president delegated significant responsibility to various members of his leadership team to help manage the various relationships, the president devoted substantial amounts of time to connect with each individual.

This was no small feat because, collectively, the number of board members greatly exceeds the number of individuals serving on most private institution boards. The fact that the president avoided any significant flare-ups during his lengthy tenure is a testament to the care with which he approached this effort.

Boards of many private institutions benefit from a unique blend of experience. It is not uncommon for private institution boards to include members from other academic institutions or, in the case of religiously-affiliated institutions, from other organizations of the same faith. Presidents, provosts, or even deans from other institutions can be enormously helpful in assessing and validating complicated faculty and student issues. Having academics on a board balances the skills of alumni and business leaders, who bring their expertise in finance, law, insurance, technology, etc. It is sometimes particularly helpful to gain the perspective of someone from a different institution which may be tackling the same challenge being examined by a board.

Engaging in dialogue with other theologians also can help a board tackle the sometimes very challenging issues that arise on religiously-affiliated institution campuses. There is a delicate balancing act that takes place almost daily between the principles of academic freedom, free and open expression of thought, and adherence to the tenets and values that define the character of the institution. Theologians and other representatives from different religious organizations can introduce a fresh perspective to board members.

Structuring Board Committees

One very effective board process is to use cabinet members as staff to the various board committees. For example, the chief business officer typically staffs the finance, audit, and buildings and grounds committees; the provost or vice president for academic affairs usually staffs the academic affairs committee; and the vice president for student life staffs the student affairs committee. These assignments help the president coordinate the agenda and presentation of information and provide a mechanism for fluid conversations between committees on multifaceted topics. When relying on this approach, it is valuable for the president and the senior leadership team to have agreements on how the vice presidents will interact with trustees. Additionally, there needs to be regular communication from the senior team to the president so she is aware of any important issues that may surface with a committee when she is not present.

Care must be taken with one particular issue when trustees and the president's senior staff have direct interaction. These relationships can create increased opportunities for micromanagement to occur. Committee members frequently will seek to influence the president's senior leadership team much more quickly than they would the president herself.

Identifying strong and effective committee chairs also is an important board process. The role of the committee chair is to move the committee agenda forward and make recommendations on issues to the full board. There should be substantial congruence between the committee's agenda and the institution's overall agenda. One of the committee chair's responsibilities is to ensure that the committee remains focused on its charge while considering it within the institution's broader context.

Oftentimes it also is necessary for the committee chair to invest effort in managing the other committee members. The most significant issue likely to arise is micromanagement—whether from individual committee members or the chair. For this reason, care should be taken to avoid appointing chairs or assigning committee members who are too zealous about the committee's area of responsibility. They sometimes can forget that theirs is but one committee and the institution has priorities in a wide range of areas. If a member or the chair requests extraordinary levels of detail on issues and projects, or seeks to be overly directive to institutional staff, it may be necessary for the president or board chair to intervene. The specific institutional dynamics will dictate whether the president can safely do this herself or leave it to the board chair to handle.

This concern about instances of board micromanagement needs to be kept in mind. In public institutions there often is a political agenda that makes this issue even more complex. Members of private institution boards tend to view their role as improving the institution, lending support, and being external advocates for the institution. There are times with any board, however, when well-intentioned trustees cross the line into day-to-day details that are more appropriately within the realm of the senior leadership team. Board chairs can be most effective in working one-on-one with trustees on this and providing the appropriate level of information—not necessarily more information—on the issue at hand. Setting expectations about what the board *should* do and encouraging appropriate discussion of difficult questions often is enough to reduce the urge for some trustees to micromanage an issue or area.

We are aware of one new president of a mid-sized private university who found herself wrestling with a plan to establish an engineering school. The plan had been developed by the previous president, under the direction of the board, and enjoyed ardent support from the board's chair and vice chair. The plan was not supported by formal financial statements but, rather, was based on very rough cost estimates. Compounding this situation was the fact that the former president presented to the board very preliminary cost estimates that were not very well understood, thus leaving them in the dark about the most critical information.

The new president set about hiring experts to provide input into the essential issues such as finances, faculty, and accreditation. What she learned in the process was that the costs were huge, resulting in deficits of $4 million in year one and $9 million in year two. Deficits of this magnitude could not be absorbed in a tuition-dependent institution with insubstantial reserves available to cover the losses. The primary cause of the deficits were the plan to hire 45 faculty and start construction of a new building to house the engineering school.

It was clear to the president that this plan had the potential to seriously impair the financial health of the institution. By the end of her first year in office, the president knew that she had to attempt to persuade the chair and vice chair that the plan for the engineering school simply was not feasible. Although she sensed that others on the board were beginning to realize that there was more involved than originally stated, she realized that she had to convince the chair and vice chair first.

To say that the chair and vice chair were angry when she presented her argument against the engineering school would be a significant understatement. The conversation prompted the vice chair to contact all trustees two days prior to the next board meeting stating that senior management was out of line in dismissing the engineering school plan. The e-mail further alleged that management was mismanaging the institution's finances. In the e-mail he proposed that the university proceed with the engineering school and that the chair and vice chair take over management of the institution's finances.

This, of course, led to an intense weekend of politics and drama. The chair decided to schedule an emergency teleconference for the night before the board meeting to attempt to negotiate a solution. At this point, the president realized that the engineering school was not the real issue. Instead, it was a lack of effective board governance and the "old boy's network" that were railroading the rest of the board into a project that would imperil the university's economic stability.

The president decided to prepare a presentation for the board that would put all the facts on the table in support of her position on the matter, while at the same time defending the reputations of her senior management team. She clearly understood, of course, that, by the end of the meeting, she would either be in a stronger position with the board or out of a job.

In the end, there was a unanimous vote to reject the establishment of a engineering school. Equally important, the vote was followed by a second resolution in support of the leadership team. The latter resolution included an explicit statement that the board would refrain from micromanaging the university's finances. Immediately following the meeting, the president began the process to rebuild her relationships with the chair and the vice chair.

Board Interaction with Stakeholder Groups

The nature of periodic board meetings when trustees are on campus for only an agenda-packed day or two makes meaningful interaction with stakeholders a challenge. Yet the failure to create opportunities for such interactions can sometimes lead to board members failing to recognize what is most important for the institution's overall success—the engagement of faculty with students.

Some institutions routinely incorporate student participation in board meetings, whether in the form of presentations by student competition winners, attendance at a student performance, or simply dialogue with members of a student club. For other institutions, student participation is more cyclical and keyed to specific campus events such as introduction of new student government officers or announcement of a graduating class gift.

Some boards have adopted the tradition of inviting faculty to dine with trustees. One president shared with us her institution's practice of encouraging faculty to host board members in their homes for small dinner parties. The institution reimbursed the faculty for their expenses, creating an inexpensive mechanism for faculty to have direct, informal interaction with board members. This practice has the added benefit of a two-way exchange of viewpoints that might not otherwise have the chance to occur.

Another strategy is to create the opportunity for constituencies to meet trustees informally at planned social events. It always is valuable for trustees and members of the institutional community to have some knowledge of one another, their general hopes for the institution, and their ongoing challenges. Building this into the board's agenda in a systematic (formal or informal) way was found by many presidents to add positively to the process and provide board members with real connection to the culture and campus life.

The President's Performance Assessment

Prior to the start of an academic year, it is important for the board chair and the president to agree on the goals and priorities for the coming year. An effective annual performance appraisal process is part of a regular cycle of review of the progress toward the president's goals, and often includes assessment of the senior leadership team's accomplishments as well. There is value in charting these accomplishments toward the attainment of strategic institutional goals. The president's annual review can be conducted by the executive committee or an ad hoc group of three to five trustees. We tend to favor reviews that involve more than just the board chair to ensure that multiple perspectives are available. This is especially important in situations when the president and the board chair develop a close personal friendship. Such relationships can sometimes make it difficult for the chair to fully recognize the president's strengths and areas of needed improvement.

It is not uncommon for boards to solicit feedback about the president's performance from members of the board, from faculty representatives, from the president of the student body, and from members of the senior leadership team. The performance review should include all major areas with the opportunity for both quantitative and qualitative comments. Potential topics include leadership, administration (including financial management), donor and alumni relations (including fund-raising), quality of internal personal interactions, strategic planning, and the relationship with the board of trustees. Additionally, questions about personal strengths and suggestions on how to face challenges are often asked.

The gathering and analysis of information ideally leads to an open and candid dialog with the president about his accomplishments, as well as a discussion about the challenges and opportunities for the upcoming year. At the same time, there should be attention to his ongoing personal commitment to the role, opportunities for his professional development, and his aspirations. With this conversation as background, the chair should be in a position to work with the board's compensation committee to determine the president's compensation package for the upcoming year. The final part of the process is the confirmation of the upcoming year's goals against which the president will be evaluated in the succeeding year.

Board Development and Assessment

In a private institution board development starts with a focus on the institution's mission. The mission is what distinguishes one institution from another. It helps provide purpose for the institution and articulates its uniqueness among the broad range of higher education institutions. The current marketplace for higher education includes vocationally-focused community colleges, public four-year institutions focused primarily on teacher education, highly selective elite liberal arts colleges, and the largest and most complex public research institutions. The importance of mission and purpose is conveyed through new trustee orientation, and is echoed in strategic planning goals. Focusing on mission is a powerful way to connect trustees to campus and culture.

Many models of board orientation have been developed to provide the background and information a trustee needs to perform his fiduciary duties. Among the many areas addressed through orientations, it is critical for new trustees to be grounded in the historical and current sense of mission. Both a new trustee orientation and an ongoing mission formation program provide value to boards. Providing regular opportunities to engage in discussions around mission and planning also help maintain the board's long-term focus.

Orientation is just as important for public institutions but, unlike private colleges and universities, public institutions frequently have their mission defined for them by the state. Although most private institutions are subject to some form of oversight by a state agency (e.g., education department or coordinating board), they have much more latitude than public institutions. It is rare that a public institution can unilaterally alter its mission. Therefore, it is important to focus orientation on the mission to provide context for public institution trustees, although this is less critical than for trustees at private institutions. Instead, the former will focus more energy on the state-mandated current initiatives and priorities. This will be supplemented with any institutionally unique plans and priorities, but there is an expectation that the public institution trustees—many of whom are appointed through a formal state-mandated process—will emphasize the broad state initiatives.

Board development for both public and private institutions can be relatively informal or very formal. Informal board development may take the form of retreats organized by the institution with no outside expertise. Alternatively, some institutions have very formal, structured educational programs for their boards. In some cases, these sessions are facilitated by those who specialize in organizational development generally. In other cases, institutions rely on consultants who specialize in development and education for higher education boards. Irrespective of the method chosen, it is a good idea for boards to devote some attention each year to improving their effectiveness.

Many institutions have gone a step further by implementing a routine assessment process for the board and its individual members. The approaches can vary widely but they usually focus first on the board as a whole. Such assessments examine the effectiveness of the board's processes related to such matters as decision making and conflict management. On a smaller scale, they examine issues such as the effectiveness of board meetings, the quality and timing of materials provided in advance of meetings, and the number and importance of issues covered during the meetings.

These assessments are supplemented by the examination of the ongoing commitment of individual trustees as evidenced by their personal participation and engagement. By monitoring and assessing these issues routinely, any personal frustrations are identified early. The data supporting participation and engagement will be reviewed periodically with the board chair. She then can have a conversation with members who have not been attentive or whose commitment and meeting attendance has not been consistent.

Board Succession

Board succession is a fairly routine matter at most public institutions. There is a minority of institutions for which board members are elected. Term limits in these situations vary from state to state, but they serve to force automatic transition among board members. For public institution boards with appointed board members, it is also typical to have term limits. A common limit is two four-year terms. In many cases, board members at public institutions are appointed by the governor. The governor usually has the authority to reappoint board members who have not reached their term limit, with or without input from the institution. Even when a governor has the authority to appoint board members, it is common for the board's officers to be elected by the members of the board.

In some instances, the governor has total discretion when selecting board members while, in others, the institution is involved in the development of a slate of candidates from which the governor chooses. The latter approach is preferable because it minimizes the impact of cronyism. Too often, governors are repaying political favors with higher education board appointments. If the institution has no input to the process, it is entirely possible that the board will lack essential skill sets and expertise. Although the appointees may be potential donors—as evidenced by their financial support during the governor's campaign—there is no guarantee that their interest in the institution extends beyond attendance at sporting events.

The tenure for private institution board members tends to be longer than that of public institution board members. It is becoming increasingly more common, however, for private institution boards to establish term limits—both for service on the board and for service in officer positions. This raises the question of how private institution board members are selected and, for boards with fixed membership numbers (the vast majority), how members cycle off.

The ideal situation is to have self-perpetuating boards. In such a situation, the board identifies and selects replacements for board members who resign or whose terms have expired. The president's role in this process is of crucial importance because it will be her responsibility to work with all board members. It is also possible that any board member appointed to a board could eventually serve in the chair's role—or at least chair a committee. As such, this is an area in which the president should seek to have a formal role. The goal should be to serve on the nominating committee for board appointments but, if that is not possible, she should at least have informal influence over the appointment process.

The president of a large private institution began his presidency under the board chair who chaired the presidential search process. That chair remained in place for the first two years of the presidency. As the time came to identify the next chair, the question of open-ended terms needed to be addressed. The president's past experience and working knowledge of his current board led him to seek a term limit of three years as board chair. The plan calls for the next chair—the first subject to a term limit—to hold the position for three years, ending in 2008.

As he thought about the many talented trustees on the board, the president realized that there are several individuals who would be strong candidates for the next term as chair (2008–2011). It was in the midst of considering these individuals that the president, with the support of the board's executive committee, decided to tentatively identify and groom the next several board chairs. This succession plan for the position of board chair is unique in its deliberate correlation to phases of the institution's capital campaign and to the life cycle of the presidency.

With this succession plan in mind, the president formed a small committee to identify the third chair who would work with him during the early years of the public phase of the capital campaign. The goal is to select a trustee with the personality, connections, and time to assist with facilitating the public phase of the campaign.

Once this person had been identified, the president began to work on the identification of skills and personality traits for a board chair to serve during the final phase of the campaign. He also considered one who might even be a good chair for the transition to the next president (after about ten to twelve years).

This type of planning is not typical but it is very effective in grooming leaders and providing continuity. The relationships can be established and have time to grow. It also creates the opportunity for the president to work with the current board chair to steer projects and assignments to those designated as future chairs. The only cautionary note applied to this approach is to ensure that backups are identified. It is possible that a board member's personal situation could change causing the need for a shift in plans.

At the end of the day, a new president's relationship with his board—especially the board chair—is crucial. Ultimately the board's judgment about the president's performance determines whether he is successful in his role. Developing and maintaining a strong relationship with the board—one built on trust, honesty, and effective communication—will serve well both the president and the board and, therefore, the entire institution.

PAY ATTENTION TO THE FACULTY

Second only to the board, a new president's establishment of an effective relationship with her faculty may have the greatest impact on her long-term success in the presidency. Constructive faculty relationships are essential to any president's success, but more so for new presidents because the faculty will be watching more closely in the beginning than at any other time. Faculty members play an important and unique role in any institution because they are at the core of the educational process. Every president needs to have a disciplined and thoughtful approach to developing authentic faculty relationships on her campus.

For a new president, positive faculty relationships start during the search process. Ideally, the search committee includes several credible faculty members who ask tough questions about academic excellence, teaching quality, research emphasis, and other topics of special interest to faculty. The answers new presidents provide will go a long way toward shaping faculty perception in the initial months of their transition. New presidents should of course prepare well for these interviews, but they should pay particular attention to faculty questions, so that initial impressions are favorable and supportive.

As the new president comes on board, faculty should have a meaningful presence in the learning network and help educate the president about faculty perspectives on aspirations, culture, governance, and politics. The president also should ask to be invited to faculty senate meetings so that she can begin to build relationships and engage in dialogue with the faculty. The last thing a new president needs is to be summoned to faculty senate meetings only when there is a difficult problem to solve or they are upset about a decision she made.

Establishing a connection with the faculty senate chair and executive committee members is an important step to take early in the transition process.

Several presidents we spoke with have instituted an informal breakfast
meeting for faculty leaders every couple weeks or at least a couple times per
semester. This gives the president an opportunity to discuss issues and build
relationships with key constituents. The tenor of these meetings should be
collegial, open, and honest. If a faculty member has a concern, this should be a
safe place in which to raise it. The president need not respond immediately,
but should acknowledge the issue and communicate her intention to look into
the situation. Then, without fail, she should do so. Whenever possible, a
response should be provided before the end of the next business day—either
the final answer or an indication of when one will be provided. This sort of
follow-through demonstrates the president's sincerity and reinforces to the
faculty that she recognizes their importance to the institution.

What is important to remember is that the tenor of these breakfast meetings
must be positive. These meetings should not evolve into an opportunity to gripe
or dump issues in the president's lap. The president must set the tone and
expectation for the meetings and impress upon participants that they represent
opportunities to informally discuss challenges, initiatives, and other issues of
the day. It also is important to talk about the positive things that are occurring
on campus.

When selecting the attendees, care must be taken to invite faculty with
credibility, who care about the institution, and who are willing to speak the
truth to power. The president should suggest some topics for discussion so that
the dialogue becomes two-way and not focused solely on issues of concern to
the faculty. It is just as important for the president to learn from the faculty as
it is for them to learn from her. Some presidents do some gentle brainstorming
about an issue just to stimulate discussion and see where faculty sit on a given
issue. Holding these meetings early in the morning (e.g., 7:30 or 8:00) tends to
ensure that only the dedicated will attend.

Other presidents use an open breakfast or even brown-bag lunch meeting for
faculty on a monthly basis. This kind of gathering is much more informal and
serves primarily as an opportunity to build connections with faculty as opposed
to addressing substantive issues. On the other hand, it can be a very effective
forum in which to float trial balloons on complex issues. The key is for her to
make it very clear that she is sharing preliminary thinking solely for the purpose
of obtaining input.

It is important for the president to communicate an openness and respect for
faculty in as many ways as possible. Attending faculty events (e.g., colloquia,
lectures, symposia) is important and should be scheduled into the president's
calendar to the extent possible. When a faculty member is awarded tenure, a
personal phone call or note is a much appreciated gesture. When a significant
grant or award is earned by a faculty member or department, once again, personal acknowledgement by the president is important. Personal contact is always

better than a note or phone call, so whenever that can happen, he should seize the opportunity. A president should not worry if he cannot acknowledge every worthy event or action. Having the reputation of doing it when possible further demonstrates his respect for the faculty.

When a self-study or strategic planning process is undertaken, extensive faculty participation should be encouraged. All three authors have been involved with strategic planning processes in higher education. Typically, a diverse and highly credible steering committee is created to help manage the complexity of an institution-wide planning process. The failure to include adequate numbers of faculty is sure to damage the president's reputation and, even worse, produce suboptimal results.

We believe strongly that 50 to 60 percent of the steering committee members should come from the faculty ranks because, if faculty do not trust and buy into the planning process, it will not succeed. The ideal scenario is to have a highly credible faculty member serve as co-chair of the steering committee along with a high level administrator (e.g., provost, chief business officer).

Two of the authors have worked with several institutions at which the new president insisted on complete transparency with the budget process. When the money is a mystery, cynicism grows widely and wildly. These presidents put faculty at the table when budget issues are discussed and insist on clear and accurate information from administrative departments, especially if there is bad news. They also provide an outcomes report via an open forum to present the coming year's budget and respond to questions. These presidents are convinced that the transparency has helped reduce cynicism and build trust among faculty.

The bottom line for a president is to build a consultative mind-set with the faculty. This does not mean that the faculty must have a voice in every decision, because that would slow the institution to a glacial pace. It means, however, that on substantive issues, the president will seek their advice and opinion in a variety of constructive ways. Managing the level of consultation is the art and craft of leadership. When done well it conveys respect for the faculty's unique role and contribution.

BUILD THE SENIOR LEADERSHIP TEAM

A new president can use the time between the appointment announcement and her arrival on campus to form an initial sense of the senior leadership team. Typically the senior leadership team members are present at the board of trustees' announcement and early welcome of the new president.

In the best circumstances there are opportunities for the president to be on campus informally prior to officially taking office. It is important to take advantage of these early campus visits to arrange informal individual meetings with each vice president and other cabinet members. Such meetings will allow the president to gain an understanding of the particular responsibilities of the person and their unit, their background, expertise in their field, professional skills, and aspirations—both for themselves and for the institution. Very often the story of the institution as viewed through the eyes of the senior team provides helpful perspective for a new president and alerts her to sensitive issues at the same time.

Getting to Know the Team and the Issues

One of the primary goals of a new president is to learn as much as possible about the institution—both its strengths and anticipated future challenges—and do it as quickly as possible. Team members will appreciate being asked to share their individual perspectives on their unit's recent accomplishments and those of the institution as a whole. If the right climate is set from the outset, they will be completely candid when sharing the upcoming future challenges, again both for their areas and, from a strategic perspective, for the entire institution.

Asking the cabinet members to prepare a short summary of institutional challenges can provide an incoming president with a range of issues that can guide the agenda for the first year or even longer. This process is no substitute for the strategic audit but, when that process has not been followed, it can provide useful information. And, when there is a strategic audit report available, the president can compare that report with what he receives from the cabinet members to look for congruence or inconsistencies. The latter can form the basis for exploratory discussions in one-on-one situations.

One president requested each cabinet member (i.e., vice presidents, deans, and the executive assistant) to send him a brief memo prior to his arrival. Each person was asked to provide their assessment of the most significant accomplishments of the past two years, the most critical challenges in their area anticipated during the next two years, the institutional challenges on the horizon, and their advice on how to manage those challenges. This particular team had been a cohesive and stable group, with many of the members in their positions for five to ten years.

These simple questions created a database of valuable information. The memos contained a synopsis of the recent past, the challenges unique to each division of the institution, upcoming institutional challenges, and good insights on how the campus would view these challenges. Most importantly, the president received tangible helpful information at the outset of his presidency. Another by-product of this fast exercise was that the president was able to see consensus from the team and read the real enthusiasm with which this team was aggressively charting the institution's future.

The senior leadership team should not be the only source of this information. However, members of a well-developed team often have an institution-wide perspective and a personal investment in success, and can provide a multidimensional picture of the unique challenges from several vantage points.

The New President's Education

Once on campus, additional outreach to each senior team member individually can benefit both parties as they begin to know one another and understand their respective leadership styles. During the first three months in office, one president scheduled a dinner one night each week with a different member of the senior leadership team. It took valuable time, but each member chose a different restaurant and the president was exposed to different areas of the city while also getting to know his team members more directly.

It is important to assist a new president with identifying the issues to which she needs to devote attention, in both the short and long term. Each vice president can provide the factual information on issues, the history, and potential pitfalls that are essential for her to understand early in her tenure. While presidents' backgrounds vary, the transition requires a substantial investment of time to learn each area and the issues, as well as pick up on the culture and traditions.

Advancement professionals are typically the first in line to meet the president and engage her in the pleasant task of meeting alumni, donors, and potential benefactors. The nucleus of many capital campaigns is defined in these early days. Linking fund-raising to the institutional strategic plan provides a valuable exercise, as well as an exciting platform from which to pursue long-term fund-raising projects. The caution in this area is that the president not be encouraged to spend excessive amounts of time away from campus in these pursuits. Some travel will be unavoidable but, whenever possible, gatherings for alumni, donors, and others should be scheduled on campus. In addition to allowing the president to remain visible on campus by avoiding excessive travel, this approach also enables the institution to showcase itself and to allow alumni to reconnect with the institution.

In the academic arena, the provost provides background on shared governance, faculty senate issues, curriculum, and the unique aspects of each school or college. As the heart of the institution, forming the relationships with faculty and understanding the curriculum are critical in the early months of the presidency. The provost is the conduit to the deans and academic department heads. Many presidents seek to have meetings with each academic unit during their first year on the job. The provost can help establish the sequence in which these meetings should take place.

The chief business officer provides the president with a wide array of information needed to help him better understand the institution. These include the details of the budget, various audit reports, project financing approaches, debt covenants, and other significant transactions that are in progress. Additionally, it usually is the chief business officer who is most directly involved in town-gown relations from a business perspective. There are significant business interactions between institutions and their surrounding community such as key vendor relationships, payments in lieu of taxes, and various zoning issues. For this reason, the chief business officer plays a critical role in orienting the new president regarding this aspect of the community.

It is critical for the president to understand the wide range of information under the purview of the chief business officer, and particularly to become comfortable with the general approach to resource allocation. It also is valuable at the beginning to take the time to learn the important details of critical policies and procedures in areas such as hiring, procurement, expense reimbursement, and entertainment. In this way the president is knowledgeable enough about the policies to share responsibility and set expectations for consistent adherence by others.

On one campus the student life team decided to prepare a document that included their individual résumé information highlighting skill sets as well as descriptions of each department in the unit and a profile of the students being served. It was a useful snapshot for a president to have, even before getting the opportunity to meet the individuals.

Like the chief business officer, the vice president for student affairs plays an important role in town-gown relations—especially for residential institutions. One of the most vexing issues for residential campuses is the impact of students on the neighboring community. Whether it is fraternity parties, students walking to and from local entertainment districts, or violations of noise ordinances, the vice president for student affairs is the point person for the institution. The chief business officer usually tackles issues related to parking, security, and the adequacy of campus housing, but the remaining student-related issues fall under the purview of the vice president for student affairs. The president will spend a significant amount of time with both officers gaining a comprehensive understanding of the relevant town-gown issues.

As is true for the provost, the vice president for student affairs can help prioritize the president's efforts with student groups. In most cases, it automatically will start with the student government association leaders. In a few cases, however, this may not be the key group for the president to engage. For instance, at some community colleges, the most important group may be the clubs organized around career interests.

This discussion focuses on the most typical senior leaders with whom the new president will interact to obtain a sense of current issues and existing priorities. This is not an exhaustive list, however. Beyond the four vice presidents discussed here, depending on the size of the institution, its mission, and the number of cabinet members, a new president may find herself meeting with a general counsel, athletics director, vice president for research, chief information officer, chief enrollment management officer, diversity officer, mission officer (particularly in religiously-affiliated institutions), and potentially many more positions. The key for the new president is to identify the individuals within the leadership hierarchy with whom she should have one-on-one contact very early in her tenure—potentially even before her first official day on campus as president.

Composition of the Senior Leadership Team—Expectations and Fit

While the president is working to get to know the members of the senior leadership team, they also are investing energy in getting to know and understand him. The interpersonal dynamics, personality, and fit of the team members with the president take time to establish. The president will be formulating his team strategy, desired organizational structure, and working style with this group throughout the first year.

Presidents come from a variety of types of organizations inside and outside of academe, from small or large institutions, with flat or complex organizational structures, etc. A president needs to ask himself whether the existing inherited structure suits him. Are there too many direct reports? Too few? How many direct reports does he feel his own style will accommodate while still being productive? If there are many direct reports, the question becomes, is there a benefit to having direct information from a diverse group of reports for the first couple of years? Will this entail more time than he is comfortable allocating? Are there ways to utilize individuals differently to advance the president's and the institution's agenda? Is the team well established and, if so, will changes be received favorably? How will the faculty and staff view organizational shifts? Are there compelling reasons to make changes early in the game?

Personalities, length of tenure in the positions, and organizational climate all weigh into decisions about reorganization. If the team is solid and it is desirable to maintain the players for the short term, it is often best to go slowly with restructuring and utilize natural turnover to effect the desired structure over time. If there are clear gaps in the structure or there is a need for more coordination between units, it is recommended that the president announce his preferences early on. That can lead to a modified reporting structure, as he takes the time to methodically define the positions and assemble the appropriate team members. In these situations, it is important to provide careful and clear communication to the university community about changes in both the structure and the appropriate decision-making channels. This will help manage expectations and build confidence in the new administration.

Another gauge of the strength of the team is the level of esteem with which individuals are held in the community. While weighing this clearly nebulous characteristic, it is important to remember that anyone who has made decisions has made some people unhappy. The key is to seek an understanding of whether the individuals are respected and viewed as strong contributors to the mission and progress of the institution.

As discussed in chapter 2, we recommend an off-site retreat with the senior team early in a new president's tenure. Such retreats, if properly planned and executed, will contribute significantly to the effective working relationships between the president and his senior team, as well as among the team members.

Changes in the Leadership Team

With changes in leadership more the norm than not, it is important for the president—to the extent possible—to anticipate some turnover, and prepare well-managed transitions for the senior leadership team as it occurs. This is always critical, but even more so in the first year of the presidency when his own transition into the university community is still underway.

Experience indicates that the addition of a new member into a team is not always completely smooth sailing. Performance issues and incompetence should be addressed by the incumbent president prior to her departure. On the other hand, it is not always possible to anticipate that a team member will not be a good fit with the new president or that a different skill set will be required. New presidents will have to pay close attention to their cabinet members to assess whether they will provide what the new president and the institution need.

Upon arrival on his campus, one president concluded early on that one of the vice presidents was not a good match for his position. The president was not confident that this individual would be able to lead the division and carry out the aggressive plans in place, let alone the expansion of those plans envisioned by the new president. This was one of those times when it was necessary to make the difficult decision early in a presidency that someone is not a good fit. The vice president sensed the president's hesitancy during their early conversations and, after only two months, offered to tender his resignation. While it was early and somewhat abrupt, the president accepted the resignation and was able to name a former vice president as interim, thereby providing some stability and continuing progress on the plans.

Some presidents have utilized a trusted consultant who knows them well to assist with assessing strengths and weaknesses of the team members and their potential fit with the president's personality and work style. The consultant can be helpful with the process of setting initial team goals and aligning the team's process with the new president's preferred style. A consultant also can help frame the exit strategy when a team member needs to go. Other data that can assist in team analysis and assessment include climate surveys or other instruments utilized to critique institutional effectiveness. Review as much background material as possible to assist in assessing the team and its effectiveness.

If clashes develop over time between members of the senior leadership team, one thing is certain—problems at the senior level do not go away by themselves. One president relayed a situation in which two vice presidents were continually at odds with each other. This had reached the point when it had become disruptive and unproductive. He told them, "If you don't fix this, one of you won't be around next year." They fixed it. Being direct is not easy, but it usually works—one way or the other.

Often senior team members who have been in conflict on various issues over a protracted period of time simply are unable to resolve their differences. Conflict is a healthy by-product of human interaction. If managed appropriately, it can contribute significantly to the quality of outcomes. When not managed well, and especially if allowed to continue for long periods of time, conflict leads to dysfunctional behavior within a team as members anticipate and try to cope with it. In the long run, this drains energy and interferes with the effective resolution of issues.

When conflict produces dysfunctionality, it takes strong negotiation skills or the intervention of a skilled facilitator to assess the situation and change behavior. While this sometimes can be accomplished successfully, we heard several examples from presidents who concluded that the removal of one person was necessary to enable the team to move forward. It is difficult to do this and there are many risks attached to the first new hires a president undertakes.

When it becomes necessary to replace a member of the cabinet, the president must ensure that a credible search process is conducted. Extra care must be taken if the president leans toward hiring someone with whom he has worked previously. There will be a natural tendency on the part of the institutional community to question whether the selection was merit-based or cronyism. A new president should consider carefully whether the former colleague being hired really is the best person for the position. If not, he would be wise to pass on selecting someone just because they represent a known commodity.

Individual Relationships with Team Members

The new president needs to maintain a balance of empowering his vice presidents, while also staying on top of issues and being careful to avoid micromanaging. It is a rhythm that takes time to develop, but it starts as soon as the president is announced. While in the learning mode, the president needs to establish how much information is desired and how often he wants to receive it. Regularly scheduled individual meetings with each team member can provide the setting for negotiating this balance.

If the senior leadership team is large, and includes positions beyond the vice presidents, such as deans, the athletics director, general counsel, and others, it is conceivable that presidents will incorporate additions to the senior leadership team almost annually as the result of normal turnover. Under this scenario the team is continually re-framing itself to accommodate the new personalities and styles. One desirable practice that some presidents utilize in hiring new team members is to have the search committee chaired by a current member of the team. They frequently also arrange for the other team members to be part of the interview process so that they will feel comfortable with the selection. It is always a good process for senior position hires to be made with significant input from the cabinet. This approach may take a little more time, but it leads to a more collegial environment among the senior staff and smooths the transition of new members.

Many presidents tell us that they utilize regularly scheduled one-on-one meetings for authentic consultation and as an opportunity to focus on the critical topics. The timing of the one-on-one meetings varies from weekly, to biweekly, to monthly. The president's schedule typically is the constraining factor. With a large number of direct reports with whom the president must meet, and the normal complexity of his schedule, ad hoc meetings are almost out of the question for most presidents. The goal for one-on-one meeting cycles is for the president to gain an understanding of significant issues, provide counsel to the cabinet members, stay on the same page with them, and ensure that the agenda keeps moving.

Not all presidents are comfortable with standing one-on-meetings. Because of the challenges with the calendar described above, some presidents prefer not to have so much time taken up with standing meetings. Although this may ease the burden on the president's calendar, it adds complexity to the cabinet members' professional lives. They are put in the position of competing with everyone else for time on the president's calendar. It also means that the president and the cabinet members must rely on other forms of communication such as e-mail or memoranda. Although this is acceptable for many routine matters, there are occasions when it is essential to have face-to-face communication. When these situations arise, it can mean significant disruption to the existing schedule for both individuals.

It is important to negotiate annual goals with each direct report and ensure that each has the resources and support needed to be successful. This process provides the framework for setting institutional goals as well as individual personal and professional goals. It is an invaluable practice, enabling the president to ensure that his priorities are reflected in each cabinet member's goals for the year. It also is the most direct way to maintain accountability.

Individual and team relationships also are strengthened when the president hosts social gatherings involving spouses and partners. It is a way of building relationships and setting a tone of camaraderie that pays dividends when facing the daily difficulties of managing a complex organization. Such relationships prove even more valuable when crises arise.

Senior Team Process

It is typical for the president's senior leadership team to include the provost, vice presidents, and, in some cases, academic deans as well. But there are many other valuable voices to have in the room, and it is up to the president to determine if she wishes to expand the group either permanently or periodically. And, if so, she must determine the regularity with which the expanded group meets.

While the size of the institution often dictates the number and scope of positions, it is not uncommon for the president to invite others to participate periodically. Examples of individuals who may be at the table include the athletics director, budget director, general counsel, senior communications officer, diversity officer, and faculty governance representatives. Many presidents include a combination of these individuals in their ongoing leadership team; others only meet with an expanded group periodically (e.g., monthly or quarterly).

There are several meeting models that presidents utilize to leverage the strengths of the team and avoid a silo mentality. We learned of weekly meetings, biweekly, and monthly meetings. Presidents use formats ranging from extensive information sharing on a long list of discussion items to very focused attention to a limited number of topics. One president holds a weekly cabinet meeting on Monday mornings and also attends Wednesday lunch gatherings that are optional for his cabinet members. They attend whenever they are able because the luncheons are helpful in addressing issues that arise. The luncheons usually include a low-key informal agenda, focused on whatever issues are of greatest interest or concern.

Another popular configuration of the senior leadership team is a two-tier model wherein the president and vice presidents meet more frequently—say biweekly, and then are joined periodically (e.g., monthly) by the expanded senior leadership team. While not always popular with academic deans, it focuses the agenda more sharply and can be a better use of time. Often budget issues, new policy formulation, board of trustees' strategies, and crisis intervention are the types of topics handled separately with the vice presidents prior to including the expanded group in the conversation. If a two-tier system is in place, it is vital to communicate the outcomes of the vice presidents' discussion to the larger group. This can be done either by sharing minutes or by providing a summary at the start of the larger group meeting, in order to avoid duplication, division, resentment, or outright miscommunication.

Other presidents have told us that they avoid standing meetings altogether because there is a lack of energy and focus, preferring to have meetings only when there is a specific agenda item that warrants it. Part of the rationale for this is the complexity of the president's calendar described above. One president relying on this approach indicated that it is much more efficient for him to obtain information through reading than listening. When necessary, he follows up with personal interaction to supplement the written information. Irrespective of the method chosen, keeping the team connected and interacting with one another is the goal.

Once the meeting attendees are determined, the president will need to develop a format and regular meeting cycle for the senior leadership team as she charts the course of her first year. Decisions to be made include who contributes to the agenda, how often meetings are held, their format, and who keeps the minutes. An appropriate balance of time spent on informational items, decision topics, and future planning is desirable. At this stage, the president's goal is to identify new ways for the team to work together that meld with her style and personality.

When considering ways to work with the senior leadership team through meetings, it is helpful to begin by examining the way it has functioned in the past. First, consider productivity. Do team members feel that the time allocated to meetings is well utilized? Is there always an agenda with suggested times indicated? Are there clear expectations for the outcome of each topic on the agenda (e.g., information, input, decision)? Is the time well spent on substantive items? Enough information shared? Or too much time on information sharing and not enough on decision making? The goal should be to develop a collective sense of ownership, avoid silos, and leverage the time and talents of the participants.

The next consideration is the group's collective skill sets and expertise. Is there a blend of people who are creative and innovative, as well as people who observe process and seek closure? Do their strengths complement each other? Or are there several financial experts and no one who promotes student needs? Does the group work on strategic issues as well as operational, short-term decisions?

Third, an essential element of team process is trust. Is there a high level of trust and openness within the group? Can individuals challenge one another without rancor? Are there regular productive exchanges of ideas? Is anyone isolated or unwilling to participate?

Strong teams tend to have explicitly stated expectations around decision making. A president often seeks wise counsel prior to making decisions, and also reserves the right to give other team members her input on decisions that she is delegating. One president informed the team that he would utilize a three-option model: your decision with my input, my decision with your input, or my decision alone. When each decision is approached from this vantage point, it is relatively straightforward for team members to understand the process and recognize when input from them is expected. Avoiding surprises around important decisions is essential for effectively forming new relationships to produce a smooth-functioning team.

Another valuable way to manage the agenda productively is to create cross-functional teams. These are particularly useful on issues that require input and cooperation from several units. Typically several cabinet members come together to study an issue and develop recommendations which then are shared with the full cabinet, including the president. These cross-functional teams generate critical levels of understanding from the different areas of the institution, and often bring the best skill sets to the challenges at hand.

We talked with a president who relies on an interesting technique to ensure that the team members are appropriately engaged with one another. On an irregular basis he will assign an issue to a cabinet member, without providing any guidance about which other units need to have input to the issue. Once the due date for the response arrives, the president pays close attention to how much collaboration is indicated by the solution or proposed approach. If he feels there is insufficient collaboration, he will counsel the individual about the need for it. This approach has worked well and the president finds himself experimenting in this way much less frequently than when he first assumed the presidency several years ago.

Organizational Structure Considerations

Operationalizing the day-to-day work of the institution should lead the president to identify the second in command so that there are clear understandings of how things will operate during the president's absence. This clear assignment of responsibility naturally leads to a regular consultative process of decision making on an ongoing basis.

In many institutions the provost traditionally is designated the number two. Because the academic agenda is paramount, the provost can be a natural fit for leading the institution whenever the president is away. Other institutions employ a model which utilizes an executive vice president position. When this position is not filled by the provost, it typically has responsibility for coordinating the administrative and financial activities within the institution. It is not uncommon for the executive vice president to fill the number two role at the institution.

Large research institutions often utilize the chief operating officer model to coordinate the inside matters, freeing the president to focus more externally. Often the person in the chief operating officer position previously served as the provost or chief business officer. It is somewhat rare for new presidents to be comfortable with this approach because it can interfere with their ability to establish themselves within the institution. Once they have had sufficient time to learn about the institution and its issues, and have developed effective internal relationships, it can be an attractive model at particularly complex institutions.

The final approach that seems to be employed at a number of institutions is rotating responsibility. This is common at small to medium-sized institutions, when the president prefers not to give one individual the added authority that comes with being a designated number two. In these situations, the senior leaders either rotate or share the responsibility during the president's absence. In a rotational approach, the assignments are tracked so that, each time the president is traveling, the person next in line is assigned the acting president's role. In a shared approach, the provost handles academic issues, the chief business officer takes care of administrative issues, the chief student affairs person handles any student problems that arise, and so on. If a situation arises that is not clearly within one of these areas, the principals usually will discuss the issue and reach a decision together.

Cabinet Members' Interaction with the Board of Trustees

It is valuable to set ground rules on communication with trustees. Some models utilize individual vice presidents as staff to board committees and they often provide information for the executive committee as well. It is important at the outset of a presidency to be explicit about expectations regarding who will communicate with whom and how the president will be kept informed. If the communication is shared with the president and he is continually updated on the conversations taking place, there is less likelihood of divergent agendas or conflicting information reaching the board table. It also creates the opportunity to head off mismanagement before it gains momentum.

While there is a need to be responsive to trustee requests for information, presidents should take time to review information with the senior leadership team (or at least inform them) prior to sharing information at a board meeting. The failure to do so can result in the president being embarrassed because of an oversight or other error.

We found that there are many approaches to preparing for board meetings. Some presidents rehearse every aspect, while others are comfortable with very free-flowing conversations. Either approach is fine as long as the board is comfortable with it, and each staff person knows the limits of his or her participation.

It is important for the senior team members to be well prepared and to anticipate potential questions when approaching board meetings. When strategic issues are under consideration, it is even more important to be in sync before entering the board room. The plans should be well thought out and developed with appropriate input before the meeting. Presenting information at a board meeting that members of the senior team have not seen in advance can cause consternation among team members and portray a team that is not unified and well prepared. Additionally, doing this is likely to result in suboptimal results because it fails to leverage the strengths and knowledge of the full leadership team.

Mentoring New Members of the Team

Long after the president has transitioned into the institution, new members will continue to join the senior leadership team. As new vice presidents and deans are appointed, it is valuable to provide a transition plan for these individuals. This pays dividends for the individual as well as the institution. In addition to regular communication and welcome events, it is important to provide new team members with a way for shared learning to occur.

We're familiar with one model that has functioned well for a number of years. Whenever a new senior leader is appointed, the president assigns two veteran team members to serve as mentors to the individual for the first six to nine months. This triad becomes a mini-learning network for the new team member. The veteran team members have a vested interest in assisting the new team member to be successful. The role of the mentors is multifaceted and generally what one would expect in the circumstances:

- Share institutional history.
- Provide a safe space in which to ask questions about sensitive issues or request in-depth explanations.
- Offer clarification of policies and procedures.
- Provide guidance on planning and budgeting procedures.
- Help the individual understand the nuances of the institution's mission.
- Serve as a sounding board for new ideas that the new team member may offer.
- Identify pitfalls before the team member encounters them.

The time commitment is fairly nominal—a couple hours per month (usually over lunch)—and intermittent phone calls. This gradually decreases as time passes and the leader becomes established. This mentoring process provides a foundation upon which many good working relationships are formed. It does not guarantee the successful transition of every new team member, but it typically provides a strong start. The process creates a central source of information for the new team member that might otherwise take months to develop.

Throughout this process the president checks in with the individual and the mentors to track progress and offer assistance if needed. In this way the mentoring process also provides early warning signals in the rare case when the new member is not transitioning in well.

Despite following an appropriate search process, there are occasions when the new hire simply is not a good fit for the team or the institution, is alienating a constituency, or is in need of additional professional development. Having a formal mentoring process creates a mechanism for addressing these issues should they develop.

A WELL-ORGANIZED PRESIDENT'S OFFICE CAN MAKE ALL THE DIFFERENCE

The reputation of the president's office is symbolically and functionally important to a campus. While it is rarely practical for a president to have a completely open-door policy, the ability to masterfully meet the myriad of requests for the president's time is a reflection on the president herself. As the campus is adjusting to the new president, she and the staff members working in the president's office go through their own adjustments. There sometimes is a fluid continuation of the protocols and processes set up under the previous president. More likely the new president will have her own unique way of operating along with expectations of how the ideal office should be organized.

A new president may prefer a traditional arrangement. With this approach positions are defined in a straightforward manner, utilizing one contact—typically with a title similar to the assistant to the president or chief of staff—who manages the day-to-day activities in the office. This includes overseeing the other staff members, managing incoming and outgoing correspondence, managing the president's calendar, coordinating the president's on-campus and off-campus events, managing the president's residence, and serving as the point person for contact on sensitive issues.

Other presidents prefer to rely on a cadre of staff who divide the responsibilities, with no individual serving as first among equals. This approach tends to be harder to manage because it does not provide a clear path to the president for important issues that arise. Some presidents prefer it at the outset, however, until they have developed a sense of the capabilities of the existing staff.

If the previous president's staff remain in their positions, one approach for the new president is simply to leave things operating as they did previously. The new president can simply extend existing assignments and responsibilities, while sharing her preferences about calendar, travel, correspondence, and other matters to guide the staff. As the president gets used to the staff and they become familiar with her, changes can be made to ensure a good fit.

It is not uncommon for the details to take some time to define. Some areas that may take a while to fall in place are listed below:

- Communication mechanisms. Does the president prefer to use daily check-in meetings? Does she accept interruptions for quick questions? Is e-mail preferred for particular items like phone messages?

- Correspondence preferences. Who opens, sorts, and drafts responses to incoming mail? Is the writing style and precision of correspondence meeting the president's expectations? Will a staff member monitor e-mail throughout the day? Prepare replies?

- Scheduling considerations. Does the president prefer to reserve time in the late morning and at the end of the day to return calls? Does she like her schedule to revolve around her high energy periods, or is she more flexible about this? Which meetings should take place in her office versus the conference room?

These are just a few of the day-to-day details that need to be sorted out and understood in order to provide for a productive and effective office environment.

During the course of the first year, the daily routine becomes established to meet the demands of the position as well as the new president's needs and preferences. This year will include numerous firsts such as the first full cycle of the academic year, including opening fall and spring events, first round of board meetings, first holiday celebrations, countless mandatory meetings, convocation, and commencement. It may be possible to define ground rules at the outset that will guide the office processes and set the pace.

New presidents should count on a full calendar leaving little flexibility to find time away or even quiet time in the week to reflect, write, and plan. Ideally, the president can rely on staff and senior team members to assist in protecting the president's time. This involves reserving the president's attendance for only those times when it is absolutely required, and not for every event or opportunity for which she receives an invitation. Allowing the president to remain informed, without requiring her to be continually present, is a difficult balance to strike. Success in this area can make the competing demands of the position more manageable.

The goal should be for the president's office to be welcoming, while at the same time assuring that the president's time is protected and effectively used. The demands of the first year typically are heavier and more time-consuming than anticipated, and a smooth-functioning office is one key to success. Factors that contribute to this include filtering communication, managing the travel and meeting commitments, and enabling the president to be responsive by effectively managing the workflow.

The president and her staff should assess progress on the details regularly (perhaps monthly at the beginning) to prevent frustration from building up. A formal assessment of staffing levels and position descriptions after six months, and again at the end of the first year, will ensure that the right structure is in place. As these reviews occur, the necessary adjustments can be made to match the preferences and the personality of the president.

***

This chapter highlights the criticality of the president's relationship with four important constituencies: the board (or system office), the faculty, the senior leadership team, and the president's staff. This is not to suggest that other relationships are unimportant; just that these are the ones that most directly influence the president's ability to have a successful tenure. Failure to pay attention to any of these may cause the president to find himself engaging in ongoing crisis management as opposed to planful leadership.

Presidents must attend to numerous additional constituencies and stakeholders including students, alumni, donors, athletic boosters, elected and other local and state officials, business partners. Each of these groups has a particular interest in the institution and what takes place on its campus. At different times, each of them can become a priority.

When a campus seeks to expand its borders, the neighborhood activists, mayor, and local business owners take on tremendous significance. If the institution seeks to offer a new degree program, and the state education regulations require approval from the department of education, those officials become a top priority. Obviously, while in the midst of a fund-raising campaign, every alumnus and past or prospective donor becomes a target of attention. The difference between these examples and the four constituencies mentioned above is that their importance varies based on the institution's agenda at a point in time. For the former group, there is no cycle; they remain critically important at all times.

GOING ON THE ROAD TO CONNECT WITH TRUSTEES
DONALD R. EASTMAN III, PRESIDENT, ECKERD COLLEGE

In accepting the presidency of a small, young, underfunded liberal arts
college with a recent history of budgetary overruns of mammoth propor-
tions, I knew the future of the college and the success of my tenure with
it depended upon a strong, supportive and engaged board of trustees. This
was the same board, by and large, that had presided over these monstrous
budgetary overruns. It was clear to me that I needed to understand where
the board was on the major challenges facing the college, and where they
thought we needed to go. I had my own ideas, but I needed to know
which ones were going to be immediately embraced, and which were
going to require a longer campaign of persuasion.

But a board of trustees is an abstraction. One does not persuade a
board; one persuades *members* of the board. So I quickly concluded,
despite my concern about the perception of my being off-campus for the
first four weeks of my service as president (Would they think I was lazy?),
that I needed to visit the college's trustees right away, individually, on
their turf (e.g., office, house, vacation house, or boat).

And so I did, visiting our out-of-state trustees from California to
Connecticut over a two-week period, and the in-staters in the two
weeks which followed. Those visits, the relationships I established, and
the things I learned gave me the best possible start on what is now a
six-year term of office full of challenges and successes.

I developed a questionnaire, which included questions about perceptions of the strengths and weaknesses of the college programs, staff, institutional positioning, budgeting process, communications, trustee
meetings, and trustee involvement. I asked how they ranked the college
among their philanthropic priorities, what they wanted to give in the
future, and what was the basis of their connection to the college. I asked
about their own educational background. (I had briefings before I went,
but I wanted to see and hear them relate their life's stories. Sometimes
the briefings missed the most important themes, even though the details
were correct.) I also asked about their families, spouse, hobbies, and hopes
for the college.

I asked for their advice, and for their support in what we both knew was
going to be a tough year, if not a tough decade. (It was, and is, and they
have been wonderfully supportive.)

The results of this odyssey were extraordinary. Within a month of
becoming president, I knew more about more trustees, and about their
views of the past and future of the college, than anyone—including any
trustee. I received a truckload of good advice, and even the bad advice

showed me where there was a misunderstanding and trustee work to be done. I immediately developed the beginning of a personal relationship with each trustee, and I began to understand what each trustee valued most in his or her service to the college. I learned which staff trustees particularly valued and that a few staff needed better coaching or to move on.

Perhaps most importantly, I began to develop the kind of trust I have needed to do my job, a job which has, from time to time, required leap-of-faith level trust.

That set of visits was simply the very best I could have had.

St. Petersburg, Florida
May 2007

BUILDING AND WORKING WITH A BOARD OF TRUSTEES
RITA BORNSTEIN, PRESIDENT EMERITA, ROLLINS COLLEGE

Following my election to the Rollins College presidency I was keenly aware that, although I had many enthusiastic supporters on the board, there were a few who were concerned. I was a Jewish woman coming from a university fund-raising vice presidency—an unusual choice for a liberal arts college founded by Congregationalists and historically led by men.

It helped that one of the trustees had nominated me for the position, knowing me from the University of Miami, where I'd served as vice president for development when he was a trustee. Another trustee had his concerns allayed after receiving a glowing reference from the chair of the Miami board, whom he had known many years earlier. Because of my background, I had to work hard to gain legitimacy from all constituencies at Rollins. The strong working relationship I developed with the board was one of the most important elements in my successful tenure as president.

One of the first things I did was to strengthen the composition of the board. Rollins had a good but very local board. Further, because there were no term limits there was little turnover. I had to persuade the board to petition the State of Florida to amend the charter to increase the maximum number of trustees allowable. Then I enlisted some of the key corporate and opinion leaders in the larger community as well as influential alumni from around the country. Working with the board's committee on trustees, I was able to recruit our first two African-American trustees and add several women. The stronger our board became, the easier it was to recruit new trustees.

Throughout my presidency I played a central role in identifying and recruiting new trustees and new board leadership. To be successful, presidents need boards that share their strategic perspectives; they also need chairs that are involved and supportive. As we strengthened and diversified the board, many of the old-timers expressed their pride in being part of such an esteemed group. I also thought it important to provide visibility to trustees and gave them leadership roles at our commencements and other public events.

When I came to Rollins it was significantly under-endowed for an institution with its aspirations. A few years into my presidency, I came to the board with a proposal to launch a fund-raising campaign for $100 million, two and a half times the amount raised in the prior campaign. The board was courageous in accepting my recommendation although, shortly thereafter, a few members decided to resign or move to honorary trustee status.

The board was very active in designing the campaign, identifying prospects, and helping with the solicitation of large gifts. A number, personally or through their corporations or foundations, were also major contributors to the campaign, which concluded after raising $160 million. Their advice was vital in the design and construction of the numerous facilities projects we undertook. They were also extraordinarily helpful in decisions about the acquisition of properties and the development of several commercial ventures. These projects all contribute to the programs and financial health of the college.

While very supportive of my vision and goals, board members were mindful of community values and the college's financial health. When I became interested in experimenting with a rather bold design for our museum, trustees pointed out that it would violate our historic and consistent style of architecture. They were right. When I was attracted by an opportunity to acquire a nearby law school, they advised that such a venture would be costly in terms of finances and administrative time. Although I was disappointed, they were correct about this as well. The accumulated wisdom of the board helped us achieve our goals while also helping us see the pitfalls of certain decisions.

Over the years we developed a thorough orientation program for new trustees, which also served as a refresher for continuing trustees. I maintained frequent and open communication with trustees, especially my chairs, alerting them to developing problems and negative press so that they would not be blindsided. I tried to make board and committee work more interesting and more strategic. We streamlined administrative and committee reports by including more material in the board books. We also began to include at least one strategic discussion in every meeting.

When I came to Rollins, I was frequently referred to as the "first woman president." I was pleased when, after several years, I became simply "the president." Nonetheless, I believe my gender influenced my relations with trustees, faculty, and other constituents. It took awhile for both men and women to understand how to relate to a female leader (and a male spouse). My relationships with trustees were cordial, respectful, but rather formal. We rarely socialized outside of college events. Since I do not play golf, I did not have the relaxed interactions available to those presidents who do. Most women presidents I know are less likely than their male counterparts to have these experiences.

The board found many ways of supporting my presidency. They paid me well, took opportunities to publicly indicate their enthusiasm for my leadership, and ignored the occasional negative voice. I recall a nasty, unsigned letter that came to all trustees during my early years asserting that the financial vice president and I were destroying the college. The trustee leadership responded immediately by telling me to ignore the letter. I was grateful.

During the last two years of my presidency I wrote a book about presidential legitimacy. I made a strong case for presidents not holding on to their positions for too long. Taking my own advice, I decided that 14 years would be a good run and that I could leave knowing that I had led a transformation of Rollins. The endowment was up from roughly $38 to nearly $300 million, we had established 23 endowed chairs and significant financial aid resources, and we had completed 24 construction projects. We had significantly more and better-qualified applicants, increased numbers of students, and a higher graduation rate.

When I announced my intention to step down, one of the nicest gestures the board made was to allocate an annual $10,000 stipend for a new "Bornstein Award for Faculty Scholarship" to be announced each year at commencement. There were also a series of memorable events and testimonials to mark the accomplishments of what was called, "The Bornstein Era." I felt good about my final contract and by the Board's assignment of an endowed chair for me, "The Cornell Chair in Philanthropy and Leadership Development."

At my last meeting, I recommended a series of changes that I thought would strengthen the board, including term limits. That idea sank like a lead balloon because trustees so enjoyed their close connection to the college and their ability to have an impact on its development. And, indeed, it is still an outstanding board. I was proud to have a well-functioning board to bequeath to my successor.

No relationship is more important to the success of a president than that with the governing board. I could not have accomplished as much as I did as president, and had as much fun doing it, without such an enthusiastic, supportive, and engaged board.

Winter Park, Florida
April 2007

THE FIRST FACULTY CONFLICT
TIMOTHY R. LANNON, S.J., PRESIDENT, SAINT JOSEPH'S
UNIVERSITY

There are several firsts that each president experiences that stay with you in a poignant way: the feeling of accomplishment after the first successful board meeting, the extraordinary pride in students after the first commencement exercises, the excitement (and relief) of the first seven-figure gift. There are other firsts that stay with you just as strongly, but are on the opposite end of the emotional spectrum. One of these is the first significant conflict with the faculty.

I was appointed president of Saint Joseph's University in 2003 and arrived in late July. As I set about engaging all the stakeholders of Saint Joseph's in conversations, I asked about their aspirations for the school and thus began to really know the campus and the issues.

By the fall of 2003 an issue arose—one that pre-existed my tenure as president. Back in the fall of 2001, as part of the regular annual cycle of discussions to develop the next faculty compensation package, members of the advisory board on faculty compensation had requested a form of paid family medical leave. Our faculty is not unionized, and the annual conversations about the compensation package take place as a give-and-take dialogue, sometimes resulting in a joint proposal for the budget committee and sometimes the outcome is a separate set of proposals from the faculty committee and the administration.

Faculty had asked the former provost and president for a policy that would allow paid time off to be used in the case of maternity leave, adoption of children, illness of children or aging parents, or other family emergencies. The faculty stated that both former senior officers agreed to the development of policy language, and in fact the faculty had been engaged with the director of human resources on the task. It was their contention that this was unfinished business that needed a resolution. When the draft policy was presented to the administration during the annual compensation discussions, there were so many critical issues unanswered that my uneasiness began to grow. The next question was raised by the brand new CFO who had just started shortly after I arrived three months prior. He asked to see the document that indicated the agreement of the administration to pursue the policy and the goals of the proposed policy. No written document could be located—by either the faculty or in the administrative offices.

When contacted, both the former president and provost recalled the request for paid family medial leave and both stated, independently, that they had asked for a list of items to be included in a policy. However, neither former administrator recalled agreeing to a particular version of a formal policy, and in their minds, the request for paid family medical leave was still at the early discussion stages. A cost analysis had not been performed, leave-time impact on colleges had not been assessed, the effect on the tenure clock for non-tenured faculty had not been decided, ramifications for other employee groups had not been identified. In short, there were many details that needed in-depth study.

The chair of the faculty advisory board concluded that the administration was not dealing in good faith. After all, she had a draft document that had been eighteen months in the writing, and she had discussed the topic broadly with faculty members. The provost and I felt like we were being pressured into a decision we were not ready to make. There was no documentation to indicate that there was a pre-existing agreement by the former president. There were simply too many unresolved issues and I was not willing to pursue this proposal or any other until all of the details were sorted out and verified.

This did not sit well with the faculty. The chair of the advisory board made a written report to the faculty senate declaring that the administration was not acting in good faith and would not honor the commitment to a paid family medical leave policy. She broadcast the message via e-mail and thus began a hailstorm of criticism leveled at the former and current leadership.

I must admit that both the venom and the method surprised me. I struggled with how to handle such an assault. Eventually, the provost and I made a list of the most important open issues surrounding the policy recommendations. I then contacted the chair of the advisory board by phone to discuss my position on the issue. I was honest in conveying my disappointment at this turn of events and the style with which it was handled, but more importantly I conveyed the strong message that I did not want this to become our method of dealing with one another. I asked the faculty member to agree to a process of talking one last time before reacting. That is, I asked that if she had an issue with me in the future, to pick up the phone and discuss it before going public. I gave her my cell phone number and told her to use it whenever needed. I was trying to set the stage for future, more productive ways of working together, and most importantly I wanted to empower her as a leader to deal effectively with the administration. It also took away some of the steam from the issue.

Many details were studied and solutions were developed. The provost and the CFO jointly provided support. The more critical topics included the development of options that would count toward alternative work arrangements when a faculty member returned in mid-semester from a family medical leave. Then the policy on rank and tenure review was amended to state that faculty members who utilize paid family medical leave would automatically have the tenure clock postponed one year, with the option of applying to have the original timetable remain in effect. After several revisions and amendments, with assistance of legal counsel, and including direct discussion between the administration and the faculty advisory board, a satisfactory paid family medical leave policy was adopted the following year.

In areas such as governance, contracts, and policy development, it is often the case that we wait it out, since there are typically processes in place that facilitate topics to their conclusion. However, it is sometimes necessary to stop in midstream and confront the oppositional issues by meeting face to face. This approach is not easy, nor necessarily pleasant. But given the opportunity, both parties can vent their frustrations privately, prioritize their concerns, and move forward to negotiate a solution and avoid the consternation caused by public criticism and extended conflict that rarely lead to a productive solution.

Philadelphia, Pennsylvania
April 2007

NOTES

1. McLaughlin, Judith Block, ed. *Leadership Transitions: The New College President.* San Francisco: Jossey-Bass, 1996.

2. American Council on Education. *The American College President.* Washington: American Council on Education, 2007.

CHAPTER 4

Avoiding Mishaps and Self-inflicted Wounds

It's not only what new leaders *do* when they get to the top that gets them into trouble; it's also what they *don't* do.[1]

Plagiarism, infidelity, substance abuse, intemperate remarks, sexual harassment, lavish spending, and the list goes on. These represent just some of the reasons presidents have involuntarily left their positions in recent years. It seems that nearly every issue of *The Chronicle of Higher Education* includes a story about a president who has been fired, forced to resign, or is suffering the fallout from a vote of no-confidence.

And far too often the reasons these situations occur seem unimaginable. Could a president really believe that his marital infidelity with a coworker will go undiscovered? Is it possible that a president can make an inappropriate remark and expect to have it go unnoticed? With all the attention focused on presidential compensation, is it rational to expect that no one will notice when a president is reimbursed for what clearly are personal expenses? The answers to these questions seem obvious to those of us who spent any period of time working in higher education. Yet there are numerous examples of each of these transgressions—and many others—that have brought down accomplished scholars and, but for their character flaws, potentially great leaders.

There are at least two major categories of missteps of which presidents must be mindful. The first, and most difficult, category includes those issues that evolve from honest misjudgments and mistakes that occur in everyone's professional life. When not managed well, they can become a snowball rolling downhill that cannot be stopped even with a massive bulldozer. The second, and more damaging, category consists of failures of character. Although one can hope to survive the former, it is nearly impossible to move beyond the latter. This chapter examines the issues and actions that have led to involuntary departures and then provides advice on what presidents can do to avoid these situations.

When one looks closely at the specific situations surrounding involuntary presidential departures, several themes emerge. Presidents' careers have been derailed because of problems in the following areas: plagiarism/overstated credentials, financial impropriety, sexual impropriety, and various misdeeds involving intercollegiate athletics. Apart from these themes, presidents also are finding it difficult to retain their jobs during times of crisis. Naturally, expectations of leaders are highest during these situations. All too often presidents are found to be incapable of providing the leadership demanded by the situation.

There is one other theme that is harder to pinpoint because it usually is code for a wide range of somewhat ambiguous issues. Nevertheless, one cannot ignore the series of problems described simply as philosophical differences between the president and the board. The following examples in each of these areas are instructive because they demonstrate the extreme behaviors of some presidents.

PLAGIARISM/OVERSTATED CREDENTIALS

Given the importance of original scholarship in the academy and the emphasis on protecting one's academic integrity, it is hard to imagine that anyone in higher education would succumb to the temptation to claim another's work as their own. It seems even more unlikely that such actions could ever involve a president. Yet there are numerous examples of presidents presenting others' work as if it were original material. There also are cases of presidents obtaining their positions by overstating their credentials, claiming degrees that had not been earned or publications that did not exist. With the emphasis now being placed on the inclusion of formal background checks in the hiring process, these situations may become more rare. As the following examples illustrate, however, some individuals have been willing to cut many corners.

Plagiarism

A small liberal arts institution in the south found itself in hot water with its regional accrediting agency. In an effort to comply with the agency's procedural requirements, it provided corrective action plans that had been plagiarized from another institution. When the matter came to light, the president initially denied involvement. Eventually, the circumstances resulted in his accepting responsibility for the situation, forcing him to resign his position.

One would expect an institution's strategic plan to be unique and closely tied to the culture, character, and particular market in which the institution operates. Yet, in one recent case, a midwestern comprehensive university was found to have included in its plan substantial portions of another institution's plan. The individual involved previously worked for the other institution, and had contributed to the development of that institution's strategic plan. Nevertheless, following the release of an investigating committee's report, the chancellor was asked to vacate his position seven months prior to the scheduled termination of his contract.

Overstated Credentials

There have been numerous instances in recent years of college athletic coaches losing their jobs because of mistakes or outright lies in their résumés. With the increased attention focused on several of these situations, various faculty and campus administrators have been subjected to more intense scrutiny of their credentials. Faculty members at several institutions were forced to resign or were removed, and at least one college president resigned over this issue. The case involved a small liberal arts college on the East Coast, and once the issue arose, it dragged on for several years before culminating in an untimely resignation.

FINANCIAL IMPROPRIETY

Relatively few presidents come into the position with previous experience or education in finance or related subjects. Based on a recent study by the American Council on Education, more than 70 percent of presidents studied education or higher education, social sciences, or humanities/fine arts. The study does not indicate the percentage of presidents with academic background in finance or related subjects, but it discloses that only 7.5 percent of presidents responding had served in a financial or administrative position immediately prior to becoming president.[2]

Certainly many presidents have worked with budgets and/or financial information before taking on the position, but higher education finance at the institutional level is very complex. Whether a public or a private institution, there are challenges related to such topics as tuition discounting, deferred maintenance, grants management, compliance with donor restrictions, financing of capital projects, and investing endowments. Apart from these challenging individual topics, there is the larger issue of simply balancing the budget. Most boards establish a balanced budget as the minimally acceptable level of performance. With all the factors that affect the budget, it is not surprising that a number of presidents have been fired or forced to resign because of financial difficulties.

It is not always problems with balancing the budget that cause presidents to lose their jobs over financial matters. Lavish or otherwise inappropriate spending by the president frequently results in his dismissal. Strikingly, even with the publicity that such problems generate, they continue to occur. In the post-Enron era, with the advent of the Sarbanes-Oxley Act of 2002 (SOX), boards are paying significantly more attention to presidents' compensation and expense allowances. Although SOX is not directly applicable to colleges and universities, many trustees' background is in the corporate world. It stands to reason that they would be comfortable utilizing the same principles even though they may not apply technically. And any president who tries to rationalize practices that seem aggressive to their board will have a hard time doing so in the current climate.

Additionally, *The Chronicle of Higher Education* runs two issues each year high-lighting presidents' compensation (including benefits and deferred compensa-tion). One issue focuses on public institution presidents and the other on private institution presidents. In both cases, the coverage provides details about individual presidents by name. Although most people acknowledge the difficulty of running a college or university, few believe that it justifies salaries in the high six figures—or even higher. Appearing in the *Chronicle's* lists with a salary deemed excessive is a sure way to incur the wrath and watchful eye of new critics.

Lavish Spending

The most celebrated case of lavish spending in recent years involved the president of an eastern university. The situation drew widespread attention in the popular press and resulted in Congressional inquiries to the institution, as well as an audit by the Internal Revenue Service. Based on concerns reported to the board, an independent audit of the president's spending habits was conducted. The audit disclosed questioned costs in excess of $600,000 over a three-year period. In addition to extravagant meals and entertainment, it was alleged that the president had billed the university for tens of thousands of dollars for what represented personal expenses. The president's initial response was one of outrage and defiance. Ultimately, however, he resigned his position, albeit receiving a handsome severance package in the process.

The president of a large southern research university was fired for lavish spending barely more than a year after he took office. Not unlike the situation described above, this president was accused of charging the university for personal expenses. These included plane trips via the university's plane to visit his girlfriend in another city, nearly a half million dollars in unauthorized reno-vations to the president's residence, and another quarter million dollars in what were deemed to be excessive entertainment expenses. Part of the reason he was fired was the suggestion in the audit report that he had violated a number of state laws. Interestingly, subsequent investigations by state officials determined that no prosecutable offenses had occurred. This conclusion did not win his job back, although it did allow him to retain a sizable severance package.

Presidential Residence

At least two other presidents have lost their jobs in recent years because of issues related to the president's residence. Not unlike the case described above, one president of an eastern comprehensive university was forced to resign after being on the job for only nine months. The sole issue leading to his dismissal was the excessive cost of renovations to the president's residence. In another case, the president of a southern comprehensive university was accused of spend-ing nearly $650,000 over seven years for personal expenses, a sizable portion of which related to the president's residence. Because the board fired her for cause, the president's contract specified that she was ineligible for her severance package. Litigation will determine whether she qualifies for severance but, even if she receives it, it will not change the fact that she was fired in a very public way.

Fraud

Two community college presidents were forced to resign in the same week because of a wide range of financial improprieties. This situation, which occurred in a southwestern community college system, represented a fairly massive fraud. In addition to the theft of college-owned property and funds, there were allegations that enrollment reports were falsified. One of the presidents was accused of overlooking thefts from the college's athletics department. Additionally, it was alleged that both presidents traveled overseas at college expense to promote academic programs that failed to produce any enrollments.

SEXUAL IMPROPRIETY

In recent years, it seems that sexual improprieties have displaced poor financial performance or lavish spending as the number one reason for presidents losing their jobs. There is nothing unique about higher education that causes this to be a particularly difficult issue for presidents. Yet, because of the high standards to which presidents are held, these types of indiscretions simply are not tolerated. Whether a matter of sexual harassment, extramarital affairs, or sexual assaults, the principals are tainted and the damage to their reputations inevitably adversely affects their institutions as well. For these reasons, such charges—even when not provable in a court of law—usually result in the termination of presidents' contracts.

Sexual Harassment

Allegations of sexual harassment plague colleges and universities. The issue reached major levels during the 1990s when campuses established various internal policies and procedures designed to protect students, staff, and faculty from being subjected to harassment or exposed to hostile workplace environments. Claims of harassment are taken very seriously and investigations are routinely conducted. As one might expect, many claims prove difficult to substantiate. In other cases, however, ample evidence of the harassment is uncovered. Such was the case for the president of a midwestern community college. Although he denied the charges, he opted to retire rather than attempt to fight them while continuing to serve as president.

Harassment of a different type cost another president his position recently. It turns out that the sex scandals affecting the Catholic Church were not confined to parishes. The president of a midwestern university, a priest, resigned after admitting to inappropriate sexual behavior with a student at his former institution.

Extramarital Affair

The president of a major southern research university was never proven to have engaged in an extramarital affair but, in the end, the lack of proof did not matter. Several actions caused many to question his motives and involvement with a colleague, whom he had helped obtain a position at the university. He also intervened to help her obtain an even higher-paid position after a short period. And in at least one instance, questions were raised about her qualifications for the position. This led to an investigation by the local media. As news began leaking out, the president resigned for personal reasons.

In an even more serious matter, the president of a midwestern comprehensive university was forced to resign after trustees learned that he was the target of a police investigation of a sexual assault. The alleged assault occurred in the president's residence on the campus.

ATHLETICS

Athletics is a lightening rod for problems at many institutions. Clearly, for the so-called big-time programs, athletics activity consumes a substantial percentage of the operating budget. (Although there are a handful of institutions that generate a surplus from athletics, these are very much the exception. At most institutions, athletics is subsidized by other revenue sources.) Moreover, because of its importance to students, alumni, and in some cases the community, the stakes are very high. Apart from the importance the teams represent to the various stakeholders, it is also a high risk area for those institutions that are members of the National Collegiate Athletic Association. There are numerous instances of well-intentioned individuals who have run afoul of the complex rules that the NCAA imposes on institutions. The following examples, however, clearly represent instances of something other than good intentions.

Unethical Behavior

At one of the south's football powerhouses—a large land-grant university— the current coach was not producing the number of wins expected for the program. Of equal concern was the poor performance against the major instate rival. The president decided to take matters into his own hands. Along with the athletic director and two trustees, the president embarked on a clandestine trip to recruit a replacement coach. The fact that the target of the recruitment was under contract to a different institution was of little concern to the group. Nor did they feel it was necessary to inform the current coach or the prospect's employer of their interest in hiring him. Not surprisingly, despite initial denials, evidence of the meeting surfaced and it had to be acknowledged publicly. Within less then two months the president was forced to resign.

Academic Fraud

The pressure to win at one small northern liberal arts college led the president to become directly involved in matters affecting a star player's academic credentials. With the president's full knowledge, the athlete—who had completed a community college program leading to a welding certificate—was credited with the completion of an associate's degree. An associate's degree qualified him to play intercollegiate athletics. The matter came to light and triggered a series of events that ultimately led to the president being forced to resign.

PHILOSOPHICAL DIFFERENCES

This is a somewhat vague category because it is rare for the president or the board to offer specifics when a departure is triggered under these circumstances. We believe that these situations generally develop for one of two reasons. First, there are situations in which the search process was ineffective and insufficient attention was paid to the president's fit with the culture of the institution. Alternatively, problems arise when there is turnover within the board and new members push for a different direction. It is rare, in our experience, that a president decides unilaterally to depart from an agenda that had been developed collaboratively with the board.

Although "philosophical differences" is a vague term, which may represent all manner of disagreement between the president and the board, the situations are no less serious or destructive than when the issue is more concrete. Without question, institutions suffer from departures of this type. There are rare occasions when a president can leave unscathed, but it is just as likely that the president will be tainted, at least until a sufficient period of time has passed. If the president is able to obtain a significant position at another institution, or with one of the many higher education associations, it is possible that she can eventually obtain another presidency. Obviously that is much less likely in the situations described earlier.

The following examples are just a few of those that occurred in the months leading up to the publication of this book.

Board Interference

To some, the above caption may appear strange. Given the board's overall responsibility for the institution, in what ways might they interfere? What areas are off limits to the board? Actually, there are many ways in which a board can interfere with the president's efforts, especially when it comes to operational issues. In an ideal structure, boards focus on governance and policy while the president focuses on leading and managing the institution. There clearly are situations in which it is sometimes difficult to draw a bright line between policy and operations.

Such was the case for one southern community college. A small number of board members decided that they did not like the way the president was managing the institution. They inserted themselves in various operational issues to the point that the president concluded he no longer could lead the institution. Even though this was a minority of board members, it was a sufficient number to create a dysfunctional situation that the president chose not to tolerate.

The situation at one Ivy League institution did not rise to the level of micromanagement described above, but it still resulted in a premature departure. After a brief two-year tenure, the president abruptly announced his decision to resign the presidency. The reasons cited were somewhat vague, and it was suggested by the president and the chair of the board that it was a lack of agreement on the specific strategies to pursue toward achieving the institution's vision. Although there was agreement on the vision for the university, the president decided that he did not have the necessary latitude to lead the institution toward the vision.

A Poor Fit

An elite northern liberal arts institution experienced a very short presidency after making a nontraditional hire. Rather than select someone from within higher education, the board opted to hire a government official. This was the first presidency for the individual and his selection represented a departure from the board's past selections. During his two-year tenure, the president attempted to implement changes in areas that represented institutional sacred cows for various stakeholders. After being stymied and realizing that he lacked the board's support, he abruptly resigned the position.

AVOID PROBLEMS

Given that presidents are smart people who typically have spent many years building a career that resulted in them being selected for a presidency, how is it that so many have experienced such public troubles? For one thing, presidents are in the spotlight at all times. No matter how much one would like to take a day off from the job, it is just not possible for a president to do that. Even when traveling on vacation, they never know when an alumnus might be nearby. Or in the case of public institution presidents, it could be a taxpayer who recognizes them. And in this day of camera/video phones, the Internet, and blogging, the smallest incident can trigger a firestorm that could cost a president his job.

Beyond the alumnus or taxpayer who might take issue with something observed in an unguarded moment, there is a possibility of problems developing even closer to home. It is an unfortunate reality that there are malcontents within any organization. Some believe that they may be even more prevalent on college campuses simply because there are so many competing agendas and priorities. For this reason, there are individual members of the institutional community who scrutinize everything the president does—just waiting for the opportunity to pounce. These individuals include students, faculty, and staff.

Presidents must be mindful of all constituents and avoid giving them ammunition that can be used against them. The nature of the job requires presidents to make decisions that will be unpopular. Nothing can be done about that. But it is the truly foolish president who engages in the activities described earlier, thereby issuing an invitation for trouble.

New presidents must recognize that they have assumed a different role than any they've had before. A much higher performance and behavioral standard is established for them than for anyone else on campus. They are the face of the institution and they set the tone for how the institution operates. They must be mindful of this responsibility. The responsibility is somewhat offset by the personal satisfaction that comes with the opportunity to lead a higher education institution and to have such significant influence over so many futures. There are various perks and benefits as well. Managing one's appetite for such perks and benefits is a challenge, but it must be done.

Self-awareness

There are several general steps that a president can take to minimize the likelihood of significant problems developing. First, presidents must be incredibly self-aware. "Self-awareness means having a deep understanding of one's emotions, strengths, weaknesses, needs, and drivers."[3] Recognition of weaknesses is particularly valuable because it can help an individual remain grounded. It also can stimulate them to rely on others with more expertise in given areas. This accomplishes several things. It brings different thinking into the room and it reduces the likelihood of the president forging ahead in an area in which she has limited expertise.

Presidents must recognize that they are not infallible. There are going to be mistakes—some of their doing, and some that are the responsibility of others within the institution. The most important consideration with respect to the mistakes is to not attempt to hide them or cover them up. History is fraught with examples of situations that developed into major crises when a cover-up was discovered. In many instances, the transgression being covered up was minor compared to the firestorm that was created when the cover-up was discovered.

The decision about how public to be about mistakes must be made on a case-by-case basis. Some mistakes need only be acknowledged internally—for instance, within the cabinet. Others, however, require that the institution be very public about a situation, potentially even issuing a press release. Hank Brown, a former U.S. senator and currently president of the University of

Colorado, suggests that institutions "Be as frank about your blemishes as you are about your strengths."[4] This is excellent advice. We never have trouble touting our accomplishments, but it is much more difficult doing so with embarrassments. A better balance would serve presidents and their institutions well.

One note of caution though: It is important for the president to seek counsel from his or her cabinet, support group, or other trusted advisors—potentially even outside professionals—before deciding how to proceed when a significant mistake occurs. The more input, the better—especially to ensure that the response is commensurate with the issue.

Communication

Along similar lines, presidents can avoid many problems simply by communicating. There is no such thing as over-communicating when you are a president—especially with the board. The president should have regular communication with the board chair using whatever medium is desired by the chair. Many presidents with whom we spoke talked about regularly scheduled teleconferences with their chairs, ongoing e-mail exchanges, and even informal reports on various subjects. Establishing this sort of routine communication—covering both good news and bad—will make it considerably less difficult when a serious problem arises.

Of paramount importance is informing the board of anything that might appear in the media—whether positive or negative. One thing that was shared with us during our research is that boards do not like surprises of any kind. One might not think that a surprise about something positive could have unpleasant repercussions, but we learned that it can. Board members do not want to appear uninformed if someone approaches them and mentions some good news that was reported in the local media. Presidents should keep this in mind and share even seemingly small items with the board to ensure that, if they become big items, the board is not caught off guard. Additionally, sharing bad news is particularly important because it allows the president to frame the message in the most appropriate way.

Further along these lines, one president indicated that he always focused on the fact that the board members are volunteers. They are not being compensated in tangible ways and their affiliation with the institution puts them at risk of embarrassment. No one wants to be embarrassed and it is a wise president who goes out of her way to prevent it from occurring.

In addition to the board chair, the president should communicate frequently throughout the entire institutional community, using various media. Many presidents are comfortable with informal conversations, with the dialogue driven by the other participants (e.g., faculty, staff, students). Others prefer more formal means of communication such as prepared speeches on various topics, open letters to the community, periodic e-mails, and—for a few presidents—blogs. In the best of circumstances, the president will use multiple methods of communication and seek to connect with multiple constituencies. The main objective is to ensure that whatever message is being conveyed is widely distributed and reaches people through whatever mechanism works best for them.

It is not enough, however, merely to communicate widely and through different mechanisms. Presidents need to establish mechanisms to assess whether the communication is effective. Is it reaching the intended audience? Does it address their concerns? Are there opportunities to provide feedback about what is being communicated? The president must ensure that his communication is not going unnoticed or generating more questions that go unanswered. It must be a two-way process.

Another aspect of communication is dealing with the media. The first rule of thumb is to recognize that a president is never off the record. This may be the agreement with the reporter, but there are numerous instances of presidents being injured by offhand comments. Great care must be taken with any comments uttered to a reporter, a microphone, or a camera. It is impossible to unring the bell. Some reporters have very short attention spans and, as one communication expert shared with us, they are looking to make a splash at the president's or institution's expense. Generally speaking, they are not the president's friend and should not be thought of as such.

The most important advice in this regard is that the president should never attempt to interact with the media if he is not fully prepared to do so. If a cold call comes in from a reporter, the response must be to request information about the nature of the call and indicate that a response will be forthcoming. Then the president can respond once he is fully informed regarding the issue. Ideally, the president will consult with the public information officer to ensure that he is as well prepared as possible. At a minimum, he must have all the facts before embarking on a discussion with the reporter. Of course, the earlier advice applies as well. Honesty is the best policy.

Honest Feedback

There are several specific steps that presidents can take to reduce the likelihood that problems will arise. The first is one that sounds easier than it is. Presidents must establish relationships with individuals who can serve as trusted advisors and sounding boards. It is not hard at all to find individuals who are willing to tell the president what she *wants* to hear; it is very difficult to find those with the courage to tell her what she *needs* to hear. "It takes a concerted effort to cultivate subordinates who will advise and coach you. It also takes patience and some relentlessness."[5] Without access to this information, it is very possible that a president may unwittingly open the door to criticism that could have been avoided.

One of the first things a new president should do is identify one or more credible colleagues who can be empowered to share feedback that the president needs to receive. It could be the provost, the chief business officer, chief of staff, or someone who is not even a member of the cabinet—a senior faculty member for instance. The individual's position is not important. The critical thing is that they be able to pay attention to how the president is performing and, equally important, how the president's performance is being perceived throughout the campus. They must then have the freedom to share this information with the president without fear of backlash from the president.

Another important element of feedback comes through a formal evaluation process. Too often we hear about institutions that have an informal presidential performance assessment process that consists solely of an annual conversation between the board chair and/or executive committee and the president. Given the complexities of the position, this simply is not adequate.

The president should benefit from a formal evaluation process that includes opportunities for broad-based input to ensure that a complete performance picture can be painted. Informal feedback should be provided by the board throughout the year, and there should be a more formal process conducted at least once annually. Moreover, we advocate conducting a 360° feedback process at the outset of a presidency and every few years thereafter. It will be necessary to rely on former colleagues and others who know the president well for the initial effort. The new colleagues will not be able to provide meaningful feedback this early in the president's tenure. The results of the initial 360° feedback process can serve as a baseline. Future results can be benchmarked against the initial effort, providing objective evidence of changes that will have occurred. The other benefit from this is that it will help the president spot problem areas that may be developing. This will create the opportunity to address them before they become too serious.

Financial Matters

Beyond creating a climate in which honest feedback can be received, presidents can be proactive in other ways that will help prevent problems from arising. One of the most dangerous areas for a president involves finances. As described above, presidents get in trouble for not paying adequate attention to the institution's finances and for being careless when it comes to spending institutional resources.

As mentioned earlier, relatively few presidents have sufficient financial education or experience to fully comprehend the complex issues surrounding higher education finance. This is no excuse for a president not to invest the time needed to become fully aware of her institution's budget and overall financial health. We are not suggesting that the president supplant the chief business officer as the person with primary responsibility for the institution's finances. But we believe it is important for the president to devote sufficient time to understand the budget and the major assumptions that were made in its development. The president also should be able to explain the important institutional priorities being supported through the budget.

If the president does not possess the training or experience necessary to achieve this level of knowledge on his own, then he should spend sufficient time consulting with the chief business officer and/or chief budget officer to develop the necessary knowledge. Similarly, few presidents are sufficiently knowledgeable to fully understand or explain their institutions' audited financial statements. The same advice applies to these situations. The president should spend time with the chief business officer gaining an understanding of the financial statements. In fact, this can be a good practice session to ensure that the chief business officer can explain the information in ways that board members without extensive business expertise will understand.

Additionally, one of the requirements of SOX is that the chief executive and the chief business officer certify the accuracy of the financial statements. Although not required of college and university presidents, we are aware that this practice is being adopted by many institutions—especially private colleges and universities. If a president wants to take this step, he had better invest the effort to become sufficiently comfortable with such a certification.

By virtue of their position, presidents are presented with both opportunities and obligations to engage in entertainment in various settings. These situations can involve donors, alumni, government and elected officials, vendors, and others who can impact the institution's well-being. Naturally a president wants to do everything in her power to make these individuals feel good about the institution. This can create temptation to go overboard in lavish spending and gift buying.

In the best situations, a president would operate in exactly the same manner as a junior faculty member when it comes to spending institutional resources. Reality suggests that this simply is not possible. To avoid running into problems, presidents should take the time to learn the institution's policies governing such matters. All well-managed colleges and universities have established financial policies and procedures. Presidents should be familiar with what is allowable. With this knowledge she is in a position to make a judgment about exceptions to standard policies.

There will be times, however, when the president risks fallout if she grants an exception for her own benefit. One way to avoid this situation from occurring is for the president and the board chair to have a discussion about the latitude she has with respect to policy exceptions in this arena. Obviously every potential exception cannot be anticipated. On the other hand, if she and the board chair take the time to discuss this and then develop a short written document summarizing the general approach, it will prevent many problems from occurring. This sort of document can be revisited annually and, if necessary, updated to reflect changing circumstances.

The president can prevent problems from arising by adopting an institutional policy requiring a board member to review and approve her expense reports. In some institutions, a vice president is asked to perform this function. This is a suboptimal arrangement because, as a subordinate, this person may not feel

comfortable challenging a questionable expense. Any board member can perform this function, but most institutions that utilize this procedure assign the
responsibility to the board chair or the chair of the audit or finance committee.

A typical practice is to have the individual conduct an after-the-fact review of
all reimbursements that were processed during the previous quarter. The individual would flag anything of concern, discuss it with the president, and, if it is
determined that the item should not have been reimbursed, she can deduct the
amount from future reimbursement requests or simply repay it. There is another
advantage to this procedure. By subjecting reimbursements to this type of
review, the president and the institution minimize the risk that an Internal
Revenue Service review would conclude that the president received an improper
benefit.

Special mention needs to be made regarding presidential residences. On some
campuses, the president's residence is a special structure that makes a very positive statement about the institution. Many of these residences are more mansion
than house and provide space that is ideal for entertaining, while also creating a
comfortable environment for the president and his family. As with most structures, however, they require maintenance and, occasionally, repairs. And
because many presidential residences are older properties—even historic in
some cases, there are increased costs of maintenance and repair. Because it represents an institutional asset, it is important to properly maintain the structure.

The president, however, should not be involved in these decisions. Like any
other institutional physical asset, it is the chief facilities officer and the chief
business officer who should make decisions about repairs and maintenance. In
fact, it is generally a good idea to establish a formal schedule for conducting
maintenance on the residence. Such a schedule can be reviewed with the board
to ensure that it is deemed reasonable. When it comes time to address painting,
carpeting, or similar issues, it would be appropriate to consult the president
(or spouse) on colors, alternative wall coverings, and style. In fact, consultation
should occur whenever personal taste reasonably could be considered.

A special challenge is created when a leadership transition occurs and a new
president will be occupying the residence. Frequently, especially if the previous
president was in office for an extended period of time, there will be a backlog
of repairs and upgrades that need to be undertaken. The most important consideration in this situation is to conduct a thorough condition assessment of the
residence as soon as it becomes known that there will be a leadership change.

There is a temptation to defer addressing any of the issues discovered in the
assessment under the theory that the new president may wish to make some decisions regarding the residence. In our experience, this is a major mistake. There
will be tremendous scrutiny as the new president takes office and the residence
typically is a lightening rod for attention. Rather than defer decisions (and facilities work) until the new president has been selected, all of this work should be
undertaken before he or she arrives and, if possible, even before the successor is
identified. This is the time to upgrade major building systems, replace any

outdated appliances, install wireless networking, upgrade the entertainment center, repair the swimming pool, etc. There may still be a need to invest some effort with the house after the new president arrives, but the more that can be completed under the incumbent's watch, the less scrutiny there will be.

Blogs

There is one other issue that needs mention in this chapter—blogs. A blog is "an online diary; a personal chronological log of thoughts published on a Web page."[6] This is a relatively new phenomenon that already has had significant impact on some presidents and institutions. In fact there is an assertion, reported in the *Chronicle*, that a blog was instrumental in the removal of a president from one institution.[7]

The term blog, though harsh, sounds somewhat benign. And it can be. Many higher education participants engage in blogging. It is a wonderful tool to promote the exchange of information and personal views. The process turns malignant when it is used as a tool to attack presidents—especially when done anonymously.

One of the authors has seen firsthand the effect an anonymous blog had on a presidency. Like the president referenced in the *Chronicle* articles, this president struggled with whether to respond to the blog or simply ignore it. At the end of the day, the decision was to ignore it. As explained in the supplement at the end of this chapter, this was not the correct approach. Presidents should pay attention to the guidance in the supplement. The key is to be proactive.

Managing Crises

Higher education is no different from any other industry in that crises occur. In fact, because of the breadth of activities that take place on a campus, there may be greater potential for crises to occur than in most other endeavors. One would like to think that, as leaders, presidents inherently have the skills to respond in a crisis. Unfortunately, this is not always the case. For this reason, new presidents should ensure that their institutions have an established institutional response team (IRT). The IRT's charge is to manage the inevitable mishaps and tragedies that can occur on a campus. On any given morning, a president can wake up to find that there has been a student death, an incident at an athletic event, the arrest of a high-level administrator or faculty member, or a severed cable that shuts down the technology infrastructure. No one can predict when a crisis will strike, but when it does is *not* the time to start getting organized.

The IRT must be a high-caliber team, headed by the person most qualified for the role. This will vary from campus to campus. It might be the chief financial officer, chief advancement officer, or even someone at the next level of management. The key is to ensure that the individual is empowered to handle sudden, large-scale unexpected problems. This group needs to be kept relatively small and capable of being assembled or linked together at a moment's notice. The IRT chair can bring in others as needed (e.g., head of public safety, chief information officer, vice president for student life) to lend their expertise for a particular situation. If the chair is out of town, there must be a clear chain of command so that people know who is in charge of responding, with the appropriate decision-making power for the situation.

The IRT has several primary responsibilities:

- Gather relevant and accurate information so that they understand what the situation is. This presupposes that IRT members have good communication networks that they can access easily.

- Problem solve the situation and craft an effective response.

- Create a communication plan to deal with the media as well as inform board members and the general institutional community. The board should have identified a communication liaison to ensure efficient information flow without complicating things for the IRT.

It is helpful to have the IRT engage in training for problem solving, effective communication, and scenario planning so that they are fully prepared for the situations that will arise and the surprises that will accompany them.

***

It is difficult for some presidents to accept the reality that they entered a fishbowl when they accepted the position. Everything they say, do, or touch will be scrutinized by a diverse set of stakeholders. It is the diversity of the stakeholder groups and their interests that make the job interesting and challenging. Possibly most challenging is the fact that, in so many instances, the objectives of one stakeholder group are in conflict with those of another stakeholder group. Although all stakeholders have the best interests of the institution at heart, their views on what is best for the institution can be wildly different. Successfully balancing these diverse sets of desires is something that every president should strive to do. Even so, presidents would do well to recognize that they cannot please everyone and that attempting to do so is likely to lead to problems in the long run.

COPING WITH FINANCIAL CHALLENGES WHILE RETAINING THE BOARD'S SUPPORT
R. KIRBY GODSEY, CHANCELLOR AND FORMER PRESIDENT, MERCER UNIVERSITY

The relationship between the president and the governing board turns out, I believe, to be the relationship that, more than any other, defines the capacity of an institution to initiate creative change and to sustain institutional equilibrium during economic downturns or major shifts in institutional priorities. My experience has been that strong boards tend to select strong CEOs and relatively weak boards are inclined to select weaker leaders. The combination of a weak board of trustees and a weak chief executive officer seems to lead inevitably to an unstable relationship between the two.

In my own situation at Mercer University, I came to the office of president, following a period of relative stability, perhaps some stagnation in reviewing institutional priorities, and even some decline in academic competitiveness. At the time I assumed office, the university was located in two cities with four colleges—two in each city.

When the trustees elected me as president in 1979, they were well aware that the university was, in a sense, "neither fish nor fowl." Mercer was not a comprehensive university, nor could it be described as a baccalaureate institution. With the support of the board, the new leadership and the new administration began to work with university constituencies to "re-imagine" the future of the university and clarify its priorities. This clarification was made more complex by the fact that the discussions were underway for the idea of beginning a medical school in Macon.

With considerable debate and widely divergent opinions, the university, in full concert with the board of trustees, charted a course of becoming a genuinely comprehensive university, and over the next 25 years, opened eight schools and closed one for a total of 11, and implemented one major institutional merger.

The costs of redefining the course and purposes of the university were significant, especially for medicine and engineering, and the resistance to these initiatives among the faculties was monumental. In the fall of 1987, the university realized that the 1987–88 budget would experience a significant deficit. Faculty members from the long-established colleges were quick to raise voices of "I told you so" and to condemn the new initiatives as wasteful and ill-fated. Emotions ran high and academic tempers flared.

My response to this financial crisis focused in two directions—first internally addressing faculty anxieties and, second, with the board of trustees. Let me speak to my relationship with each of these constituencies—both of them vital in charting a course through the difficult waters of this crisis.

First, the board of trustees. The critical issue for maintaining the confidence and support of the board was their involvement and understanding of charting a new and clearer course for the university as a comprehensive university. The trustees were fully informed of the choices being made. They debated and were very aware of the disaffection of some members of the university community toward the creation of medical and engineering schools. Therefore, the impending deficit was not perceived as a failure of direction, but a failure to adequately analyze and assess the immediate costs of starting up these programs. Cost estimates were not on target and these revenue shortfalls and expenditure overruns caught administrative leaders, including the president, by surprise.

The chief challenge of working through the anticipated deficit was that the entire matter was played out in the media and the media were quick to publish the fears of the least informed. The administration could not confront the fears with immediate assurances, and indicated instead that we would seek an independent analysis of the situation and make a fuller report when better information was in hand. We engaged one of the major accounting firms to study the university's finances and we chose not to offer conjectures until the report was completed. That hiatus, of course, created an opening for critics to offer daily commentary without rebuttal. Not all trustees understood why faculty who were employees could not, in effect, be silenced. We tried to make clear to the board that, even as uncomfortable as the bad publicity was, the better course was to endure the unchallenged interpretation and the misinterpretations rather than challenge those views before we had documented and accurate assessments of the university's financial condition.

The assessment revealed an anticipated $8 million deficit on a total budget of $100 million. The big question was how was the university to address this dilemma. Two of the 45 trustees believed that the president had failed, having been persuaded by able colleagues on the faculty. The two resigned as a voice of protest. Other trustees were more reflective of a comment made by a fellow trustee following receipt of the auditor's report. "OK Kirby, you got us into this. How do you plan to get us out of it?" We said to the board that the administration would make proposals in a timely fashion. In about 30 days, we asked for a special "called" meeting of the board.

At that meeting, we presented alternative plans for addressing the deficit, following which I met with the board in executive session. The atmosphere was tense. In all candor, I was trading on whatever reservoir of respect and confidence that I had achieved over the previous ten years. We made clear that it would be possible to eliminate the deficit quickly by declaring financial exigency and closing several of the new program initiatives. While spelling out this alternative, I recommended against these actions. I advocated a plan that would include immediate budget reductions, but would phase out the deficit over a five-year period. Looking back, their underlying support for me, built up over a decade, probably caused them to vote to support the plan. (As an aside, the plan was implemented, and the deficit was eliminated in only two years.) The external auditors made clear to the board that, while the deficit was real and serious, the economic stability of the university was not and had not been at risk.

In the executive session, which I had requested, I told the board that I could understand how a crisis of this kind could shake their confidence in the presidential leadership. I explained that the board, and the board alone, were responsible for evaluating the work of the president, and determining the best course for the university with respect to continuing presidential leadership. I also indicated my extraordinary disappointment that we had failed in our systems and models. It was my responsibility and I had failed to comprehend or to anticipate this financial crisis. At the same time, I also affirmed my continuing conviction that the university was essentially on a sound and constructive course. And I added that now, perhaps more than ever, the university needed a strong president and they should not approve this plan or sustain my leadership with any restrictions that would inhibit my ability to lead the institution during this difficult period. I could understand why it would be tempting to weaken the president's hand, to abridge the president's authority in this situation. But I also believed that the institution, especially now, required strong leadership, whether from me or a new individual. In effect, I asked for an affirmation of their confidence. I posed this question knowing that I could have been silent on the matter of my continuing leadership. However, I believed that the strength of the office was so important in meeting the challenges ahead that the board should deliberate and make an explicit commitment regarding their willingness to support me as their president and to support the plan for overcoming the financial challenges. The board voted to sustain the plan and the president and, while they were regularly informed of the progress, they steadfastly respected the boundaries between governance and administration. Without that support, I could not have successfully overcome this crisis.

This chapter of Mercer's history and my presidency turned out to be a critical era in the university's development. The identity of Mercer as a comprehensive university was clearly defined and enunciated. It survived the fires of debate and financial difficulty and, in years to come, the university has reaped the benefit of making these creative initiatives and having the courage to stand firm in the midst of financial challenge.

Macon, Georgia
April 2007

WHEN CONFIDENTIALITY TRUMPS CONSULTATION
SUSAN RESNECK PIERCE, PRESIDENT EMERITA,
UNIVERSITY OF PUGET SOUND

During my years as department chair, dean of a college of arts and sciences, and academic vice president, I prided myself on working collaboratively with colleagues. And trying to make sure that all the pertinent voices were both around the table and actually heard. I of course also observed confidentiality, for example, when it came to personnel and legal matters. I began my presidency in 1992 at the University of Puget Sound determined to continue to work this way.

A year later, however, I was confronted with an unusual situation which—in my judgment and that of Puget Sound's board of trustees— required that I involve only a very few people in making a series of critical decisions. The situation required that I not consult with those who would be most affected by these decisions and that I commit to absolute confidentiality.

In the early 1970's, Puget Sound had created a law school in a renovated department store in downtown Tacoma, a fifteen-minute drive from what was called the "main campus." Over time the law school grew to 800 students. Although everyone, including the ABA, understood the value of integrating the law school physically with the rest of the institution, the university had neither the funds nor the space to do so.

In 1979, the board decided that Puget Sound would be best served by returning to its liberal arts roots and that it would strive to join the ranks of the national liberal arts colleges. To that end, the institution phased out an MBA program located in Seattle and closed satellite campuses on nearby military bases and at the federal penitentiary.

During my interviews, several trustees said that, even though the law school was financially self-sufficient, it would be one of the biggest challenges facing the new president, primarily because the law school was inconsistent with Puget Sound's mission. I soon learned that some trustees simply wanted to close the law school. Others wanted to reduce its size by half, in the interest of quality. Yet others proposed benign neglect.

Once appointed president and recognizing that none of the proposed alternatives were desirable, I asked the board to give me a year to gain a fuller understanding of the institution before I turned to the law school. Just as that year was coming to an end, Seattle University President Bill Sullivan, S.J., and I had a phone conversation that proved to be very important. We discussed Puget Sound's decision to define itself as a liberal arts college and Seattle University's wish, as a Jesuit comprehensive urban university, to have a law school.

Within days Bill and I met to talk about this possibility. We recognized immediately that we could in fact transfer sponsorship of the law school from Puget Sound to Seattle University in ways that would benefit each. We agreed to talk immediately to our trustees about this option. Both groups embraced the idea with enthusiasm, seeing it as a win-win situation and they charged the two of us with negotiating the terms of the transfer.

From the outset, the Puget Sound trustees and I struggled with the conflict between confidentiality and consultation. We knew that if it became public that we were exploring transferring the law school to Seattle University, there would be a firestorm of criticism from the Tacoma press and from the legal and business communities. We anticipated that some members of the law school faculty who had earlier brought suit against the institution over salaries would bring suit again. In such a scenario, student and faculty recruitment and retention would be compromised as would be fund-raising. If the negotiations with Seattle University failed, I feared that we might even be forced to close the law school.

The board leadership and I particularly worried about whether to confide in the law school's acting dean, someone whom we respected and who had a great deal of integrity. In the end, we decided not to ask him to carry the burden of confidentiality. We also worried that if we told him about our efforts, his knowledge ultimately would tarnish his relationship with his faculty colleagues.

The negotiations went smoothly, in part because we were making a mission rather than a financial decision. Seattle University immediately agreed to the following major issues:

- grant tenure and rank to all members of the current faculty
- offer faculty and staff comparable salaries and benefits
- fire no one other than for cause, and
- remain in its current location for five years before moving to a new building on their campus.

Three months later on the same morning, both boards overwhelmingly approved the transfer. When the board chair and I announced the decision (in meetings with the law school faculty, the faculty as a whole, in a meeting with the editorial board of the local newspaper, and by e-mail and letters to the campus community, community leaders, and alumni), we also announced that the proceeds from the transfer would be placed in an endowment for financial aid for students from Washington State.

The expected firestorm of criticism erupted. Despite our meeting with its editorial board, *The News Tribune* vilified the board and me personally (and continued to do so for years). The legal community was dismayed that in five years it would lose free access to the law school library and to a large pool of future employees. The business community worried that once the law school moved to Seattle, the building would be empty and therefore become a blight on the downtown. Our Congressman asked for a special meeting with the board to urge that it reverse the decision. Some law school faculty members did bring suit. The law school dean, untainted because he had been kept in the dark about the negotiations, was able to provide great leadership during the transition.

Although a great many members of the faculty as a whole supported the decision, they were understandably uneasy that I had not consulted them. I thus knew that moving forward it would be critical for me to be, in today's jargon, as transparent as possible so that I could earn the faculty's trust.

To that end, I walked around even more than I had previously. My husband and I began a series of small dinner parties for faculty. I met often with faculty groups. During our May board meeting, I encouraged small groups of faculty members to host dinners for board members and, if pertinent, their spouses and partners (my office funded these). We also made it a point to involve faculty and students more fully in board meetings. I initiated four-hour Fall Faculty Conversations during which—outside of faculty meetings dedicated primarily to faculty business—I shared with the faculty what I was thinking and, as importantly, I listened to them. I did something similar with the staff. I began sending out periodic campus-update e-mails. As in the past, I kept an open door policy.

The board leadership and I also hosted a series of breakfasts at the president's house for community leaders to explain why we had transferred the law school to Seattle University and why we needed to keep the negotiations confidential. I visited alumni chapters around the country for the same purpose.

From the vantage point of nearly 14 years, I continue to believe that transferring the law school was the right thing to do. I am now even more convinced that without maintaining absolute confidentiality, it would not have happened. Puget Sound did enter the ranks of the national liberal arts colleges. The number of applications rose dramatically to roughly 4500 for 650 freshmen spaces. SAT scores, which had been 1067 in 1992, were 1254 in 2003 (re-centering was part of this gain but by no means the bulk of it). Over these same years the endowment grew from $68 million to over $200 million. We spent $85 million on new and renovated facilities. The Carnegie Foundation reclassified us as a national liberal arts college rather than a regional comprehensive university. The Watson Foundation added us to its list, and our students won an impressive number of Watson Fellowships. Major private foundations—like Mellon, Luce, Starr, Gates and Murdock—funded us generously.

We sold the building to the State of Washington so that it could co-locate state office workers in one place rather than in offices scattered throughout the area. This infusion into the downtown of working people who were making and spending money rather than students who were paying tuition helped revitalize the downtown. With the advent of a new publisher and a new managing editor, the local newspaper began writing favorably about our accomplishments.

The law school is also thriving. Its faculty take advantage of partnerships with Seattle University's business school. They are delighted to be on the center of the campus. The school's size, rather than being viewed as a liability, is a plus. A number of the law school faculty have told me that the decision was clearly the right one for both them and us. I was especially pleased when several of them invited me to see their impressive new building and gave me a tour.

So what are the lessons that I take from this? I continue to believe that broad consultation, careful listening and transparent decision making are in most instances not only desirable but necessary. At the same time, I've also learned that leadership requires judgment, decisiveness, resolve, risk-taking, a thick skin and a focus on mission.

Boca Raton, Florida
April 2007

BLOGS—DEALING WITH THE NEW PR STING
CHRISTOPHER SIMPSON, CHIEF EXECUTIVE OFFICER AND PARTNER, SIMPSONSCARBOROUGH
HAILEY PROCTOR, MARKETING STRATEGIST AND COMMUNICATIONS ADVISOR, SIMPSONSCARBOROUGH

In pre-Internet days, one of the easiest ways to sting a political opponent running in a local election was to take a colleague and head to the tallest office building in town. You looked for one that housed banks, law and accounting firms and the like—home turf for folks who were connected politically. Your trip began between 7:30 and 8:30 a.m. by riding up and down in elevators packed with hushed workers heading to white-collar jobs. In each crowded elevator, you discussed loudly the latest tale, revelation or bombshell about the political opponent. The juicier the better, and the better the tale, the louder you talked. By noon, word was all over town effectively, expeditiously and anonymously.

Today that same underhanded tactic has a new name. In the analog world gone digital, we call it blogging. The original blog began in 1994 as an online personal diary. By 2001, dozens of blogs were being read by more than one million readers each day, far outpacing the circulation of the largest newspapers in the United States. The numbers of bloggers and readers continued to soar, with the former soaring exponentially, due largely to the ease of starting a blog and the simplicity of viral marketing to grow audiences. Today, an estimated 100 million blogs populate the Internet, covering everything from gardening to composting, life for a single guy to good empty nester living, current events to politics, and all points in between.

In more recent years, a new kind of blog was born: one with a slant toward the negative. These blogs aim to change public opinion about individuals or institutions and ultimately ruin reputations and remove power. Their impact and effectiveness in doing so is evident in several recent events.

When U.S. Senate Minority Leader Trent Lott attended the 100th birthday of U.S. Senator Strom Thurmond in 2002, he suggested the nation would be better off had the long-time South Carolina senator won the presidential election in 1948, when he ran on a segregationist ticket. Specifically, he said "...if the rest of the country had followed [Mississippi's] lead, we wouldn't have had all these problems over all these years." Lott's remarks were recapitulated from remarks he gave in 1980, but this time, his statement was seized by bloggers. They said, in effect, that Lott endorsed racism. Lott was forced to resign his leadership post, illustrating bloggers' power in the political world.

In subsequent years, bloggers on the opposite side of the political spectrum drove the downfall of TV journalist Dan Rather, whose 60 Minutes story questioned President George W. Bush's military service, and badly wounded the presidential run of Massachusetts Senator John Kerry.

Higher education became a ripe target for bloggers intent on venting opinions about college and university administrators. In recent years there have been growing instances in which bloggers attacked university presidents, chancellors, provosts, faculty members, athletic directors, coaches and student athletes. Blogging in many ways is talk radio gone digital and self publishing at its height.

So, how can you prepare for the advent of negative blogs against your institution, and what can you do to ensure your bases are covered if a spiteful enemy starts a blog and sets you squarely in their sights? Here are our five top tips for preparing for, handling and surviving a negative blog.

1. Launch your strategy by segmenting and prioritizing your most important audiences. Begin your PR/media/marketing tasks by compiling a list of the most important internal and external audiences for your institution, those you must reach each day for your institution to be successful. For most institutions they are

   - Board members, faculty, staff and students

   - Prospective students and their parents and counselors

   - Alumni and donors, the lifeblood of higher educational institutions

   - Business and opinion leaders

   - Elected officials

   - Higher education leaders nationwide

Your job is to communicate continuously and effectively with these audiences in a manner to enhance the image and reputation of your institution. In a time of crisis, you should focus on the audience, not the media or the bloggers. You cannot stop a negative blogger, but you can mitigate the damage. Focus first on key audiences, then the hit and run Internet artist next.

2. Know your opponent. In past years, the media and marketing office labored over press releases, view books and Web sites. Today, they are also responsible for daily monitoring of blogs that carry information about their institution. Blog monitoring sites such as www.technorati.com allow you to search for keywords in posts from millions of blogs. Type in your institution's name and with one click you can find out who is talking about you online anywhere in the world, in any language. Determine which blogs have the most authority, and designate those as your "key blogs."

Develop a strategy to know them, monitor them and eventually infiltrate them strategically. Your goal is to control the message and flow of information from your institution to key constituents listed above. Do not let the bloggers derail these communications.

3. Reach out to those key bloggers. Have key staff in your institution get in touch with them through their blog or by e-mail—electronic methods of communication are most likely to be received. Establish open and ongoing conversations with the bloggers so that information flows freely between you. Offer them the facts just as you would traditional news sources. Listen to their opinions and consider seriously their point of view. Respond personally, don't just send your latest pitch or press release. Treat them with respect because they hold a lot of power.

4. In a less candid fashion, have associates or employees enlist in blog conversations on particularly challenging blog sites. Having allies in the blog chatter long before a crisis erupts can help to shape public opinion. Have them check the blogs daily and respond to negative comments on your institution anonymously. Monitor your allied bloggers to ensure they take the high road and are posting thoughtful and influential blog pieces instead of emotional backlashes. Make sure their blog entries are integrated with your institution's marketing messages.

The bottom line is the worst strategy is to hope the bloggers have no impact, readers or influence. Hope is always a bad strategy. Instead, be proactive and aggressive.

5. Start your own blog. Launch a blog for someone at your institution to share his or her thoughts. Choose a person of power and authority—someone with a voice that your key audiences will respect, like the president or a vice president. Have them post valuable and informative content. Send the link to your key audiences, and your blog may become a more popular source for information than the negative blogs you are combating.

Gartner, Inc., an information and technology research firm, speculates the life of the blog has crested and will only decline. Those blogs on the low end of the totem pole no longer host significant numbers of visitors. Until a new communications tactic makes blogs obsolete, however, a negative blog against your institution may still be a force to be reckoned with. Employ these tactics and you and your organization should be able to ride out any blogging storm.

Williamsburg, Virginia
April 2007

NOTES

1. Kramer, Roderick M. "The Harder They Fall." *Harvard Business Review* 81,10 (October 2003): 58–66.

2. American Council on Education. *The American College President.* Washington: American Council on Education, 2007.

3. Goleman, Daniel. "What Makes a Leader?" *Harvard Business Review* 82,1 (January 2004): 82–91.

4. Brown, Hank. Recorded interview. *The Chronicle of Higher Education.* http://chronicle.com/media/audio/v53/i29/hankbrown/audioplayer.htm (accessed June 3, 2007).

5. Kaplan, Robert S. "What to Ask the Person in the Mirror." *Harvard Business Review* 85,1 (January 2007): 86–95.

6. Webster's New Millennium Dictionary of English, preview edition (v 0.9.7). http://dictionary.reference.com/browse/blog (accessed June 3, 2007).

7. Read, Brock. "Attack of the Blog." *The Chronicle of Higher Education* http://chronicle.com/weekly/v53/i04/04a03501.htm (accessed June 3, 2007).

CHAPTER 5

Managing the Twilight—When a President Leaves

"Few events in the life of an organization are as critical, as visible, or as stressful as when a leader leaves the institution."[1]

everal years ago, one of the authors was asked to meet with a well-respected, successful university president. The president was familiar with an article the consultant had written and wanted to talk about leadership issues. The conversation turned out to be about something quite different. The president talked about his sense of uneasiness. "I have been here for 10 years and feel very good about my senior team and what we have accomplished, but I think we have hit a plateau. The focus and excitement just aren't there anymore. I would like you to interview my cabinet and find out what they are thinking and feeling about our current situation. I don't believe they will tell me the truth because they like me too much." He was right.

The consultant spent several days on the campus, interviewing each senior leader for an hour and a half. It was obvious that a great deal had been accomplished over the past decade. To a person, they felt proud about their accomplishments and had great affection for the president. They also were afraid to tell him that he had been "psychologically out the door" for more than a year. Almost half the group suggested, reluctantly, that it might be time for him to leave.

The consultant sat down with the president to communicate the findings from the interviews. When the conversation focused on the president being seen as ready to leave, the president readily agreed. He talked about his commitment to the job, but also the burden of familiarity that had rendered it routine and, in part, boring. He discussed his uncertainty about his own desire or willingness to go on to something else. The president was grateful that the interview information was honest and caring. Knowing what his colleagues were thinking and how they felt about him created a defining moment for him as a leader. He would need to reassert his leadership or leave.

Over several months, many telephone conversations ensued between the president and the consultant. They discussed how difficult it is to let go, the fragility of the president's legacy, his concerns about the future, and the power of the presidency. At the end of the academic year, he announced that he would be leaving. In his heart he knew he needed to apply his passions and time elsewhere. He created a transition process that was well-planned, respectful of the institution, and enabled the board to choose an effective president for the future.

Over the years, we have witnessed scores of senior leadership transitions in higher education. We believe discussions should take place among board chairs, other trustees, presidents, and other senior leaders on campus as they plan how best to manage their own presidential transitions.

When a president leaves an institution, history is made. The way she performed in special and/or difficult circumstances, the endowments she attracted, the buildings she saw built, and her impact as a scholar in her field or in higher education all become the stuff of campus mythology. The ripples that result from her departure can leave the institution shaky and fragile, or the foundation she leaves behind can provide solid ground for a new administration.

It is our hope that by understanding the dynamics of this complex event, senior leaders can manage the transition period and allow the institution to remain healthy and intact.

UNDERSTANDING THE "PSYCHOLOGICAL LANDSCAPE" OF THE PRESIDENCY

It can be difficult to say goodbye. It is nice being a president. The presidency has many responsibilities and many attractions. People tend to be respectful and deferential. One can have great impact on the life of an institution and make a real difference in the lives of students. A president is likely to meet famous people and become a political player. The list goes on and on. It is difficult to give up power, status, and an attentive staff. These perquisites can create a strong psychological pull. Feeling needed, important, and well liked, why leave when everything is going so well?

"To be able to endure the pain of letting go takes deep and abiding affection."[2] The real affection the president has for the institution can be manifest in the discipline to ask herself the tough questions. Do I still have energy for this job? How attached am I to the title and all of its perks? Are there signs I should be letting go? For instance, do I lack the enthusiasm needed to respond to important campus issues? Do I find that issues unrelated to the college routinely prove more appealing than in the past? And then there are the scary questions. What else can I do? Have I been away from my field too long? Will I be able to function effectively in a different environment?

A first step in answering these questions can come from asking those to whom one is closest—a spouse, significant other, longtime close friend, trusted colleague—for honest and caring feedback about performance, connection, and interest level. They often know where an individual is psychologically even before the person does. It is important to pay attention to this feedback.

In the flurry of campus life, it is hard to create the time to reflect on contributions and continuing interest in the institution. It is affection for the institution that can provide the rigor to consider these issues honestly and authentically.

There are times when reflection seems to come naturally. Some presidents conduct a reflective review on their birthday, the anniversary date of their appointment, at the end of the spring semester, or during the holidays. The choice is up to the individual, but it is important to do it annually and to do it thoroughly.

Legacy Issues

Presidents often struggle with legacy issues that are deeply personal in nature. How will I be remembered? Did I have a positive impact? Did I focus on the right things? Why didn't I accomplish more? Is the institution in a better place now than when I arrived? Am I respected? What did I miss?

The answers to these difficult questions become the substance of a president's legacy. Most presidents want to leave with a positive contribution behind them. This is true in the corporate world[3] as well as in higher education.[4]

Defining a legacy within a higher education institution is inherently difficult. A president begins afresh with each new crop of students and each new group of faculty. Whatever has been accomplished in the past becomes the basis for future expectations even before he has had a chance to complete fund-raising for the last task. The perception of the value of accomplishments will vary depending on the beholder—president, board of trustees, faculty, students, staff, donors, or members of the local community.

Unfortunately, we have found that presidents tend not to engage in these discussions. If these conversations are not taking place, the president may stay too long, trying to complete an agenda few people understand or support. He may have deep regrets about what he was not able to accomplish, leaving behind disappointed colleagues or a demoralized campus.

ONCE THE DECISION IS MADE

"Once you have decided to leave, your only job is to say thank you over and over again to all those who made it possible for you to leave."[5]

The process of selecting and installing a new college or university president is often a long one, usually running to about a year or more.[6] Higher education institutions are, for the most part, governed and managed by consensus, and the hiring process for senior positions requires the input and participation of many individuals and groups.

This period of time should be worthwhile and productive for the president and the institution. During this transition, the president and the board separately can focus on actions that will ensure the time is well spent and the departure leaves a positive mark on the institution.

Three Key Responsibilities of the Departing President

When a president decides to leave, it is important for her to initiate three informational processes. These actions will enable the institution to choose the new president through an informed process and enable the new leader to transition onto the campus effectively. The president needs to commission a "strategic audit report," an in-depth study of the strengths and weaknesses of the institution. She also needs to create a "future challenges report," which looks at the challenges the institution is likely to face in the future. Finally, she must oversee the development of a "relationship map," to ensure that critical relationships are managed during the transition process.

Strategic Audit Report

This type of audit should go beyond the summary observations of institutional self-studies or accreditation reviews created for external audiences. It should drill deeper than the traditional briefing books and transition documents that are most often created for new leaders. A confidential strategic audit report should provide a clear and honest assessment outlining the issues the new leader is likely to encounter.

We know of several presidents who had critical information withheld from them during the search process. Once they were on board, these challenges were revealed in an offhanded manner. Unfortunately they were enormous problems, the existence of which might have influenced their decision to accept the position.

Marlene Ross and Madeleine Green found that 80 percent of presidents they studied discovered at least one significant problem that was not disclosed during the search process.[7] Financial and budgeting problems were the most common undisclosed issues. E.K. Fretwell supports these findings regarding interim presidents cautioning "count on being surprised."[8]

A strategic audit report should neither sugarcoat problems nor undervalue strengths. It should encompass the hopes, fears, challenges, and aspirations of the institution. The audit should provide the kind of unique qualitative analysis to which new leaders rarely have access.

We realize that there is a complication for some public institutions due to the open record laws and/or freedom of information acts. Even with the potential for discovery, it still is important for the report to be candid to have real value.

To the extent possible, however, care must be taken to prevent it from becoming public. If done properly the report will contain very sensitive information. It requires a closely controlled distribution.

One approach to gathering this information might include the results of a brief, *anonymous* questionnaire sent to a significant number of stakeholders (50 to 100) representing a variety of perspectives. Be expansive when defining stakeholders. Ensure that the survey is distributed to students, faculty, staff, trustees, alumni, donors, volunteers, community leaders, and any other groups involved in the life of the college. This type of survey is not meant to be statistically reliable or valid. It is designed to provide a new president with a broad and qualitative view. The following list contains the types of questions that typically are asked in a strategic audit:

- If you were talking to a good friend about sending his child to this institution, what would you say?

- What do you believe our college/university does best?

- Of what about this institution are you most proud?

- If you had the power to change two things that would improve this institution's overall effectiveness, what would they be? Why?

- What are two or three issues that need to be dealt with effectively, yet rarely see the light of day on our campus?

- How would you describe our campus culture? Please provide examples if you can.

- How would you rate the level of trust within our institution? (Very low, low, average, high, very high). Please explain your rating.

- How would you assess the effectiveness of the president's senior staff in performing their duties?

- How would you describe communication throughout the campus (e.g., effective, disjointed, open, secretive)?

- What advice would you give to the new president that would enable him to be successful?

The questions will source unique and important insights about the nature of the institution, the challenges it faces, the strengths it possesses, and the culture of the campus. It will be invaluable to the new campus leader.

This survey should be organized and conducted by the president's office. Other departments (e.g., institutional research) can help operationalize this process, but it must be seen as a top priority of the president. It is helpful to have a cover letter, authored by the president, explaining the purposes of the survey. A follow-up thank-you note from the president should be sent at the end of the process. Remember that it is essential to ensure the anonymity of the respondents in order to receive clear, honest, straightforward information.

The results of the survey should produce a report that can be shared with the search committee—which usually finds such a report highly educational—and a select group of campus leaders. In addition, finalists in the presidential search should receive a copy of this confidential report so that they clearly understand the strengths and weaknesses of the institution.

Future Challenges Report

Along with a comprehensive strategic audit report, an institution should conduct an examination of the challenges it may face in the future. An understanding of how stakeholders view the future helps create an analytical and strategic framework for choosing a new leader. The board can look at the institution's future challenges and define the unique set of skills and qualities their new leader must have if she is to serve the institution well.

While the future challenges report should include demographics, emerging issues, and trends, it also should include stakeholder advice. Like the strategic audit report, it should encompass and distill the perspectives of a wide and diverse group of stakeholders. A key source of strategic information about the future is the institution's governing board, whose members represent diverse interests, backgrounds, and perspectives. Senior leaders need to facilitate and conduct open discussions with them to solicit their views about the challenges the institution may face down the road.

It is important that senior leadership (e.g., president, provost, chief business officer) engage other important stakeholder groups about what they see as the future challenges facing the institution. At a minimum, faculty senate and administrative councils need to be meaningfully involved in a discussion about the future events, trends, and issues that could impact or influence the institution.

We suggest that students also be involved in this kind of "horizon thinking" about the future. Students are closer to the future than any other stakeholder group, but are rarely engaged in thinking about it from an institutional perspective. Their views will prove to be both enlightening and strategic and will give a well-rounded shape to the report.

The process for gathering the information can take many forms. The information could be generated in a series of interviews, small focus groups, or even in working lunches and breakfasts with stakeholders. We frequently utilize a horizon thinking activity—the Future Timeline—for this purpose. Participants are asked to use sticky notes to populate a large series of flip charts with issues, events, and trends that are likely to affect the institution during the next ten years. Once the individuals have individually reviewed and analyzed all of the postings to the timeline, they work in small groups to generate short lists of the impacts indicated by the issues, events, and trends. The process continues with the capture of the lists from the various groups. This is done in a very public way, usually recording the impacts on a master list so all participants can see them. If more than one group has the same item, this is noted by adding a check mark or asterisk for each time it is mentioned. Because there tends to be significant duplication among the groups, the process of recording the impacts on a master list helps create a clear sense of the most important impacts likely to affect the institution in the future.[9]

Relationship Map

As a president leaves a campus, thoughtful consideration and planning needs to take place about managing the complex network of relationships that she has nurtured and developed over time. Many of these relationships are essential to the institution's success and need to be identified and appropriately maintained. These relationships can be with organizations and institutions as well as with specific individuals. Many of these relationships are formal and easily identified. Others are informal and may be difficult to identify yet they are often just as important as the formal relationships.

It is important that there be broad participation in the process to assist the incumbent president in identifying these key stakeholders. The main reason a relationship map is created is to maintain, if not strengthen, the complex relationships the new president will inherit once he is on board.

In many cases the outgoing president will not be able to effectively maintain all these relationships. Much of his time will be consumed by focusing on the culminating agenda of the last year, saying goodbye to hundreds of people, and attending many goodbye receptions and events during the transition.

The new president's schedule during the first six months, even if effectively managed, can be overwhelming and makes it difficult to connect with all the key relationships. This could leave a situation in which key relationships have no real connection to the institution for a year or more. This should be avoided at all costs.

There is no shortage of critical relationships for a president. The following represent examples of just some of the relationships a typical president will have established.

Local school districts

Many institutions—especially community colleges—have long-standing and important relationships with local public and private schools. These could be schools in which the university assigns its student teachers, engages in community service, conducts research, maintains practicums for nurses and psychologists, or even charter schools that are fully managed by an education school. Although the president may not have personal relationships with specific schools, he usually has relationships with the school superintendent in the community. This kind of relationship needs to be maintained throughout the transition by an appropriate representative (e.g., provost, dean, senior faculty member).

Foundations

Many institutions have beneficial relationships with local, regional, and national foundations. Often these relationships have significant financial commitments attached to them that help support aspects of the institution's overall operations. The key contact people at these foundations need to be identified and the right member of the cabinet or senior staff needs to be assigned to maintain the relationship during the transition.

Local community activists

There may be various highly influential community members who are essential to positive town-gown relations. These individuals may be connected to a local organization or work independently. What makes them important to the future president is their political and relational power within the community. It is not necessary for them to have a large, complex organization behind them for them to be able to affect the community's relationship to the institution. It is important to identify these key community leaders and assign a respected senior leader to manage the relationships during the transition.

A process for developing a relationship map

Identify the key relationships

Soon after the outgoing president has announced that she is leaving, a meeting needs to be conducted with the president and her senior staff. The purpose of this initial meeting is to identify the numerous formal and informal relationships, maintained by the president, that enable the university to pursue its mission.

The president needs to provide a little history and context about each relationship as well as describe its value to the institution. All of this information needs to be captured in writing because it should be shared with the incoming president after things settle down.

Prioritize the relationships

After the initial list has been created, along with a rationale for each, the relationships need to be prioritized so that the most important ones are clearly identified. This could be done with a smaller group working with the president.

Establish relationship assignments

After all the relationships have been identified and prioritized, a member of the cabinet/senior team or a highly credible senior faculty member should be assigned as liaison to maintain the relationship during the upcoming transition. It is important to choose the right individual for each assignment so that the external relationships feel respected, paid attention to, and most importantly so they can connect to the assigned representative during the transition. Just randomly assigning names can actually damage a valued relationship. This needs to be done very thoughtfully.

Conduct monthly reviews

During the transition of the incumbent and the new president, all of the liaisons should meet monthly to report the status of their assignments. During these monthly meetings key issues can be specified for each relationship, problems or challenging relationships can be discussed, and strategies for meaningful engagement can be developed. If necessary, reassignments of liaisons can be made.

Sample Relationship Map

The abbreviated list below indicates the types of assignments that typically would be made to the specified individuals.

Outgoing president

- Trustees and former trustees
- Other local/regional campus presidents
- Selected alumni and major donors
- Local business leaders

Vice president for advancement

- Alumni association president
- Mayor
- State representatives for institution's district
- Selected alumni and major donors

Provost

- State department of education
- Faculty senate officers and other key individual faculty members

Chief business officer

- City/county officials
- Selected neighborhood organization representatives
- Community development district members
- City district representatives/ward leaders

Vice president for student affairs

- Student leaders
- Selected neighborhood organization representatives

Public information officer

- Local newspaper education reporters

Another important benefit from identifying the president's key relationships is that it helps create the beginning of a communication plan for the transition process. It is important for the president or board chair to personally contact the high priority relationships. They should not learn about the president's leaving by reading it in the newspaper or hearing it through the grapevine. Personal contact conveys both importance and respect for the key relationships. They need to be engaged throughout the transition process and they need to know that a key member of the institution will be in contact with them throughout the process.

The development office plays a key role in the transition process, especially with relationship mapping. A briefing book needs to be created for the new president that highlights the significant donors and potential gifts along with comprehensive background information for each one.

A strategy for each high level donor needs to be crafted and the incumbent president needs to personally meet with the most important ones. It is important to communicate the institution's goals during the transition; create some excitement about the future; gain a commitment from the donors to continue to support the institution's mission, goals, and aspirations; and assure that a thoughtful and planful selection process will be undertaken to choose the very best president for the future.

ADVICE TO PRESIDENTS
Be an "Owner" of the Transition Process

Being an owner does not mean dominating the process, but being directly involved in the transition process. The president needs to be seen as being proactive and helping to design the process. The perception should not be of something done to her. The following are some ownership responsibilities.

The outgoing president needs to meet with her cabinet and board chair to assemble a transition team to manage the complexities of the transition process. This group should consist of credible and knowledgeable individuals who have an appetite for a lot of work.

Appoint a Transition Manager

John Moore and Joanne Burrows suggest that institutions appoint a transition coordinator to manage communications and orientation activities.[10] Although we agree, we strongly believe that the individual will have many more complicated and complex responsibilities beyond coordination and logistics. This individual will be involved in highly sensitive conversations with the outgoing and incoming leaders. The transition manager will have to manage board communications and relationships, keeping them involved and informed appropriately. He will need to interact with internal and external stakeholders and be personable, flexible, and very well-organized. In addition, he will have to know how to deal with power, egos, nervous stakeholders, and delicate, if not conflictual, situations.

Highly effective transition managers come in different shapes and sizes. We have worked with several of these managers, including a provost, a vice president of operations, a chief of staff, a respected former provost, and a chief financial officer. This individual performs an invaluable role. Choose carefully.

The transition manager's role

Foremost, the transition manager has to be seen and respected as a highly credible individual throughout the campus. He has to be someone who deeply understands the institution's history, culture, and complexity and be trusted by everyone. He might be, as we call it, a "cultural traveler"[11] who is able to cross boundaries within the campus, have access to the rumor mill, be privy to many highly confidential conversations, and effectively deal with politics and power. No small task indeed.

The transition manager is primarily responsible for high quality and efficient communication throughout the transition process. He should be *the key* communicator about presidential schedules, campus events, search committee updates, and board communication. The last thing an institution needs is several voices speaking for the institution on these important matters. Quality control around communication is essential for a smooth transition process. Other responsibilities of the transition manager are listed below:

- Create an outreach plan for internal stakeholders (e.g., presidential events to say goodbye, meet and greets for the incoming president).

- Ensure that any ground rules that have been agreed upon are protected and enforced.

- Communicate regularly with stakeholders to generate excitement about past accomplishments and build anticipation for the future.

- Manage the orientation of the new president (e.g., briefing books, learning network, culture surveys, strategic audit report).

- Oversee the schedule of events and meetings the new president will need to attend with critical stakeholders during the first six months to a year.

- Keep the board fully informed about events and progress so they have an opportunity to be involved and know that the transition is well planned and moving forward.

It is apparent that this represents a significant responsibility—one that will absorb considerable amounts of the individual's time and energy. As such, it is advisable that the transition manager be relieved of some of his normal day-to-day duties to ensure that he is able to adequately perform in this critical role.

An adept transition manager will provide the appropriate balance of information and activity to engage the campus while also using the opportunity to tell the broader world of the university's past success and future hopes.

Establish the Transition Team

The president and cabinet should work together to create a transition team that will steer the campus through the process. Their responsibilities include:

- Creating an effective communication process to keep the institution's community informed and engaged

- Creating a series of celebratory events for the outgoing president

- Planning for the installation of the new president

- Providing a learning network and support network for the new president.

The members of the team should be chosen for their specific representative areas (e.g., faculty from each school, staff from each major division), and also should be respected for having balanced viewpoints—no axes to grind—and be good communicators. The primary reason for a thoughtful transition process is to alleviate anxiety and promote positive anticipation of the next chapter in the institution's history. Members of the transition team should be chosen with great care as this group is very important.

Make the Announcement

There needs to be an official announcement to the campus community. It should be a planned event presented with dignity and respect. The purpose of the announcement is to signal the beginning of the transition process and to outline what stakeholders can expect will happen over the next year. It is important to convey that business will continue, important work still needs to be done, and that the search and selection process will be done with great care.

The following letter was used by Nicholas S. Rashford, S.J., president of Saint Joseph's University in Philadelphia to announce his retirement.

Letter to University Community—February 22, 2002

Dear Colleagues,

Over the past few months there have been thoughtful and ongoing conversations regarding the eventual transition of leadership at Saint Joseph's University. With my final term as president due to expire in 2004, and the executive vice president assuming the University of Dayton presidency, we have reached the point at which we are ready to address Saint Joseph's transition process more closely.

This afternoon, a deliberate transition plan was begun. I informed the Board of Trustees of my intention to step down as president at the conclusion of the 2002–03 academic year. This 12-month acceleration of my term allows the Board to authorize a presidential search immediately. The timing of a number of current initiatives at the university make it more critical that my successor be in place to help shape the issues that will affect the next administration.

There are three primary goals of the overall transition process. The first goal is to assure the continuing strength of the Catholic, Jesuit mission of Saint Joseph's University. The second is to continue the tremendous advancement of the university through an inevitable period of change. The third goal is to assure that stable leadership is in place across the institution. The transition plan is timed intentionally so that each of our major searches is given singular attention and that there is ample input from faculty, staff, alumni, and trustees wherever appropriate.

In order to best continue the momentum of recent years and to assure the smoothest transition possible across the university, the Board of Trustees also has agreed to the following proposed timetable regarding several key leadership positions:

- As noted above, the presidential search will begin immediately and extend through the 2002–03 academic year. A search committee will be named by the Board, representing all of Saint Joseph's primary stakeholder groups, and I will appoint a "transition team" to help guide the many inter-divisional initiatives that are underway.

- All agree that the new president should select the permanent academic vice president. I have learned, especially while working hand-in-hand with Dan Curran, how important this relationship is to the institution. To that end, my successor will then lead a national academic vice president search.

- Therefore, an interim academic vice president will be named. This individual will not be part of our vice presidential search pool, but will instead serve as a bridge between the two administrations. We have identified a highly qualified external candidate for this important role who will serve Saint Joseph's extremely well. We expect to announce this appointment next week.

- The next step in the plan involves the College of Arts & Sciences. The dean of the College of Arts & Sciences informed us in December of her desire to take a sabbatical year and then return to the faculty. I am happy to announce that the associate dean, who led our successful Phi Beta Kappa candidacy, will serve a three-year term as dean as part of this overall transition plan. This allows the incoming Academic Vice President the freedom to conduct a search for a dean in 2004–05. I thank the dean for her outstanding service and also recognize the great respect with which the associate dean is held in the College.

A final part of the transition plan involves the departure of the vice president for mission and ministry. During this transition time, the Board of Trustee's committee on Mission and Ministry will report to the president.

While significant progress has been made toward most of the objectives of our collaborative Plan 2000, the Board of Trustees and cabinet are fully aware of the challenges that are most immediate. My focus during the next 18 months will be to bring closure to a number of projects, including:

- Completing negotiations for the purchase of property adjacent to Saint Joseph's.

- Gaining community and legislative approval to develop the perimeter properties that have been acquired over the last several years.

- Bringing new residence hall facilities online.

- Coordinating the planning of the next capital campaign, so that a successful launch can be undertaken by the new president.

It is a busy agenda, but I am confident the momentum and experience are in place to achieve these objectives. I am very confident in the ability of Saint Joseph's University to manage leadership transition and emerge even stronger at its conclusion. I am as excited about the closing years of my presidency as its beginning, and I draw continual encouragement from the members of this community who make Saint Joseph's the special place it is.

I would like to offer the opportunity for us to come together to discuss these changes and will host an **open meeting on Monday, February 25, 2002, at 3:00 p.m.,** in the Haub Conference Center of McShain Hall.

Nicholas S. Rashford, S.J.

Mark and Celebrate the Endings

William Bridges tells us that it is important to "mark the endings,"[12] and that we are often reluctant to do so because people do not like endings. In most instances, when a president chooses to leave, much has been accomplished for the institution and there is much to celebrate. The campus needs to acknowledge this in a thoughtful and explicit manner. A chapter in the history of the institution is ending and must be recognized.

It is important to plan a series of events that allow the president and stakeholders to say goodbye to each other. This can be done at formal gatherings, such as convocations, as well as informal gatherings, lunches, and dinners.

It is important for the president to thank people for their support, to acknowledge specific people when appropriate, and to talk about hopes and wishes for the institution. These events will help create psychological closure for those who participate and will be an important part of the way the president will be remembered. Consider personal gifts to key players such as a book of poems or a special picture.

Create Transition Updates

Unless it is managed well, a presidential transition will create a great deal of stress, confusion, and misinformation. The rumor mill will shift into high gear and interesting stories, usually both inaccurate and negative, will abound.

One process that should be institutionalized is a series of written campus-wide communications and face-to-face meetings with stakeholders throughout the campus. The main purpose of these transition updates is to share honest and current information about the transition process. Topics to be covered might include the selection and composition of the transition team and the search committees, what will continue as usual during the transition process and what will change, what the final tour for the president will look like, and the goals to be accomplished during the transition time.

Identify the groups that should be updated and then post a schedule on the institution's Web site so stakeholders can see who is receiving communication. Ensure that donors and alumni are included in these transition updates. These update meetings should be 45 to 60 minutes in duration, include the appropriate information, and—most importantly—allow time for questions and answers. Transparency is important. Explain what is known and get back with people if answers to particular questions are not readily available. It is a good idea to have the updates transcribed and posted to a campus Web site to fully inform stakeholders.

Develop a Communication Plan

There are several goals of a presidential transition process. The primary ones include the following:

- Assure the continuing strength of the mission of the institution

- Continue the momentum and advancement of strategic goals

- Ensure that stable leadership is in place across the institution

- Provide opportunities for input and alleviate anxiety on the part of faculty, staff, students, alumni, and trustees through communication opportunities and routine information sharing.

Communication plays a significant role in achieving these goals. Developing an effective communication plan helps ensure that nothing important is missed and that the community is aware of the key events taking place.

Step 1—pre-planning

Identify to the extent possible the plans of senior leadership team members during the time of the presidential transition. Develop the search strategy and select the chair of the search committee with the board of trustees. The president and board chair also need to identify plans for an interim president, if necessary. They also must communicate with the senior leadership team and the board to set expectations.

Step 2—formal announcement

After consulting with the board of trustees, the president provides a written communication informing institutional stakeholders of his plans and the upcoming change in leadership. A Web site should be established to begin posting official notifications throughout the transition. Use this as a defining historical moment to recap the institutional advances during the presidency. A revised version of the announcement letter would go to a large group of individuals including alumni and donors, friends and former colleagues, local government officials, business affiliates, and other external constituencies. This usually is supplemented with a press release.

Step 3—open forum

The president personally conducts an open forum to facilitate interaction with members of the institutional community. This is an opportunity to convey the confidence of a well-planned leadership transition process and to honestly answer questions.

Step 4—announce the search

The board chair should announce the members of the search committee, identify the external search consultant if applicable, and detail the steps in the search process. This should be the first in a series of regular communications on the search progress. This also is an opportunity to address expectations around confidentiality in order to maintain the likelihood of a strong applicant pool.

Step 5—name the transition team

The board chair provides information to the institutional community about the role and composition of the transition team.

Step 6—search updates

The chair of the search committee, with assistance from the transition manager, provides monthly (or bimonthly) progress reports to the trustees, alumni, and institutional community. One of the early postings should include the position description and list of advertising media and dates. Later in the process, an update can inform the community of open forums with the candidates and encourage them to attend and provide feedback.

Step 7—announce the new president

The board chair announces the outcome of the search to the institutional community and widely to the regional area. This usually entails a press release.

Step 8—develop profiles of the outgoing and incoming presidents

Develop magazine-quality articles to recap the search process and provide a profile and introduction of the new president. One effective way to provide closure for the previous presidency is to cover its history in the alumni magazine soon after the announcement is made. Information utilized in step 2 above can be reused at this time, with more elaboration.

Step 9—transition updates

This is an ongoing process that starts with the announcement of the incumbent's plans. It continues with regular installments regarding upcoming events, "save the date" notices, and the new president's early public schedule.

Step 10—installation planning

Typically a subcommittee or separate inauguration committee is established with some overlap of transition team members. Each president will have preferences that form guidelines for designing the events. For example, it is not uncommon to design an event that is connected to mission (e.g., service day). He and the committee will decide whether the ceremony will take place on-campus or at an outside venue; whether it will include a student-focused event such as a fun-run, picnic, or gala; plans for an event for family and former colleagues; etc.

Even in situations involving the selection of an internal candidate, it is important for faculty, staff, trustees, and others to get to know a new president in her new role. The presidency is like no other position. It is a very different role with new relationships that vary greatly from those of prior positions.

Leave Well

"Effective leaders plan an exit that is as positive and graceful as their entrance was."[13] A graceful exit does not happen all by itself. It must be carefully planned and implemented.

The president's final year in office needs to be a good one. Solid performance, good interactions, visibility, smart decisions, and saying goodbye well all will be important. The institution needs to see its leader at her best as she leaves the campus. In the transition year, there needs to be a high level of presidential visibility throughout the campus. This is not the time to have a meek presence. She should be seen.

In times of stress and change, people need more face-to-face interaction with their leader, not less.[14] Attend regularly scheduled, campus-wide meetings such as faculty senate, administrative councils, employee recognition ceremonies. This allows the president to demonstrate her belief in the centrality of these events. Most important, it will relieve some of the stress campus stakeholders will experience during the presidential transition.

We witnessed one president's slow withdrawal as he backed out of his presidency. He missed meetings, was seen as inattentive at functions, and gradually disappeared from campus. It was awful to see. His legacy was damaged because he could have finished on a high note, but ended poorly.

Departing presidents should be generous. One departing president we talked with had several gift commitments that she kept on the back burner during the final stage of her presidency. She waited until the new president came on board so that he was able to announce these gifts. The new president reaped political and social benefits from his predecessor's generosity. It also enabled him to build his own social capital because he had such a positive beginning.

Maintain a Journal

Maintaining a journal can create a discipline for reflection that many presidents find useful. Taking the time to reflect and write helps slow down the hectic pace of campus life, which only seems to accelerate during the final year. Many conversations and events will take place, issues will be raised, memories touched, and important moments realized. There are many reasons to wish to capture these activities.

For presidents seeking another presidency, the journal can be a powerful learning tool. It provides them with strategic and personal information about what is important, it highlights achievements, it captures the regrets, and it reveals what is truly valuable personally. This will be important information as they enter their new institutions.

Fundamentally, the journal is for the president who is leaving, but it may be possible to share information from it with the new president. New presidents receiving this gift from their predecessors find it to be a rich resource in their own transitions.

Build a Bridge to the Future

As a president thinks about leaving an institution, he needs time to reflect on what he will do afterward. We have seen situations in which the president stayed several years longer than he should have because he had no bridge to the future. In these cases, he ended his tenure with several mediocre years filled with ambivalence and worry. One president advised, "Build a bridge to the future early in your career. You can't build it overnight."

Moore and Burrows tell us that one in five presidents will pursue another presidency.[15] What happens to the other four? Not everyone retires. Does the president want to travel, conduct research, consult, or return to teaching? Depending on the individual's field or background, there may be opportunities in the private sector or for speaking in a national arena. Conversations with trusted colleagues, individuals who have recently retired, and others can be enormously helpful in preparing the president psychologically for the options that may be available.

ADVICE TO BOARDS
Institutionalize Sensitive Conversations

At least annually, the board chair should have an honest and in-depth discussion with the president about accomplishments, aspirations, and plans for the future. This should be much more than a performance review. It should be used to assess the psychological connection of the president to the campus, to her senior team, to the faculty, and to the future vision and goals of the institution.

Some religious communities (e.g., Jesuits) have a disciplined annual protocol in which the head of a province (region) will actively engage his presidents in a discussion about their legacy, excitement for the job, connection to the institution, and their motivation to continue being the president. This is considered a normal practice and is important for the professional development of the individual as well as the long-term health of the institution.

The board chair must be able to assess the level of excitement the president has about helping the institution move forward, how well she understands campus issues, and what kind of relationships exist between her and the faculty and senior staff. It is also important to assess how much physical energy she has to carry out her job responsibilities, whether stakeholders have access to her, what she is learning, and what she sees as the critical issues facing the campus. Obviously, this is not a short conversation. It needs time, structure, and attention to have real meaning. It is essential that the board chair and president trust each other. Without this, little will be accomplished.

Senior leaders (e.g., provost, chief business officer, board chair) should pay attention to what the president talks about. A fully engaged and effective leader must focus on the future, including the short-term issues confronting an institution. If the president is not involved in future or "horizon issues," and focuses most of her attention on the short-term challenges, it may be time for a sensitive conversation.

Openly Talk about Succession Planning

The board needs to have an annual in-depth discussion about succession planning. This is even more important when a successful, well-respected president with impressive accomplishments or a strong personality is at the helm. We worked with one "larger than life" president who seemed to fill a room when he entered. The board never discussed succession planning because they were afraid of his strong reactions. When he decided to leave, he gave little notice to the board, and left an institution with little capacity to change and deal with the future.

This candid discussion requires full trustee participation in the absence of the president. Other senior positions (e.g., provost, chief business officer, chief information officer, deans) also should be discussed on an annual basis.

Interact with the Senior Team

The board chair should appoint a trustee to meet with the senior team to review progress toward goals, to evaluate the president's leadership effectiveness, and to assess the well-being of this key group. In the collegial and non-confrontational atmosphere of higher education, it is often difficult to get to the heart of operations and interactions at the senior level. It will take a trustee with enormous skill and care to create the sense of safety needed to have this honest and delicate discussion. When done well, it can become a routine to which senior members look forward.

Negotiate the "Culminating Agenda"

Because it can often take a year or more to select a new leader, the president may be perceived during this time as a lame duck. This should not be the case, and it does not have to be. After the official announcement, the board chair needs to negotiate with the outgoing president the top two to three priorities for the transition period.

It is a time for focusing on meaningful goals that align with the institution's mission, vision, and strategic plan; not for new initiatives or important decisions that will greatly impact the incoming president.[16] They must be important enough to engage the president and be worthy of his commitment. These priorities need to be communicated within the institution, so that stakeholders understand the focus of the president's work.

On the other hand, some presidents use their departure as an opportunity to tackle a vexing problem during their final year as president. This will take courage, careful planning, tremendous board support, and discipline as stiff resistance will be encountered. Typically, presidents who elect this approach enjoy significant social capital that they're willing to spend for the benefit of the institution. Even when they're successful with this, it usually results in some tarnishing of their legacy.

We know of one campus president who chose to deal with the sensitive and complex issue of post-tenure review. He met with a great deal of resistance and made some enemies, but persisted anyway. The institution benefited greatly from having this issue resolved, but the president got bumped and bruised in the process.

The Importance of Ground Rules

It is essential that a few important and explicit transition ground rules be negotiated and agreed upon by the board, the incumbent president, the cabinet, and the transition team. These ground rules help ensure a smooth transition and should be sacred. Each campus needs to create their own ground rules, but some generic examples might be helpful.

The Role of the Incumbent in the Search Process

"In most cases, the role of the incumbent should be limited to providing guidance to the board, the search committee and the candidates regarding the nature of the position and the condition of the institution."[17] We strongly agree with this advice. The incumbent should be a resource *when asked* and not have a proactive role in the search process. Furthermore, the incumbent should have *no* role in the selection process.

The departing president can add value in many ways such as focusing on his culminating agenda, paying attention to his own transition process, and saying thanks to the many people who have helped him. These activities are much more valuable to the institution than any unsolicited contributions he might attempt to make to the search process.

Communication

This was mentioned in the discussion of the transition manager's role, but it is worth repeating here. It is essential to have the institution's leadership agree on who will be in charge of communication regarding the transition process. Quality control is crucial here and only one person—ideally the transition manager—can be the focal point for all communication.

Stakeholders will have many questions, even anxieties, about what is taking place during the transition and rumors may be rampant. The last thing an institution wants to have is multiple voices and representations sharing different perspectives and information. Agree on the communication plan *and* the institutional spokesperson.

The Authority/Role of the Incumbent

During the transition process, the incumbent should focus on the few priorities negotiated with the board chair. Complex new initiatives generally should not be undertaken. If there is a sticky personnel matter—especially one involving a senior level individual—it should be resolved either by the incumbent or the board, *before* the new president arrives. Hiring decisions for cabinet-level positions should be deferred so that the new president can choose her own person and not have to deal with a recent hire who is someone else's choice. If positions become vacant, they should be filled through interim appointments until the new president is ready to undertake searches for the positions. The incumbent should not make promises she will not be around to keep, or create new initiatives that will need the incoming president's approval and commitment.

Requests by the Incoming President

The new president might ask for significant amounts of information before he comes to campus or he might want to talk or even meet with cabinet members. This is a fairly routine expectation on the part of the new president, but there are times when it might not be desirable. How will this situation be handled? It is important to ensure that requests are handled appropriately but, at the same time, it is important to avoid overwhelming current staff or placing them in awkward positions.

A meeting between the board chair, transition manager, and the incoming president is helpful to review the requests and negotiate what is acceptable. The transition manager then is charged with implementing the agreed-upon processes with others and keeping the outgoing president informed to avoid surprises.

Engage in "Career Mapping"

When a president leaves, a sense of uneasiness and uncertainty can pervade the senior leadership group or cabinet. People often become preoccupied with their own futures and spend time worrying about potential outcomes. Career concerns can become paramount and some may begin to look for options outside the institution. This can create stress and institutional vulnerability that needs to be managed quickly and effectively.

The board chair should assert leadership and appoint a trusted colleague such as a faculty member, a former administrator, or the transition manager to engage in a series of highly confidential discussions with each of the senior leaders in the institution. The purpose of these discussions is to identify their concerns and determine how each senior leader views his or her current career choices. At this time, it is essential to learn who is considering leaving, staying, or is unsure about their options. By being proactive, the institution can quickly and clearly define what to do to maintain the stability of the institution. This also is the time to allay people's fears over major changes that might occur.

It can be a useful discipline to institutionalize this process on an annual basis to anticipate major career moves among senior leaders. Sudden exits can be costly in terms of reputation, prestige, and institutional stability. There are usually warning signs that presage these moves. An annual conversation helps surface these signals and enable the board to be proactive and strategic with their leadership.

We know of one institution whose very charismatic and well-respected president left after a decade of wonderful achievements. Once she announced she was leaving, four of the seven vice presidents began to search actively for new positions. The board chair had to meet individually with the vice presidents and talk about what all the transitions could do to the institution. He enlisted the support of the outgoing president to address people's fears about the future. He crafted a search process for the incoming president, one which provided the vice presidents with key roles in helping choose the new president.

The combination of an inclusive search process, increased responsibility assigned to the vice presidents, and enlisting the participation of the respected outgoing president, helped prevent a potential crisis. Only one of the vice presidents left, thereby minimizing the potential disruption to the campus.

As a general rule, boards should make it clear to presidential candidates during the search that the executive team should be kept in place during the first year. If the vice presidents know this, they will not feel the pressure to start looking for new positions immediately after the president announces her impending departure. This does not mean that if an intense problem emerges with a particular vice president that he will not be let go. It means that communicating a sense of stability in the first year is essential.

With the luxury of planning, a presidential transition can be healthy for leadership and positive for the individual, and provide a series of proud moments for the institution. The following scenario is taken from an actual transition involving one of the authors.

In the fifteenth year of his presidency the flame was waning, other interests were crowding his day, and teaching was becoming a greater focus. The power and passion for the school were at an all-time high but the drive to do the job had greatly diminished. The successes were numerous: the enrollment was growing steadily, the strategic plan accomplishments were mounting, and the capital campaign had come to a successful conclusion. To those closest to him, it was evident that this was the time to conclude on a high note. This is often the case. Close colleagues and friends often know it before the president does. Those who can speak the truth to the president find themselves rehearsing the conversation in their minds so that when just the right time presents itself, they will seize the moment and offer their assistance.

The president at this mid-sized comprehensive institution listened. He readily agreed that he was amenable to planning an exit strategy, but was not truly willing to leave the institution. The thought of becoming the first chancellor was appealing—however, it was not a realistic ambition for many reasons, most of them political. Advancement to the role of chancellor was tied to naming his successor as well. The scenario called for the current executive vice president to become the institution's first lay president. The president was confident he could negotiate this with the board.

While the plan was not successful, it did stir the pot. The executive vice president subsequently accepted the presidency of another institution. The professional partnership with the executive vice president and other close members of his team had played an important role in the last several years of the presidency. The president realized that selecting the next executive vice president while he had intentions of departing soon was not in the long-term best interests of the institution. He realized that he had the luxury of time and decided to use it well.

One of the authors had developed the strategic planning process with the senior leadership team and was called upon to facilitate an in-depth discussion. The president was honest and forthright. He laid out for the team a two-year plan to complete his presidency, provide time for a full search, and transition the new president into the institution. He had one overriding concern, however. Because many members of the team had been in place for several years, he was concerned about too much movement out in a short period of time.

The facilitator asked each member of the team if they would be willing to discuss their own plans and goals. He designed a process for confidential individual consultation by one of the team members. This individual would ask several direct questions and develop a summary of the information that the president could use to understand the range of transitions facing the institution. The team agreed to participate honestly and, to the best of their ability, maintain the positive institutional momentum and minimize the negative impact of whichever potential transitions were identified. A framework is presented below for such a conversation with senior leaders.

Given the president's plans to complete his term in office, it is likely that a search will begin in the coming months. The senior leadership team members' plans are key to a successful transition. Please reflect on each of the following questions during our conversation, and the ideas will be summarized and shared with the cabinet to provide valuable input as we work on the details of the transition plan.

Given the upcoming transition, what are your plans? Do you see yourself in your current position in three years? Still at the institution? In a different role?

Describe the worst case scenario for this transition. And the best case scenario. How does either of these influence your choices?

What advice can you give for this transition period? What needs to be done well? What should be avoided?

Please share your recommendations for people to serve on the leadership transition team.

It was discovered that one vice president was seeking a presidency and would most likely be leaving and one dean was ready to return to the faculty, but that the remainder of the team intended to be stable for the next two years. With that sense of stability, the president proceeded to develop interim leadership plans. He prepared to inform the board with a plan to make the internal announcement the following month.

A TOUGH ISSUE: THE INCUMBENT'S FUTURE RELATIONSHIP WITH THE INSTITUTION

"Take a vow when you step down, that you will absent yourself from the campus for awhile and that you will never respond to complaints about your successor."[18]

The future relationship with the departing president and where she will reside are two of the most complex and potentially thorny issues in a presidential transition. The outgoing president often has many long-standing connections and relationships with people throughout the institution. If she has been an effective president, she has contributed much to the institution and many will have great respect, even admiration, for her.

Where the complexity really emerges is the need for the new president to establish his own light and not be dwarfed by the shadow of the former president. There is no pat answer to this sensitive topic because each institution must reach an understanding that meets their unique needs, institutional history, and the personalities of the incoming and outgoing president.

There are some interesting stories regarding this subject and we'll share just a few of them to stimulate thinking and discussion.

We talked with a president whose predecessor lives across the street from him. This by itself does not present a problem but, unfortunately, the former president visits the campus frequently and tries mightily to stay connected to campus politics. A steady flow of campus visitors to the former president's home can be witnessed daily by the current president. The former president's campus presence and very visible residence constantly undermine the current president's role.

We talked with another president whose tenure lasted about 20 years. He was fortunate to have the same board chair for more than 15 years and they developed a strong collegial and personal relationship. Together they had accomplished a great deal for the institution they loved, and they had genuine respect and affection for each other.

The president enjoys telling the story about his going-away party, which was filled with celebration and many wonderful stories. At the end of the evening, his dearest colleague, the board chair, cornered him and said, "You've been great for this place and I love you. Please don't come back to campus for at least a year!"

The president knew that his great presence and the affection people had for him could easily undermine the new president if he were around too much. The board chair was wise enough to know this and courageous enough to deliver the strong message to his friend.

We know of two institutions in which the former president lives on campus and contributes positively to campus life while fully supporting the incumbent president. At Saint Joseph's University in Philadelphia, the former president, Father Nicholas S. Rashford, served as president for 17 years. He now lives on campus in a student residence building contributing to campus life, saying Mass for students, and teaching a course in the executive MBA program. His relationship with the current president is cordial and non-interfering.

At one private institution, the first lay president was viewed by the outgoing president as a perfect fit. Both the incumbent and the new president met with faculty and were seen together around campus prior to the start of the new president's official term. The impression these actions created was very positive. One faculty member remarked that they seemed almost like brothers. The former president has returned to the faculty to teach and resides on campus.

If an outgoing president is going to have an official relationship with the new president, and have an official role on campus, the following elements need to be in place:

- The board chair and the incumbent president must meet for an open and honest discussion about the potentially positive and negative impacts and influences the incumbent's presence could have on the campus. They need to agree on the future role and create some specific ground rules for future behavior.

- The outgoing president must see himself as a resource to be utilized *only when asked* by the new president.

- The outgoing president must commit to stay out of campus politics and never discuss his successor's problems. This is an essential promise to require because some people will complain about how things are going and actively solicit the previous president's opinion about the direction the new president is taking and the decisions being made. He must keep his opinions to himself.

- After the board chair and incumbent have reached agreement, a meeting with the new president needs to occur. This is when various scenarios can be discussed (e.g., What happens when the president of the faculty senate solicits the former president's advice?). All three need to understand each other's roles, agree to adhere to the ground rules, and create a mechanism for dealing with problems that might surface *before* they occur.

This might sound like a lot of work but it is worth the effort because the odds are against a successful relationship between the incumbent and the new president.

Approximately 25 percent of former and sitting presidents felt it is unwise for former presidents to continue residing in the community after leaving the presidency. Twenty-five percent of former presidents and about 45 percent of the sitting presidents were uncertain about the advisability of staying in the community. Only 25 percent of both groups found it advisable for a former president to be formally affiliated with or employed by the institution after their term in office. Most had reservations about this option.[19]

In the end, such an arrangement will only work if the outgoing president has deep affection and respect for the institution and its mission, and possesses the emotional (not intellectual) maturity to be on the sidelines. If he has never exhibited these characteristics while he was the president, he surely will not after he leaves.

We believe that the new president must have the opportunity to establish his own light and not be consumed by the shadow of the former president. This does not mean that the outgoing president has no role in campus life. There will be plenty of occasions (e.g., commencements, graduations, alumni dinners) when he will be most welcome.

DEALING WITH UNTIMELY DEPARTURES

Up to this point in the chapter, the discussion has focused on planful transitions taking place as the result of a voluntary decision reached by a president after many years of successful service. As much as we wish this were the case in every situation, we realize that there are instances when the president's departure is unexpected or involuntary. The approaches outlined earlier in the chapter may not always be workable in those situations.

One of the most difficult situations occurs when a sitting president dies. Unless this follows a long illness that allowed the institution to plan for this unfortunate circumstance, the community will be shocked by the sudden loss. The grief and tragedy that accompanies an untimely death is one thing; it is quite another when the death is completely unexpected.

The same situation can arise when a president becomes seriously ill very suddenly, or suffers the death of a spouse or child. Any of these situations can prompt a president to resign the position without the benefit of a planful departure. As difficult as this is for the institution, no one can fault an individual for placing their needs or those of their loved ones ahead of the institution's under such circumstances.

There are other situations in which the decision is taken out of the president's hands. There are at least two general categories of what might be termed involuntary departures. The first and less common type involves situations in which the president's performance has been unsatisfactory and the president is being terminated for cause. It is highly unlikely that much can be done to effect a smooth and graceful departure in these situations. Instead, the institution must be deliberate in its actions. The board of trustees must act in accordance with established institutional policies and procedures to remove the president. This should not occur until after the board has identified the internal individual who will serve as interim president (or at least defined the process to select that person as quickly as possible). Once these steps have been taken, the institution can begin the process of recovering from what undoubtedly will be a tumultuous period.

The other type of involuntary departures are those resulting from changed circumstances—either institutional conditions or board expectations. In these situations the president's performance, though not unsatisfactory, is deemed to be out of sync with the current needs of the institution. It is rarely a case of incompetence on the part of the president. Rather, these situations frequently occur when the institution has evolved to a new level and the president has been unable to keep pace with this evolutionary change.

For instance, more and more public institutions have shifted from reliance on funds provided by state legislatures to increased reliance on support from private sources. For many presidents, the shift from a governmental relations focus to a development focus is second nature and made quite easily. Others, however, find it extremely difficult to ask individuals, foundations, or corporations for financial support. It is much harder to request funds when one is unable to point to benefits that will be received by the legislators' constituents.

Another common situation that leads to involuntary departures is changing expectations on the part of the board. This is more common among public institutions with board turnover frequently mandated by state statute or regulations. As new board members are appointed, they bring a new perspective of what the institution should be (or should become). A president who might have been highly successful in leading an institution focused on undergraduate liberal education may not be as adept at leading one shifting its emphasis to professional schools and graduate education.

When changed circumstances dictate that a president's tenure must come to an end, care must be taken to accomplish this with as little disruption as possible. In fact when done well, there is no reason that the primary guidance in the chapter cannot be followed.

There are two key elements when addressing situations involving the involuntary departure of a president. The board must be deliberate in its actions and it must make provisions for the president's future. If the president is not meeting the needs of the institution after years of successful service, it no doubt will be difficult to convey the message that his or her services no longer are needed. Yet this must occur. It should not be left to chance for the president to come to the realization that circumstances have changed. Either the chair of the board or another board member who enjoys a solid relationship with the president must explain the need for the change. Keep in mind that this will be much easier if the institution has established a pattern of annual presidential performance reviews. If this is a routine practice, the discussion can occur naturally as part of this process. But, even when this is not the practice, the president must receive the message that a change is needed. At that point, the planning for the transition can begin.

As mentioned above, there is a second element to involuntary departures of presidents who have served well for a number of years. The institution must assure a smooth and comfortable transition to the president's new role. Depending on the president's age, the new role may be that of a faculty member or the head of a new center or institute within the institution. Or it may be the negotiation of an appropriate severance period to enable the president to find an appropriate position with another institution—maybe even another presidency.

On the other hand, if the president is ready for retirement, the new role can take many forms. For instance, a new position (e.g., chancellor) might be created to enable the president to transition to a role as institutional goodwill ambassador or fund-raiser. In this capacity the president may be called on to participate in key institutional events as she transitions to full retirement. Alternatively, the president may be appointed to a role in community relations or development. In any case, a president who has provided many years of loyal and effective service should be allowed to depart gracefully and with her dignity intact.

***

The end of a president's tenure has a major impact on the life of his institution. With proper planning, care, and execution, this presents an opportunity to write a positive chapter in the campus history. Appropriately addressing the anxiety that accompanies major transitions—both for those leaving and those staying—requires forethought and preparation. If the right processes are in place as a routine activity, the board, senior leadership team, and the campus as a whole will be well positioned to respond to the challenge that change of this magnitude brings.

A SECOND CHANCE
NICHOLAS S. RASHFORD, S.J., UNIVERSITY PROFESSOR AND FORMER PRESIDENT, SAINT JOSEPH'S UNIVERSITY

In the life cycle of a presidency there are five stages. Donald Hambrick and Gregory Fukutomi[20] of Columbia University have studied the seasons of CEOs in many industries and their life cycles. The first phase begins with the president assuming his role based upon a particular paradigm or frame of reference from prior experience or executive positions.

In my case, I was formerly the dean of a business school; my format was utilizing live case studies. I came to the presidency in 1986 with a strong commitment to educate future leaders, and I felt that these future leaders would need to hold a master's degree at a minimum. The baccalaureate degree was no longer going to be sufficient. I felt that this paradigm was most likely to take hold in the business school, so I pressed hard for new master's programs there. I was also interested in starting what was, for them, a new format—the executive MBA (EMBA). My idea of how a university should operate was open and entrepreneurial.

The next phase is the experimentation phase, in which the commitment to the original paradigm varies based upon its perceived success. This is when the president's knowledge of the job is moderate, interest in the job is very high, and power is beginning to grow. Most importantly the president's information continues to flow from numerous sources, but is well filtered by the time it reaches him.

In my presidency, I was anxious to experiment. The graduate programs had begun to take off and the new EMBA program had been established. I next focused on the international arena. I felt that the horizon had to be wider than the local region. In terms of content, the modern leader would need to be savvy in international culture and business processes. The concept of a two- to three-week study tour within a program was expanded and made mandatory for the master's programs. I also believed that it was beneficial to recruit international students more heavily to diversify the campus experience and extended a long-term contract with a language school partner, ELS (English Language Schools).

The third phase is the defining phase of the presidency. It is characterized by the president's level of commitment to his paradigm. At this point the knowledge of the job is strong, rate of learning declines, interest is still high, and information begins to come from fewer and somewhat more filtered sources. During this phase the president's power continues to grow.

In my case, I was committed to sustained growth (in a very tuition-driven institution) in order to get to a critical mass that was necessary to provide the resources needed to improve programs and the physical plant. The undergraduate student body was growing steadily, the quality indices were up, and the rankings were improved. The graduate programs were still not fully embraced by the faculty and there were no new programs in the arts and sciences college. I was energized by all the change and could clearly see where the institution was headed, even though the planning committee was no longer active. The board of trustees was supportive. However, at this point in time, the faculty began to feel I was not listening to their concerns about the stress of growth on resources (human and financial). They feared that the increased size of the undergraduate program and the new emphasis on graduate programs would change the culture.

The fourth phase is a convergence phase, as a president pursues a series of steps to reinforce the major changes that have resulted from his commitment to his paradigm. By this time in the life cycle there is a strong knowledge of the job, interest is starting to diminish, and information is highly filtered and from very few sources. The president's power is strong and ever increasing.

In this phase, I looked like a textbook case. I was in my seventh year, I was confident, we were in the midst of a successful capital campaign, but I was hearing from fewer people. I held weekly expanded cabinet meetings and realized that there was serious dysfunction in some of the interactions at the vice presidential level.

Reaching the fifth phase is postponed. It was at this point that the faculty gathered together their concerns and asked me to meet with them. The provost joined me for a session with about 20 faculty leaders. They asked why I wasn't listening to them, told me what was going wrong from their perspective, asked where the institution was going and why there was no agreed upon strategic plan. They suggested that we hire an outside facilitator to process these issues and help reconcile the parties. I agreed. While I was terrified that the faculty would not understand and embrace my paradigm, I also realized that this could provide an opportunity for a fresh start. But in the meantime, other administrators became skittish and backed away from the conversations.

This became a very stressful intervention. Significant changes in leadership took place. After three two-day off-site meetings, a series of agreements were developed that included regular communication and future planning. The consultants facilitated discussions of scenarios for the future. The faculty embraced the graduate programs as I conveyed my understanding that it was part of the university's mission to form men and women who would be leaders and these leaders would really need to have a master's degree.

A new planning process emerged. The process was designed for real input from all constituencies, with the ability to shape the goals and identify the steps to achieve them. Lastly, the institutional planning committee was reformulated to lead the planning and implementation processes.

The experimental phase revisited...the knowledge of the job is moderate, interest in the job is very high and power is beginning to grow. In this second phase, the knowledge of the job was high, and we were experimenting once again.

A new way of operating was established. It was not always easy for me, but the faculty kept me honest. There was a strategic plan adopted and this agreed-upon agenda formed the basis for the accomplishments of the next several years. One of my goals was to move into the doctoral level—not to become a significant research institution, but to provide the Ed.D. for local educators in the Philadelphia region.

The defining phase revisited...knowledge is strong, rate of learning declines, interest is still high, and information begins to come from fewer and somewhat more filtered sources.

This time around, the defining phase really was descriptive. The planning process took hold and a culture of planning was gradually embraced by the community. The cabinet finally worked well, with the right people in leadership positions.

The convergence phase revisited...there is a strong knowledge of the job, interest is starting to diminish, and information is highly filtered and from very few sources.

I prefer not to think about diminishing interest. Rather I describe it as diversifying interests. I was comfortable, I was seeking new creative projects, and I began working with a technology company, serving on their board and facilitating meetings. It was during this time that the Y2K issues were causing institutions to rethink their major administrative systems and I was active in the analysis and process of identifying and implementing a new enterprise system for the university. The undergraduate programs had grown and student interest in on-campus housing was at an all-time high. We were able to acquire units, build a new residential quad, and provide apartment-style options for upperclassmen. There were still things undone, and I began to think that the need to renovate the science center and expand the student center would become part of the next strategic plan.

Phase 5—at last. This final phase is defined as dysfunction. During this part of the cycle the president's effectiveness is seriously diminishing. The commitment to a given paradigm is solidified, and interest in experimentation is seriously weakened. Information is from a very few, highly filtered sources. As interest ebbs, energy for risk and change disappears too. Paradoxically, the president's power and ability to lead are at an all-time high.

During this time my interests began to shift—I had energy to spare and I put that energy into learning conversational Spanish. My passions involved all types of new technology. My hobby of photography became a consuming daily quest. Once again, my colleagues tell me that I was almost a textbook case—with one exception. I felt safe in asking the cabinet for their advice about an exit strategy and timing. They felt safe in telling me what I needed to know. I did try the denial route for a bit of time while I settled into the idea of leaving the presidency, its power, and all its perks. However, when my long-time colleague and provost was offered and accepted a presidency, I realized that it was not my place to hire the next chief academic officer. That belonged to the next president. With that realization, I began to work with my staff, the cabinet, and the board to plan the transition to the next presidency.

Philadelphia, Pennsylvania
April 2007

NOTES

1. Hesselbein, Francis. "The Challenges of Leadership Transition." Leader to Leader 6 (Fall 1997).

2. Levinson, Harry, and Stuart Rosenthal. CEO: *Corporate Leadership in Action*. New York: Basic Books, 1984.

3. Ciampa, Dan, and Michael Watkins. *Right From the Start*. Boston: Harvard Business School Press, 1999.

4. Moore, John W., and Joanne M. Burrows. *Presidential Succession and Transition: Beginning, Ending and Beginning Again*. Washington: American Association of State Colleges and Universities, 2001.

5. Showalter, Shirley H. "When and How to Leave a Presidency." *The Chronicle of Higher Education*. http://chronicle.com/weekly/v51/i35/35c00301.htm (accessed June 3, 2007).

6. Moore & Burrows. *Presidential Succession and Transition*.

7. Ross, Marlene, and Madeleine F. Green. *The American College President*, 2000 Edition. Washington: American Council on Education, 2000.

8. Fretwell, E.K. *The Interim Presidency*. Washington: Association of Governing Boards of Colleges and Universities, 1995.

9. Goldstein, Larry, and Patrick Sanaghan. "Looking Beyond the Moment." National Association of College and University Business Officers *Business Officer* 81,10 (June 2003): 26–30.

10. Moore & Burrows. *Presidential Succession and Transition*.

11. Sanaghan, Patrick, Larry Goldstein, and Susan Jurow. "A Learning Agenda for Chief Business Officers." National Association of College and University Business Officers *Business Officer* (May 2001): 42–49.

12. Bridges, William. *Managing Transitions*. New York: Addison-Wesley, 1991.

13. Hesselbein. *The Challenges*.

14. Weisbord, Marvin R. *Productive Workplaces*. San Francisco: Jossey-Bass, 1987.

15. Moore & Burrows. *Presidential Succession and Transition*.

16. *Ibid*.

17. *Ibid*.

18. Bornstein, Rita. *Legitimacy in the Academic Presidency*. Westport, Connecticut: Praeger, 2003.

19. Moore & Burrows. *Presidential Succession and Transitions*.

20. Donald C. Hambrick, Gregory D.S. Fukutomi, "The Seasons of a CEO's Tenure," *The Academy of Management Review* 16:4 (1991): 719–742.

CHAPTER

Building a Bridge to the Future

Ultimately, the goal of interim service is to prepare for new leadership.[1]

n the mid-1990s one of the authors was engaged to initiate a year-long strategic planning process for a public institution. The campus climate could be described as one with low morale, contentious faculty and administration relationships, a pervasive amount of cynicism, and a silo mentality. The president was seen as distant, arrogant, aloof, and not a fan of strategic planning. In short, this was not a pretty picture.

The system board charged the campus president with initiating strategic planning processes. This president had very little enthusiasm for the effort. Despite these challenging circumstances, we embarked on a very inclusive and highly participative strategic planning process. Engagement throughout the campus was high and some real interest—even enthusiasm—was created. About two months into the process the president unexpectedly resigned his position and left the campus. This was met with a combination of surprise, enthusiasm, and celebration. Unfortunately, however, the planning process was put on hold.

Within a week of the departing president's exit, an interim president was chosen. He had been a president at two other institutions in the state and had a solid reputation for effective, stable leadership.

We met with the interim president to discuss the future of the planning process. Our hopes were not high because we assumed it would be put on hold indefinitely. We were wrong. The interim clearly communicated that it was essential to continue the hard work of the planning process and necessary to create a shared picture of the future of the university. He let us know that he would fully support the strategic planning process and asked how he could help. He attended all the important planning meetings, talked about how valuable this process was for the institution, and listened carefully to stakeholders' ideas.

He served for 18 months as the interim and oversaw the initiation of many of the strategic goals and actions of the plan. He helped pave the way for a new president to come onto the campus with some renewed hope, more positive relationships, and a shared meaning about the future.

It was our first exposure to an interim president's responsive and responsible leadership. In the short time he was at the university, he made a real difference in many lives and showed how strategic and important the role of an interim can be.

"Between 1945 and 1970 [Michael] Cohen and [James] March estimated that a college or university had a 4 percent chance of having an interim president. Our estimate for 1998 was 6 percent for the private institutions and 11 percent for public universities."[2] Given that there are several hundred presidential transitions occurring every year, somewhere between 40 and 50 interim presidents are leading our institutions at any one time.[3] The more that is known about this unique leadership position, the better institutions can utilize interims.

Interims can be utilized for a variety of reasons: as part of a planful transition process for a long-term president's departure, to provide leadership during a presidential sabbatical, or to fill the void after the sudden unanticipated departure of a president (e.g., death, health reasons, unsavory act, unexpected resignation for a unique opportunity).

For purposes of this chapter, we want to distinguish between two different types of interim presidents—external and internal. The external interims are leaders from outside the institution. These individuals often have former presidential experience.[4,5] Internal interims come from within the institution. Internal interims are often chosen because of a sudden departure.

Choosing an interim primarily is a board decision with very little stakeholder input. It is the board's responsibility to choose an excellent interim who will provide effective leadership during the transition period.

The beauty of an interim appointment is that it does two important things for the institution and creates a very special opportunity. First it creates the space and time for the development of the intelligent, inclusive, and disciplined search process necessary for finding the permanent candidate for the future.

Next, it provides a sense of stability and security in times of change. During transitions a great deal of stress and anxiety can be experienced by campus stakeholders. An effective interim can calm the waters, communicate that things are in good hands, and demonstrate that a bridge to the future is being built.

The special opportunity created is one that does not occur very often in an organization's history. The appointment of an interim allows the institution to seriously examine its strengths and weaknesses. The interim is going to be on board only for a short period of time. This arrangement encourages people to be more candid with their feedback about what works and what does not. No matter what they say, the listener will be moving on once the permanent president is hired. The information obtained by the interim through an informal assessment process can pay dividends long after he has departed.

Although both kinds of interims will have many of the same responsibilities and challenges, there are unique aspects for each that need to be considered and understood. We will address the external interim's role first.

If an external interim has past presidential experience, it enables her to move smoothly into a top leadership position. She often understands the complexities of campus life, shared governance, and other issues unique to higher education, and can deal with ambiguity and politics. This allows her to focus on the most important institutional issues and not get bogged down in trivial details that can bury any leader.

The following section provides some advice for boards and external interim presidents as they manage this unique role in higher education.

ADVICE TO BOARDS

Consider identifying a transition manager. Appointing a transition manager may not be possible or appropriate in all cases. When it is, however, the position (as described in chapter 5) can minimize the complexity attendant to transitions and make it much easier for the interim.

Be visible in support of the interim. Attend town hall meetings, athletic functions, and social occasions with him. Campus stakeholders need to see the board's support of the new leader and believe that they are committed to his success. It communicates that the interim president has the confidence of the board during this time of change. Additionally, if the board is in a position to enlist this type of support from some key faculty, that also does wonders to enhance the interim's credibility.

Do not forget the interim's family. Most institutions are thoughtful about family issues with a new president. They need to be just as thoughtful with an interim. If the interim has a spouse or partner, there needs to be some discussion about that individual's role and the expectations for him or her during the interim's tenure. The interim's family often can be a hidden resource. Too often though, they are ignored. Avoid this by paying attention to the interim's family and their needs. The interim will feel taken care of and focus his efforts on leading the institution and not worrying about his family.

Do not prolong the interim's stay. Remember that the primary role of the interim is to lay the foundation for the permanent president to be successful. He is there to allow time to search for an excellent president. Boards should avoid falling in love with the interim. He will be leaving. If he stays too long, he will get caught up in the daily activities of the institution, its complexity, and culture. The interim should not become a lame duck by being kept in the role too long. Focus on hiring the new president.

Avoid the sin of omission. In most cases search committees and boards are very enthusiastic about their campus and want to communicate all the positive things about their institution. They tend to be reluctant to share problems, challenges, or negative issues with potential interims because they are afraid they may scare away good candidates for the interim appointment. This is a natural but not helpful approach.

With an interim, the board needs to be honest about both the gifts of the institution and its potholes. The interim must fully understand what she is walking into. If there has been a sudden departure of a president, the interim must know what the circumstances were so she knows what to avoid and so she can understand the potential ripples of the departure. Honesty is key.

Watch out for end runs. In some institutions people might take advantage of the fact that the interim will only be around for a relatively short period of time. Some people might be inclined to enlist the support of trustees to further their own interests and initiatives. Private conversations with trustees could occur. This must not happen because it will undermine the power and authority of the presidency. The board chair needs to clearly communicate to the trustees that this should never happen and, if it does, he needs to intervene quickly to stop it.

Avoid the term "acting president." This term conveys the impression of a leader that merely is "holding the line"[6] versus one that continues to move the institution forward. An interim should not be a placeholder stuck in neutral. She needs to lead the institution in a thoughtful and meaningful way while progress is being made.

Interims are not just placeholders. At the University of Vermont, the board hired Edwin I. Colodny as an interim president. Colodny—the former chief executive officer for US Airways—is not an academic, but he had served as a board member and chair of the University of Rochester board of trustees. He served as interim for 13 months. The university had gone through three presidents in less than a decade and was described as being "rudderless." Colodny was given the mandate and support of the board to make some tough but necessary decisions. He eliminated five of 27 sports teams, shrank the continuing education department by cutting 36 positions, and eliminated the dental hygiene program by transferring it to Vermont State Colleges.[7]

Where does a board find an interim president? If there is not a good internal candidate, they might consider the Registry for College and University Presidents. This is an excellent source for interim candidates. The organization, established in 1992, has more than 100 former or retired presidents available for interim positions.

ADVICE TO INTERIMS

Negotiate with the board. The interim must negotiate a number of thorny issues with the board and the sooner the better. Gain clarity on the board's expectations. Do they want business as usual? Do they want a caretaker who will maintain stability until a new president is selected? Do they want the interim to deal effectively with several significant challenges? An interim should seek the answers to these essential questions because they will define his presidency.

The interim must approach the position with careful consideration for the specifics of the situation. Some interims are hired in the middle of the academic year, because the predecessor departed during the semester break. Others start in the middle of the term because of the untimely departure of the previous president. Still others are lucky enough to begin service at the beginning of the academic term. Irrespective of the specific start date relative to the academic calendar, the interim must recognize that the timing will influence what can be accomplished—and how quickly it can be accomplished.

What is the strategic agenda? It is important to manage the expectations of the board about what actually can be accomplished during the six to 18 months of the interim's tenure. These goals need to be agreed upon and made public, so that everyone on campus understands them and can begin to align their efforts toward their accomplishment. Examples might include preparing for a self-study, developing a strategy for the new campaign capital, or establishing a framework for curriculum review.

Irrespective of the specific agenda to be tackled, the number one priority for every interim is to prepare the institution for a permanent president. The interim should do everything in her power to lay the foundation for a successful transition by the new permanent president. This might mean making some difficult personnel decisions, tackling a thorny budget problem, refocusing the energies of the cabinet, or sharing some unpleasant feedback with the board. Whatever the issue is, it is her responsibility to do whatever she can to minimize the impact of the situation to enable her successor to be as effective as possible once he is on board.

The interim president should establish an agreement with the board on how they will work together. She should not assume that everyone knows what is expected of her. It is important to have several operating ground rules that help articulate the relationships between the board and the interim. How will important decisions be made? What will happen if there is a major problem or crisis? What is the interim allowed to do? Are there issues/areas of which she should steer clear? How will the interim and board communicate with each other so both feel respected and informed? What should be the frequency and format of communication (e.g., phone, e-mail, face-to-face) between her and the board chair?

There is a special opportunity in some interim situations as it relates to boards. If the previous president left because of difficulties with the board, it is possible that they were not all of the president's doing. The interim may be in a position to suggest to the board that they examine their processes. We have learned that failed presidencies usually are like failed marriages—both parties are at fault. The board's decision to remove the president may have solved that part of the problem, but it will not solve the board's problems. Given the interim's appointment for a brief period of time, he has nothing to lose in attempting to help the board work through any governance and other process issues that contributed to the previous president's difficulties.

The interim president should ask about problems that may exist. This will take some courage but it will be important for her to define the real challenges of the institution. She must be able to map out the minefield of problems so that she can strategize about them. Brutal honesty is needed from the board about what needs to be fixed. She probably cannot fix everything, but practices and protocols can be put in place to begin to deal with these difficult issues. E.K. Fretwell advises interim presidents to "count on being surprised."[8] Many of the interims in his study indicated that they had one or two major surprises that made their work more challenging. Remember, ask about problems.

Learn fast! It is important that the interim learn about the institution as quickly as possible. Obviously, reading the strategic plan, accreditation reports, and self-studies is helpful, but he should get to campus as quickly as possible. Once there, he should wander around, talk with people, and listen carefully. It is helpful for him to have some strategic questions to ask people that will educate him about the institution. For example, how would you describe the campus climate? What is done well here? What are you proud about? What are some changes you would like to see happen over the next several years? What traditions represent the institution at its best? How do people who live in this area perceive the institution? What advice can you give me so that I can be successful during my stay here?

The learning network we recommend for new presidents is a very helpful mechanism for interims also. This network is a small (six to eight people) credible group of faculty, administrators, and staff whose primary purpose is to educate the interim to help him avoid the potholes. The learning network can perform a valuable service by taking steps like the following:

- Communicate the history of the campus.
- Describe the complexity of the culture.
- Identify the important traditions that must be preserved.
- Articulate the political landscape that must be navigated.

In short, the learning network addresses the factors that make each campus unique. The interim should meet with this group several times during the first month and, if at all possible, before actually arriving on campus.

Meet with key staff and the cabinet. Within the first few days of arriving on campus, the interim should consider conducting a full-day, off-campus retreat with key staff. The interim may want to engage a trusted and experienced facilitator (e.g., faculty member, external consultant) to help manage this meeting to enable him to focus on the conversations and relationships. Some of the purposes of the retreat are to get everyone on the same page about the strategic agenda for the next year; discuss personal leadership styles, especially the interim's and how he likes to do business; create ground rules or working agreements that will enhance the working relationships within the cabinet; and clarify how decisions will be made in the future.

A successful retreat will create positive momentum at the beginning of the interim's presidency. It will communicate to others that he is leading an effective team and help move the institution into a brighter future.

It would be helpful to have a one-day retreat every three to four months to make sure everyone is still on the same page, identify any emerging issues or challenges, clarify any misunderstandings, acknowledge and celebrate successes, and continue to build effective relationships.

There is another way in which retreats can be used to help prepare for the permanent president. Along with the items mentioned above, the retreat can include time used to identify ways in which the senior staff can support the permanent president. Attention to this topic will help the senior staff think specifically about what it will take for the new president to be successful and what they can be doing to contribute to that success.

Hold a series of town hall meeting as soon as possible. These inclusive events create the opportunity for people throughout the campus to meet and greet the interim president. This is very important. These meetings should be informally structured but allow for some comments from the interim, include a question and answer period, and provide for some informal mingling. About an hour and a half should be allotted to each meeting and they should be conducted throughout the campus. They should not be held in the president's residence. The interim needs to be out meeting people on their own turf.

Schedule the town hall meetings at different times throughout a day or week (e.g., morning, lunch, evening) so that as many people as possible can be engaged. There should be frequent town hall meetings throughout the interim's tenure. Remember, visibility and connection are important during transitions. Whenever possible, have board members present at the town hall meetings to communicate visible support for the interim's presidency.

Interact with junior staff including secretaries, cashiers, and custodians to learn what they know. It is striking how much information individuals in these positions possess, but are never asked to share. Although some may be intimidated by being approached by the president, many will not. Their positions enable them to observe the inner workings of the institution in ways that senior leaders rarely experience. They also know who is contributing, and who is not; who is supportive of the administration, and who is a malcontent who seeks nothing more than to stir the pot; who will go the extra mile, and who is more inclined to throw hurdles in the path of progress. This information will be invaluable to an interim.

One interim president shared with us the importance of collecting and disposing of lingering issues. He has emphasized addressing the campus's long-standing complaints, past injuries, and poor decisions by the previous administration. The objective is to bury the past and shift the focus to the future. As a result of the emphasis on the future, he was able to engender a renewed optimism on the campus.

Create and maintain connections with external stakeholders. During the transition process, there are key groups with whom the interim must stay connected and develop a relationship. The alumni association is one such group. Interims need to convey confidence to this important group. The interim will want their work (e.g., fund-raising, volunteerism) to continue at a high pace and not be put on hold for a year or more. The interim should attend alumni meetings whenever possible, and they should be invited to the president's office for dialogue and discussion. They must be kept informed through e-mail, phone, and video-conferencing about campus events and progress.

The neighborhood community is an important stakeholder group with which to connect. It is essential that every campus have positive town-gown relations. An institution cannot afford to have the community feel disconnected for any length of time. Once the connection is lost, it is very hard to reestablish.

The interim should reach out to the community by attending some of the important community meetings. She also should invite key individuals to the president's office to obtain their advice and perspective. If she gains their trust, the campus continues to benefit and it will provide a unique way to learn amazing things about campus leadership, politics, history, and perceptions.

Local government leaders comprise another important stakeholder group with whom to connect during the interim's tenure. The senior leadership group needs to create a plan for the interim to meet with specific governmental leaders (e.g., mayor, county executive, local legislators) so that a relationship can be established. Given that an interim's tenure can last from six to 18 months, the institution cannot afford to allow these key relationships to deteriorate.

It generally is a good idea to invite these external stakeholders to campus so that they feel a real part of the institution during the transition period. Conversely, it is sometimes a good idea to visit them on their turf. This demonstrates respect for them in their role.

Identify some trustworthy people with whom to connect. There should be a small group of influential and trustworthy individuals who can act as an ongoing feedback mechanism, reality check, and sounding board for the interim president. Weekly breakfast or lunch meetings should be held with these individuals—sometimes one-on-one and other times as a group. The goal with these trustworthy allies is to see how people on campus are doing, identify the latest rumors, find out what positive things are occurring on campus, and identify any emerging challenges or problems.

At least one of these allies needs to be a respected faculty member. Obviously, these conversations are highly confidential and this has to be agreed to at the beginning. It is not a secret that the meetings are taking place. The interim should be open about this, but the content of the meetings should remain private.

Some people might wonder why the cabinet is not used for this important role. This sounds good in theory but does not work in practice. The cabinet needs to be focused on doing their jobs very well and the interim will rely on them to address many confidential matters related to running the institution. The trusted allies, however, serve a very different purpose. They are convened to speak the truth to the president, keep him fully informed about campus realities and complexities, and provide him with a real pulse of the institution. Their allegiance is to the institution and not the interim. They are there to give the essential information and perspectives the interim must know about if he is to be successful.

Walk around the campus and be visible. Visibility is important for any president, but especially for interims. People need to see and interact with their leadership in times of change and transition. It is helpful to conduct these walks with a friendly and familiar person like the provost, a highly influential faculty or staff member, or even well-known students. People will be more apt to say hello or come over to chat if they recognize a familiar face. It also conveys that the interim is connected to people who are part of the institution.

Take the walks at irregular times because different things will be seen and different people will be encountered throughout the day. Of course, having lunch regularly in the faculty dining room or student center also is helpful.

The interim should have open lunches occasionally to which people are invited to "chew and chat." It enables people to connect with the interim and ask her questions. It also moves beyond rumors and creates a real perception of the new leader.

The interim should attend as many of the institution's important ceremonies, meetings, and other events as possible. This communicates respect for the traditions of the campus and the events taking place. It also creates a wonderful set of opportunities for her to learn and discuss things.

Avoid filling key vacancies with permanent hires. Interim presidents should not make key appointments that the new president will inherit. If possible, fill important vacancies (e.g., provost, chief business officer) with other interims, leaving the permanent appointments to the new president. The interim can take steps to accelerate the process for the new president by laying the foundation for a search. This will enable the permanent president to select his own team and do it expeditiously if necessary.

Communicate often. During a transition, people will have a fair amount of anxiety and many questions. The interim should be able to supply quality information to stakeholders that communicates what is being learned and what the interim is doing. Biweekly e-mail reports from the president's office can be very helpful. The president should keep these informal and informative. He should let the campus know what his schedule has been, with whom he has met, and what is being learned about the institution. The interim also can pose a question or two to the campus stakeholders that will stimulate their interest, provide some information, and give an indication of who actually reads their e-mail.

Act as a resource. The interim president can act as a resource for the search committee and the board. She can openly and honestly share what she is learning about the institution's needs, challenges, assets, and future possibilities. Because her agenda is clear and her motivation is to help the institution, her knowledge and insights will be invaluable.

If asked, she also can have conversations with the incoming president. These conversations will be a rich source of information for the new president. She can share what she has learned about campus politics and traditions, its problems and challenges, its hopes and aspirations. She also should be able to identify key influential stakeholders with whom the new president should develop a relationship. These key influencers are those individuals who deeply understand the campus culture, have great credibility with peers, possess affection for the institution, and—most importantly—can speak the truth to power. These individuals can be a strategic resource for the new president and serve many purposes in the future.

The interim also can act as a resource to the final candidates in the search process. It is essential that these potential presidents fully understand what they are getting into. With this honest high quality information, their decision to come on board can be made with the confidence that they know most of what they need to know. Of course, there is a risk with this approach because some may decline the offer after the conversation. It still is the best way to go.

INTERIM AS CANDIDATE

The conventional wisdom and our experience tell us that the interim should not become a candidate for the permanent position. There are several reasons for this. When potential candidates realize that the interim is already in the candidate pool, they will often assume that the job is already "wired" and that it is a done deal. The institution will lose highly qualified candidates because they simply will not apply. The interim has an unfair advantage over the other candidates because he is already learning on the job, developing relationships, and presumably moving the institution forward. It is hard to compete with an established record.

If the interim wants to be the new president, he may become reluctant to take on a tough issue. One of the important benefits of an interim is that he does not have to worry about making future enemies. A potential candidate has to worry about this.

The goal is to have the interim do an excellent, temporary job and then leave. Obviously there is the rare exception when an absolutely stellar interim candidate is the right person for the job. But more often than not, the interim represents nothing more than an easy choice. Overall, the best advice is to hire the interim to do the job on a temporary basis and spend the time and energy looking for stellar candidates for the permanent position. "Simply put, if the acting president is permitted to be a candidate, the process will suffer greatly, as will the institution."[9]

Fretwell's excellent monograph on interim presidents found that an overwhelming majority of the 52 interims he interviewed communicated that the interim should not be a candidate for the permanent position. Fretwell also found an interesting trend that could use more exploration. Thirty-one of the fifty-two interims were called in to fill a vacancy on a campus where the departing president had left a troubled campus.[10]

THE INTERNAL INTERIM

Most of what has been covered in this chapter has focused on external interims. We recognize that internal interims actually are more common than external interims, but we chose to address the guidance from the perspective of external interims first. We did this because we believe the challenges tend to be somewhat greater for external interims—primarily because they arrive without the knowledge and institutional experience that an internal interim possesses.

If the institution plans to use an internal interim, it is important to ensure that the individual selected is relieved of their regular duties. It is simply not possible to hold down two full-time positions, if one is as challenging as a presidency. If it is just not possible to relieve this person completely of their former duties, there should be some support from other areas to help manage the workload. If this does not happen, it is very likely that the interim's tenure will not be as successful as it could be.

The internal interim needs to do most of the same things that are suggested for an external interim. She needs to negotiate with the board about expectations, goals, ground rules, and communication. She should meet with the cabinet/key staff as soon as possible to get everyone on the same page, agree on decision-making processes, establish ground rules, define communication protocols, and share the goals that were agreed to with the board. She should conduct several town hall meetings for campus stakeholders because she now is in a new leadership role and people need to see and experience her in this new role.

She will need to create or maintain connections with external stakeholders, walk around campus, and establish effective communication processes to keep people informed and provide feedback. She also can act as a valuable resource to the final candidates for the presidency and, if asked, the permanent president.

An internal interim can be a very mixed blessing. On the positive side, the internal leader is a known entity and has hopefully developed a positive and credible reputation as well as constructive relationships with many campus stakeholders. If she is respected and trusted, she can lead the institution effectively during her temporary tenure.

Ideally, she already understands campus culture, the political landscape of the institution, its challenges, and strengths. Her learning curve will be flattened in many areas (e.g., culture, key external stakeholders), but as steep as the external's in others that may not be in her area of expertise (e.g., finance, technology). Because she understands the institution, she can add real value by moving things forward.

The downside of an internal interim is that she is a known entity. If she has been unkind or arrogant, her reputation is well-known throughout the campus and people will not be enthused about her new leadership role. She can be wedded to "the way things are done around here" and never push for constructive change.

Even if she has not been a difficult person to deal with, it is possible that she still may be unpopular. If she has performed her job appropriately it is possible that she was forced to make difficult or unpopular decisions. This may have caused her to make some real enemies throughout the institution.

It is often difficult to be a cabinet peer one day and the president the next. Other senior leaders might find it difficult to report to someone with whom they have had a collegial relationship. The internal interim also may be reluctant to rock the boat because she will be around after the permanent president is in place.

With a sudden departure such as the death of a president, boards tend to appoint an interim (often the provost) rather quickly. They want to communicate that a senior leader is in place and ready to lead. Board policies usually dictate who will be appointed as the interim. If a board does not have this policy in place, they should consider establishing one.

***

Interims can play a vital role in the life of an institution. They can create a sense of security and hope during a time of complex change. They have their work cut out for them and they will need the help and support of others to be successful. In the best circumstances, they create the time to develop a disciplined and inclusive process for selecting a permanent president who will help the institution realize its full promise and potential.

COMING THROUGH SUCCESSFULLY—EVEN WHEN YOU'RE LEAST PREPARED
JOHN COCHRAN, FORMER CHAIR, LOYOLA COLLEGE IN MARYLAND BOARD OF TRUSTEES

Harold (Hap) Ridley, S.J. had recently completed the tenth year of a rather remarkable presidency at Loyola College in Maryland when he died unexpectedly, literally dropping dead on the floor of his residence. Despite having recently received a clean bill of health during his annual checkup, he died of a pulmonary condition—having never shown any outward sign of a problem beforehand.

The shock of his untimely death was felt by everyone within the college community. Father Ridley and the board had recently discussed his future at the college and it was everyone's expectation that he would serve for several more years before retiring, continuing work on the many new and exciting initiatives underway. Much had been accomplished already during Father Ridley's tenure, including new facilities, enhanced academic programs, and a very successful capital campaign. No one was prepared for an event of such enormous implication—and sadness.

As chair of the college's board of trustees, I was immediately focused on the process of identifying an interim president, reviewing the scheduling of memorial services and related events, and beginning the search for a new president. Of course, all of these issues needed immediate attention.

The college's vice president for administration played a key role in the days immediately following Father Ridley's death. Obviously there needed to be a press release to inform the community of Hap's passing, and to inform the school's constituents as to what they could expect next. It was important to convey to the Loyola community that, despite the tragic loss, the college would continue to operate as it always had.

The board's vice chair also played an important part in my activities following the tragedy. The two of us spent many hours on the phone and in meetings to map the process of recovery, working with the administrative staff. The first step was a carefully crafted press release informing the community of Father Ridley's passing and describing the larger accomplishments of his decade of service as Loyola's president. We also thought it important to set the stage for the quick appointment of an interim president.

The vice chair and I reviewed the potential candidates for interim president. It was important to us to appoint someone from within the college if at all possible. Our first choice for the position was the vice president for academic affairs. He had been with the college for many years, was well-known and well liked, and—especially significant—he was respected by the faculty.

Despite the urgency of the situation, we did not want to act in haste. We considered it necessary to consult with others about our plan before approaching our choice for interim president. This included contacting the school's other four vice presidents, who might soon begin reporting to their former peer. Given that Loyola is a Jesuit institution, we knew we needed to consult with the provincial for the Maryland Province of the Society of Jesus. (The Jesuit Provincial typically plays an important role in identifying candidates within the Order who may fill the role of president for Jesuit schools.) We also convened a teleconference with the full board to advise them of the plan. Throughout these consultations, everyone expressed strong support of our choice for interim president, and we were able to announce his appointment within 48 hours of Father Ridley's death.

A reasonable question to ask at this point would be whether succession or contingency plans had been in place for the college. In truth, there were no plans at all. This is somewhat ironic given that Father Ridley's predecessor, Joseph Sellinger, S.J., also had died in office after serving for nearly 30 years. Despite this history we were focused on the future, which looked very bright for Father Ridley and for the college. Needless to say, I've thought many times since then about how much easier the process could have been had we been better prepared for this possibility.

When the vice president for academic affairs was appointed as interim president, he selected the associate vice president for academic affairs to take on the responsibilities he was temporarily vacating. It was not clear how long the search process might last, and we knew it would be difficult for the interim president to perform both jobs satisfactorily. Even though it turned out to be a short appointment, separating the responsibilities was clearly the right course of action. This allowed progress to continue on many fronts throughout the transition period.

Once the appointment of the interim president was complete, we turned our attention to the selection of a permanent president. In addition to the vice chair, I asked the previous board chair to assist with the search. The three of us—all successful businessmen—decided to assemble a small yet representative search committee. Our goal was to ensure that there was adequate participation among the trustees, while keeping the group small enough to function efficiently. We also engaged a consultant to assist with the effort.

In addition to assisting the search committee, I was trying to stay closely connected to the day-to-day operations at the college. I didn't want to interfere but, under the circumstances, I felt it appropriate to stay in regular contact with the college's leadership team. During this period I spoke with the interim president and the vice president for administration three to four times per month and also visited the campus more frequently than I otherwise would have. There was less frequent contact with the other vice presidents, but somewhat more than would have occurred if we were not in a period of transition.

It was very gratifying to see the college function smoothly, despite the lack of a contingency plan. There were no major problems during the transition period and, in fact, there were some successes, both large and small.

The closest we came to any real problem was a small public relations challenge when that year's commencement speaker was announced. Many of Loyola's students come from the New York area. Because this graduating class had started their academic career around the time of September 11, 2001, Rudy Giuliani was invited to address the graduates. He accepted the invitation, leading to a minor problem with some members of the Baltimore Catholic community because of his pro-choice stance. In the end, the matter was resolved, but the incident was a reminder of the need to look beyond the institution to the college's many stakeholders—especially during times of transition.

The search for Loyola College's 24th president was completed in only five months. It helped that we were able to readily identify a good pool of candidates from within the Jesuit order. Selecting a Jesuit as the next president was very important to the search committee, as well as to the full board. Finding someone who was already part of the Jesuit tradition and well-versed in its principles and philosophy was, in our mind, a critical qualification for the school's next president. Fortunately, there was no shortage of Jesuits interested in leading our 155-year old institution. And in the end, the new president's transition was made easier because he already was familiar with Loyola. Brian Linnane, S.J., a dean at Holy Cross, was selected as Loyola College in Maryland's new president. Father Linnane had served on the school's board for five years, allowing him to hit the ground running in his new role.

In looking back on the initial tragedy and the activity that followed, a couple thoughts come to mind. First, communication was key to the college's continued successful operation during the period. With the possible exception of inadequate consultation with *all* of our constituents before selecting Rudy Giuliani as the commencement speaker, there was timely, effective communication throughout. It started with a deliberate, thorough press release issued immediately after Father Ridley's death. This was followed closely by the announcement of the selection of the vice president for academic affairs as the interim president. From that point forward, there was frequent, regular communication between the college's senior leaders and me as board chair. The board's vice chair also played an integral role during this time. Our increased involvement with the college's leadership continued up to—and for a short time beyond—installation of the new president.

The other thought that occurs to me is that you cannot overstate the importance of succession and contingency planning. Though it may at times be an uncomfortable subject to raise and a difficult one to address, especially given all the matters that require immediate attention, it must be dealt with. I know it to be a standard practice in every successful business; it should be no different in higher education.

Wilmington, Delaware
May 2007

"PITCHING MY TENT"
ROBERT VOGEL, INTERIM PRESIDENT, BETHANY
COLLEGE AND FORMER PRESIDENT, WARTBURG
UNIVERSITY

Retiring to Colorado after eighteen years as president of Wartburg College, I subsequently have "pitched my tent" at three institutions. Currently I'm serving as the interim president at Bethany College in Lindsborg, Kansas. By accepting the interim presidency, I became part of the institution, taking on its heritage, traditions, challenges, and aspirations. It means thinking and speaking as "we" instead of as "you" or "they."

It is important to be clear about the board's expectations during the interim. This is not always easy because the board has serious issues to deal with, including the launching of a search for a new president. My current tenure began in January during the college's interterm, just prior to the beginning of spring term. The chair of the board readily agreed when I suggested that I should, first, do what was needed to help the college make spring term a good term for student learning and for the college. And, second, do what was needed to assure that the next academic year would be a good year for student learning, for the college, and for the new president. It also was agreed that finances, enrollment, and morale would be priority areas to be addressed. Beyond this there were few specifics.

Before arriving on campus I asked the senior administrative officers to identify the three or four things they and their staff needed to accomplish to make spring term a good term. After these priorities were shared and critiqued, the same individuals were asked to identify the three or four things they needed to accomplish by the end of summer to assure that the next year would be a good year. All of their responses were "grist" for developing an Action Plan for my tenure.

We agreed on four broad categories to focus on during the interim: *finances, enrollment, culture* (including morale), and *opportunities*. In a retreat setting we formulated goals and proposed specific initiatives which were shared in draft form with the faculty senate, staff senate, and student congress. After another round of discussions, a joint session of these groups with the president's cabinet made changes, massaged the language, and came to an agreement that the Action Plan could be presented to the board for approval. Fortunately the board was meeting within a month of my arrival. The board spent several hours in small groups discussing the plan and then voted to approve it as a charge to us for the interim. It also served to establish the agreed-upon priorities for our work together as an administrative team.

The Action Plan not only set our course for the interim; it has provided evidence that the college is indeed moving forward during this critical time. It has piqued the interest of the wider community, as well, and I have readily agreed to share highlights of the Action Plan at a series of meetings with local organizations and alumni.

What's in the Plan? Under *finances* you can well imagine the initiatives have to do with fiscal management during the remainder of the current fiscal year and with the budget we will bring to the board for the year ahead. This is the budget that the new president will inherit. It is recognized that the new president will need to quickly lead the way in shaping a clear and compelling vision for the future along with a plan to accomplish it, including the launching of a major comprehensive campaign. A joint administration/board action team is to gather the comparative data necessary to make a case for change as background for those efforts. A second joint action team is identifying possible sources of funding for immediate and longer-range projects.

We are using action teams during the interim, identifying the can-do people on campus who will be needed to make things happen and giving them short-term assignments. Under *enrollment,* the admissions staff, of course, has major responsibility for implementing the initiatives we have identified for the rest of the recruitment year and for the year ahead. In addition, in order to develop a campus-wide effort in recruitment and retention, there is an action team working to substantially improve our first year program. Another team is fine-tuning the early alert academic support program with a specific assignment to better incorporate academic support for athletes into the program. A third team is reviewing and refining the college's scholarship and awards program. At the same time there are ongoing meetings with faculty, staff, and students aimed at developing a common language for expressing what is special about the living/learning experience provided to students at Bethany.

What started as a concern for morale has evolved into a concern for raising the bar, expecting more of the college and ourselves. The category is *culture* and it includes specific initiatives in fostering hope, trust, and pride in the campus community. In this regard, a helpful question is: What should the finalists in the presidential search find when they visit campus? We are saying they should find us hard at work, happy in our work, hopeful about the future, and with enough good things in place to believe they could be successful here.

Finally, *opportunities* describes the use of events to advance the interests of the college. The current focus is a project to create a new entrance to the campus and integrate the center of the campus with a promenade of flags, cobblestone walks, and landscaping. This is the most exciting, visible sign of progress. Moving the statue of the founder to its new place atop a fountain in the center of the campus also created excitement on campus and within the community. The move was celebrated with a pep band, cheerleaders, and a party. Announcements and events connected with the search, introduction, and inauguration of the new president will be carefully planned. There are periodic mailings to major donors and friends of the college from the board chair keeping them informed about the search and other activities on campus.

One added note. On two occasions as an interim president, my tenure began at a time when a major study was being done. In one case it was a marketing study and, in the other, it was a financial operational assessment by one of the authors of this book. Their reports provided a quick snapshot of the current situation at the college and the consultants' recommendations became a significant part of the action plans that were developed. Interim presidents can benefit from these types of reviews because they can provide a unique perspective at a critical time.

Lindsborg, Kansas
April 2007

NOTES

1. Martin, James., James E. Samels, and Associates. *Presidential Transition in Higher Education*. Baltimore: Johns Hopkins University Press, 2004.

2. Padilla, Arthur, and Sujit Ghosh. "Turnover at the Top: The Revolving Door of the American Presidency." American Council on Education *The Presidency* (Winter 2000): 30–37.

3. Perry, Robert Hastings. "When Times Call for an Interim President." Association of Governing Boards of Colleges and Universities *Trusteeship* (March-April 2003): 29–32.

4. Fretwell, E.K. *The Interim Presidency*. Washington: Association of Governing Boards of Colleges and Universities, 1995.

5. Longevin, Thomas E., and Allen E. Koenig. "The Interim President: An Effective Transitional Leader." In *Presidential Transition* by Martin, Samels, and Associates.

6. *Ibid*.

7. June, Audrey Williams. "An Interim President Can Be More Than a Caretaker." *The Chronicle of Higher Education*. http://chronicle.com/weekly/v49/i12/12a03101.htm (accessed June 3, 2007).

8. Fretwell. *The Interim Presidency*.

9. Fretwell. *The Interim Presidency*.

10. Fretwell. *The Interim Presidency*.

CHAPTER

Lessons Learned

This chapter summarizes the most important findings from our research on leadership transitions in higher education. It highlights those factors that we believe are most critical for presidents and others interested in ensuring that presidents are successful. It is unlikely that every president will be able to address each item highlighted. If they successfully address most of them, they will find this challenging position to be more manageable and more rewarding.

HIGHLIGHTS FOR NEW PRESIDENTS

Although this section focuses primarily on new presidents, we believe that most of the suggestions are equally helpful to incumbents as well.

Pay Close Attention to Relationships

First and foremost, presidents must recognize that the role is centered on relationships. This might well be the most important advice we can offer. Many presidents told us, in essence, "It all comes down to relationships." If a president cannot establish authentic and meaningful relationships with stakeholders, *especially faculty*, she simply will not be successful in the long run. She might be able to increase the endowment significantly or construct a new building. Those accomplishments may be indicative of good marketing or sales skills, but that is not leadership.

Presidential leaders build their institution's reputation, improve academic quality, enhance the quality of student life, build and maintain a positive institutional culture, and prepare their institutions for future challenges. All are complex, tough, challenging, and necessary tasks. They require the hard work, intelligence, and commitments of others to be successful.

Stakeholders must trust their leader, have a personal connection to her, and have some sense of her values and aspirations. Relationship building is a key leadership responsibility that every president must approach proactively.

Learn to Listen Very, Very Well

Listening carefully conveys several powerful messages to stakeholders: that the president is interested in what people have to say, that he is open to the ideas of others, that he is curious and a learner, and, especially important, that he respects them as individuals. These all are crucial messages to convey *authentically*.

It is important for the president to reflect back what he is hearing so that people experience that he understands what they said. A president cannot afford to listen passively because, after a while, he will lose credibility.

The president does not have to answer every question *quickly* to demonstrate his brilliance. He should pause a little—maybe even repeat the question to slow down the pace of the conversation. He should never interrupt a questioner in mid-question simply because he believes he knows where the question is going. Apart from the fact that this is disrespectful, it is also possible that he's wrong. On the other hand, there are rare occasions when a person offers a political or personal statement in the form of a question, merely to capture the president's attention. In that case it might be appropriate to gently interrupt to prompt the question. But it is likely that he will lose some credibility for having interrupted.

A president must pay attention to his body language because some people quietly, yet powerfully, convey their impatience or boredom without realizing it is happening. A president should never multitask in front of others, even if he thinks he can do this well. As with interrupting, it is disrespectful to others. The president should demonstrate his interest in what is being said by maintaining eye contact, nodding his head, and other body language. People are watching all of the time. We have been amazed to see how many presidents make phone calls during meetings, check e-mail via their Blackberries in front of others, and read reports while attending a meeting.

There is much to be learned from the Carly Fiorina story. When she first arrived at Hewlett-Packard she tried to dazzle people with what she knew—and she knew a lot. She had an answer for every question, but she never asked questions! While her intention was to convey confidence, knowledge, and brilliance, the impact was intimidation and a lack of respect for the way people interacted at HP. Fortunately, over time she learned to engage in give-and-take conversations, probed with questions, and listened to people. Unfortunately, board politics consumed her and she was forced out. As one president told us, you can solve more problems by listening than by talking.

Build a Reservoir of Goodwill

In many of our interviews with presidents, they used different terms to describe this theme. One president told us that new presidents have a "bucket of goodwill coins" that is about half full when they come on board. Their goal is to fill up the bucket as fast as possible so they are prepared for the inevitable problems, mistakes, and challenges that draw coins out of the bucket. Other presidents used terms like political capital or social capital to describe the same theme. Most agree that there is a limited amount of goodwill so it must be used very wisely.

Presidents can build capital by developing authentic and trusting relationships with campus stakeholders—especially faculty—by listening to people and reflecting back what is being learned, and by building on institutional strengths, traditions, and history. Additional desirable actions include engaging others around a vision for the institution, being willing to let others see who they really are, and owning their mistakes.

Another way to build goodwill is to create transparency in the budgeting process. On many campuses, the budget process is complicated, mysterious, and distrusted by many. We know of two new presidents who insisted on complete transparency in the budget process after many years of darkness. Although it was difficult at first because much was exposed, it created a sense of trust throughout the campus and built goodwill. Now, faculty and others are at the table when important financial decisions are made.

The capital a president develops over time will allow her to move the strategic agenda forward and change things in a meaningful way. Without it, she will be unsuccessful no matter how hard she works or how smart she is.

Seek and Maintain a Personal Balance

This might be the toughest challenge of all, especially for a new president. Expectations are high. The president wants to make a positive impression, and too many stakeholders want too much of his time. This is inevitable so a new president should plan for it. As one president told us, "The job will suck all the hours available unless you create some strong boundaries." It is important for a president to control his calendar to the extent possible, especially if he has a spouse, partner, or family. He needs to carve out time for relaxation, exercise, meditation, prayer, reflection, or other personal time. This is much easier said than done. It will take constant vigilance.

One of the presidents we met does not conduct a meeting before 9:00 a.m., which gives her time to rise, exercise, and meditate before her 12-hour day begins. Another married president negotiated with the board that he would do two social gatherings a week in the evenings that included his spouse, as well as one Saturday event, but no work on Sundays. The point is that, unless the president carves it out for himself, nobody else will.

A president should continue to pursue his interests and passions while he is the president. They will sustain him. One president kept his love for photography alive by teaching a photography course for undergraduates. Another took interesting educational trips with alumni that fueled her passion for travel.

New presidents should find a touchstone somewhere. This could be spending time with a small group of trusted friends, attending to a spiritual or religious practice, pursuing a hobby passionately, exercising with friends, reading about his academic discipline, painting, sculpting, or writing poetry. He should pursue whatever will sustain some personal core and provide emotional sustenance.

Build the Senior Team and Empower Them to Do Meaningful Things

The president's senior team enables her to implement the institutional agenda. This cannot be accomplished by the president alone, even if she is driven and charismatic. She needs the team to be successful so she should pay attention to them, nurture them, and—most importantly—hold them accountable. We mean the team and not just individuals on the senior team.

Many presidents hold one-on-one meetings on a regular basis with members of their cabinet, but rarely meet together as a senior leadership group. Others meet with the cabinet but do not devote time to regularly scheduled one-on-one meetings. Some presidents we talked with meet with their cabinet quarterly or even monthly for a few hours, but this is not enough time to build an effective team.

When presidents only connect individually with their cabinet members, a systems perspective is never developed. Vice presidents manage within their silos (e.g., finance, development, academic affairs) and do not learn from each other. They also do not understand the complexities of the larger institution. The president needs to create both the context and the opportunity for everyone on the cabinet to share ideas, resources, and support so that the talents and skills of the senior team are leveraged.

A new president should hire the strongest provost and chief business officer that she can find. These two key positions are critical to a president's success. Every senior member of the cabinet needs to be highly effective, but without an exceptional academic leader and a stellar business person, the president will face an uphill struggle for success. One of the first tasks for a new president is to focus energy on assessing the quality of these two positions and getting the right people in place. After that, building a high-quality senior team will be considerably easier.

Another important reason that a new president should focus on building the senior team is that, when she leaves, there will be enough institutional memory, capacity, and momentum to continue the progress toward the shared goals. Building people's capacity is a lasting legacy and, according to Peter Drucker, the great organizational thinker, it is the true test of leadership.

Assess the Institution's Readiness to Respond to a Crisis

If an Institutional Response Team (IRT) is not established, start the process to develop one. Catastrophic events—both natural disasters and those that result from poor judgment—do not recognize a honeymoon period. An otherwise successful presidency can be undermined if the campus is not adequately prepared to respond in times of strife.

Establish and Sustain a Connection to the Campus to the Extent Possible—Especially in the Beginning

We realize that this can be a Herculean task given the extraordinary pressures and expectations to raise money, meet with community members, attend conferences, connect with trustees, and fulfill other responsibilities off campus. On the other hand, a president cannot lead effectively if he is not visible and his impact is not felt by internal stakeholders. People need to see their leaders, talk with them, seek guidance, share advice, listen to their responses, and struggle with complex issues together. One cannot lead from afar. It needs to be up close and personal.

We related earlier the example of a new president being scheduled off campus 75 days in his first year! Unfortunately, this is not all that unusual. If the president loses or fails to make the personal connections during the first year, he will find it extremely difficult to develop them later. The new president should devote substantial energy to building connections and being seen throughout his presidency, but especially in his first year.

This does not mean that the president has to be charismatic—something that actually can be a liability in higher education—or be a salesperson. It means that he has to reach out and connect in some way with campus stakeholders whether by visiting classes, having lunch with faculty and students, or participating in social events on campus. Simply stated, he needs to be visible and available by being present. The day of the lone wolf is over. Campuses are relational by nature. The new president must build relationships with her people.

Presidents must watch out for excessive external commitments (e.g., boards of other organizations, high-level task forces, national steering committees) because they will consume his time and talent. Many offers will come because it is great to have a president of a college or university on the board, especially if he is well-known and respected. The first commitment is to his campus, so he should ask himself how being on this board will help his institution.

Build a Positive Relationship with the Board—Particularly the Board Chair

We found that the relationship with the board chair is *the* most important relationship for *any* president. If the president and board chair are not on the same page, difficult times are ahead.

The board chair relationship should begin with the search process and be attended to throughout the president's tenure. If the board chair changes during a president's term, care must be taken to ensure a constructive transition to the new chair. We interviewed several presidents who started with one chair and, down the road, inherited a very different individual. This caused them a great deal of stress. Presidents should not take this relationship for granted. They must cultivate it carefully.

The president needs to be proactive in keeping the board chair informed and connected to what is going on throughout the campus. She must share good as well as bad news and be very transparent about what is going on. One ground rule that helps is a no-surprises rule. Never surprise the board chair *or* the board with something negative that might have been brewing for awhile. Share information widely and quickly—especially negative things that have the potential to appear in the media. Several presidents have face-to-face communication with their board members between meetings, while others use a monthly newsletter or e-mail to keep them informed. Presidents should select whichever method is most comfortable for them and their board.

Many of the presidents we talked with make it a point to conduct informal, personal visits to the board chair, often visiting with the chair while they are on vacation or traveling in the area. Acknowledging birthdays, anniversaries, and special occasions is a thoughtful thing to do that chairs will appreciate.

Model Honesty and Openness, While Recognizing That the Spotlight Never Goes Out

The president must function as if he were in a fishbowl—because metaphorically he is. He must be careful about ever letting down his guard as there are critics just waiting to strike. Most importantly, the president must model honesty and openness in his business dealings with the institution.

Many perks come with the job—as well they should given the demands of the position. Care must be taken not to go overboard in the pursuit of additional tangible and intangible benefits. In this case, less is more. The president who displays reasonable spending habits sets a beneficial tone for the institution. Moreover, should budget cuts become necessary—something that is likely at some point in most institutions—he will find it much easier to implement them if he's demonstrated a touch of frugality now and then.

We ask every president we talk with to tell us who speaks the truth to them. Most readily acknowledge that they are not really sure if anyone does, or are confident that few people do. It is difficult to speak the truth to the president, especially if he is well liked, respected, critical, or larger than life.

Only the president can create the climate for true openness and candor. First, it must be rewarded whenever it happens. When someone raises a critical issue or has a different perspective or opinion, the president needs to acknowledge the effort. This will encourage others to share their differing perspectives when they exist. The president can actively solicit the ideas of others, holding his opinion until later, or share his beginning thinking about an issue and invite robust feedback.

How the president reacts to the feedback will be closely watched. If he responds appropriately, more ideas will probably follow. He must be vigilant about this because people can fall into predictable patterns of agreement. If the president has not had his ideas tested in awhile, he should pay attention because it is unlikely that he can be that brilliant all of the time.

In religiously-affiliated institutions, there is an added complexity that we call the "power of the collar." When the president is a cleric who wears a uniform, not only is the power of the presidency present, but the power of the church or order is also in the room. For many, this can be too much. Once again, self-awareness is essential and the president must create the conditions for an open climate.

Do Not Move Too Quickly!

During the first year, the president will quickly learn about the institution's challenges as well as its opportunities. Often, there is a false sense of urgency created to change things as soon as possible. This urgency can be communicated by the board, vocal campus groups, or the new president's need to show people she can lead by doing something visible. Presidents should resist this urge.

It is important that the president regulate the pace of institutional change carefully. If she moves too fast, she will lose credibility because people will not understand the rationale behind the change or accurately perceive its intended outcomes. Most people are not all that enthused about change and often see only its negative implications. Important changes must be seen in the light of institutional aspirations and not personal appetites or ambitions.

There are those times when a new president must move fast for the sake of institutional health. Tough decisions must be made. When this is necessary, the board and the president must make clear to the campus community the reasons behind the change and what is creating the sense of urgency.

WHEN THE PRESIDENT'S JOURNEY IS COMING TO AN END
Leave Well

It is most important that the president leave well and have a well-managed, meaningful final year that both improves the institution and enhances her legacy. No campus can afford a lame duck period. The outgoing president must articulate the strategic agenda for the last year and communicate it widely to the various stakeholders.

As one president told us, "I communicated that I was the CEO till the last day and that we had a lot to still accomplish." Presidents should be judicious about how much actually can be accomplished, and ensure that they keep things moving forward while continuing to lead the institution.

A president would do well to remember that, once he lets people know he is leaving, it is not about him any longer; it is about the institution. He should do whatever it takes to ensure a graceful exit, acknowledge people's contributions, celebrate, visit with important constituents, and communicate genuine interest and hope for the future.

Do Not Shift into Neutral

If there are difficult decisions to make (e.g., personnel), the departing president should make them before he leaves so the new president does not inherit a problem at the outset of his service to the institution. If the president can be generous (e.g., delaying the announcement of a major gift until the new president arrives, resolving a difficult institutional problem), he should do so. It will only help the new president and the institution and that should be his primary objective.

The president should be available when needed during the search process but should not take an active role. He should be a resource, not a driver. He should help out in any way he can to assist the new president with his transition. One way to find out what he can do is to ask the incoming president how he can be helpful. He should have plenty of suggestions.

Ensure an Effectively Managed Transition

The president should appoint a credible and highly competent transition manager and surround him with an effective transition team to help with this important institutional responsibility. As a president leaves, there are thousands of details to be considered, relationships to be mapped, meetings to be conducted, and communications that must be relayed. She should select the best people for the transition team to ensure a graceful exit.

She also should commission the work necessary to prepare the strategic audit report and the future challenges report. She should put a high-powered team together for each of these important efforts and pay attention to the quality, honesty, and clarity of the products. These reports will fully inform the board about current and future realities and help them craft the criteria for selection of a new president. It also will create a rich database for review by the final candidates, who will need to deeply understand the complexity, challenges, strengths, and aspirations of the campus they wish to lead.

ADVICE FOR BOARDS
Make Sure You Know What You Want When You Set Out to Select a President

Utilizing the strategic audit report, the future challenges report, and other relevant data, the board needs to agree on the skill set and qualities a new president will need in order to lead the institution into the future.

An emerging practice that we learned about is asking internal stakeholders what they believe will be important attributes for a new president. This creates an intelligent database that can help inform the board and the search committee. Some campuses make the selection criteria public so that everyone knows what the institution is seeking.

One of our university clients created a survey and distributed it to hundreds of campus stakeholders. The top three criteria suggested for the new president were effective communication skills, an understanding of the business side of running a campus, and an entrepreneurial spirit. These criteria created a framework for the search process and, most importantly, enabled everyone to know what was needed in a new president.

There needs to be discipline in applying the criteria to the selection of the final candidates. It is too easy to fall in love with a candidate because of his charisma, reputation, or credentials. Boards should ensure that the final candidates fit the criteria for leadership. If they do not, the board should be patient and continue to search until they find the right fit. They should never settle for an *okay* candidate.

Conduct Annual Performance Appraisals of the President

The president needs both support from, and accountability to, the board. There should be a set of clearly articulated strategic goals that the president needs to accomplish each year. Some of these goals will be multiyear in nature. Even when this is the case, there should be a rigorous review to assess progress during the year and identify any problems related to the goals. Although the performance appraisal process should include participation by several board members and result in a written report, the board chair should review progress toward the president's goals with him on a quarterly basis. This ensures that there are no surprises if he falls short of what is expected. It also allows the board chair to strategize with the president, assess his skill set, and enhance the chair's relationship with the president.

Implement a Succession Plan

The board must have a clear policy covering what happens if there is a sudden departure or incapacitation of the incumbent president. Although presidential deaths are rare, they do occur. Within a short time span during 2006, four presidents died in office. More common are rapid departures because of financial impropriety, sexual misconduct, problems involving athletics, or other such issues. The institution should know who is in charge if the president suddenly leaves. Often this is the provost, but other senior leaders (e.g., chief operating or chief business officer) might be candidates for this key leadership position.

In some cases, when a president travels extensively, there needs to be a protocol in place for making important decisions in her absence.

POSSIBLE AREAS FOR FURTHER INVESTIGATION AND RESEARCH

Over the last five years we have talked to many presidents, provosts, trustees, and other senior leaders throughout higher education about presidential transitions. As the journey began, we were not quite sure what we would find at the other shore. We found out many important and helpful things that we share in these pages. A few themes emerged and some surprises were discovered that engaged our thinking in robust ways. We were not able to explore this handful of ideas thoroughly due to the scope of the book and its timetable. The next section presents ideas that might be helpful for others to explore so there can be a more complete understanding of the unique and complex role of the presidency and leadership generally in higher education.

E.K. Fretwell wrote in his monograph that about 15 percent of presidential transitions are forced.[1] This could be due to a vote of no-confidence, board decision to terminate the presidency, non-renewal of the contract, or a scandal. When we talked with higher education leaders, we asked about this percentage. More often than not, they told us they believe that it is considerably higher—with involuntary terminations ranging anywhere from 30 to 50 percent—whether publicly acknowledged or not. They communicated that there are many departures that are quietly negotiated behind the scenes. Numerous reasons for these involuntary terminations were offered. Some were the result of a complete mismatch between what the board wanted the president to accomplish and what could be realistically delivered. Others were the result of a lack of a shared vision between the board and the president, or being out of sync about where they see the institution going and how to get there. Finally, there were the cultural mismatches between the president and campus stakeholders, especially the faculty.

Even if the percentage of forced transitions is no higher than 30 percent, this is not good for the academy. Some research should be conducted to assess more accurately what the actual percentage is and, most importantly, what is causing these terminations. Once we know the scope of the problem and the reasons for it, we can begin to strategize more effective ways to select and support our presidents.

In the 2006 study, *The Leadership Imperative*, the task force mentions that about 80 percent of campus presidents were hired from outside the institutions.[2] Interestingly, in the corporate sector, close to 80 percent of CEOs are promoted from *within* the organization. Why is this? Corporate America is not without its flaws, but it seems to do a better job than higher education of investing in grooming leaders within their organizations in disciplined and rigorous ways. Are there implications for higher education? Is it possible to be a prophet in your own land or must we search elsewhere for our campus leaders? Further investigation into this phenomenon might be warranted. Higher education might learn a thing or two about building a leadership pipeline within their institutions.

Who speaks the truth to the president? Although we briefly cover this theme throughout the book, it warrants further investigation. What is the dynamic that creates this reluctance to communicate openly with the president, push back on his ideas, or offer contrary opinions? How can a president encourage open dialogue and constructive conflict? Is this something he even wants to do?

In order to deal with both the complexity and pace of change, a president needs the strong ideas and voices of leaders throughout his institution. The best ideas need to be at the table to ensure the president is fully informed before important decisions are made.

As organizational consultants, two of the authors are often asked by presidents to share their opinions. We strive mightily to do this, *especially* if we know the opinions might not be well-received. That is our job. We realize that we do not have as much at stake as inside leaders do, but we are surprised by people's reactions to our honest responses. It is as if we have offended the president *and* the institution by being open and direct. Although this is not an everyday occurrence, it happens often enough to warrant investigation.

What are the complexities of the psychological relationship between the president and her followers? Does the president represent both herself and the institution, thus making it difficult to challenge her ideas? What happens when the president is also a rabbi, minister, or nun? Does the power of the collar make it even more difficult to share openly and offer different, even conflicting, opinions?

Another area of complexity that surfaced during the interviews is the unique experience for women presidents—especially unmarried women. In most institutions, the majority of board members are men. This sometimes creates challenges for the development of the strong interpersonal relationships we recommend for the president and the board chair. Everyone would like to believe that gender should not be an issue, but it is a reality that cannot be ignored. Men and women do not always treat each other the same way in every situation. Nor do they always react similarly to problems and opportunities. Based on discussions we have had, this has profound implications for some presidents.

On an even more basic level, unmarried women presidents—and men as well—are challenged to keep up with the personal side of their lives. Given that the job can be 24/7/365, how do they keep up with the routine tasks that are required of anyone in modern society, whether it is dropping off and picking up the dry cleaning, shopping for groceries or a birthday gift, or getting the car serviced. In large cities, there are service firms who will handle these types of responsibilities for a fee. But what about the multitude of presidents who lead institutions in rural or small town settings? Or those who are single parents? The complexity for those individuals is staggering.

Finally there is the issue of a single man or woman in a position of power attempting to have a personal social life. If he or she is lucky enough to have the time to devote to romance, what is the likelihood of being able to pursue this when there are so many demands placed on the president? And what about the all too frequent situation that arises for couples when they both have academic careers? It is not at all uncommon for a tenured faculty member's spouse to leave the area to pursue a presidency. This creates a difficult challenge for the president and the spouse/children who remain behind. These are issues that need further study to help identify the magnitude of the problem and then the solutions for it.

Many institutions are blessed with excellent trustees who care about their campuses and help the president manage the complexity of their organizations. These individuals often are successful entrepreneurs, corporate leaders, or retired individuals who may have attended the institution 40 or more years earlier. They meet several times each year for one to two jam-packed days of work. They review plans, meet in committees, listen to reports, and work very hard. Most board meetings are very, very carefully orchestrated.

One of the quieter themes that emerged from our interviews is the lack of genuine connection between the board of trustees and the campus. It is possible that they are helping manage an institution they may not fully understand. When and how do trustees interact with campus stakeholders? How often do they meet to discuss issues with the faculty? Talk with students about their concerns and aspirations? How do they get a feel for campus culture? Politics? Problems?

One of the authors participated in a meeting with several board members and faculty. Over the course of two hours, some powerful ideas were exchanged and things became a little heated. People were civil but passions were flying. Toward the end of the meeting, we created a time for reflection and had each participant talk about what they had learned from the discussion. Several people spoke about the need for more discussions like this one, others about the need for honest information sharing and dialogue. One of the trustees reflected that he finally realized that he did not understand faculty life whatsoever when he heard about course load, student-teacher ratios, or the time needed for cutting-edge research. He simply did not get it. He told the group that he was committed to learning about the faculty in more detail and would submit a request to serve on the academic committee rather than the financial committee in the future.

This is but one small story but it is suggestive of the problem that we heard about from presidents: the disconnect between the board and faculty and campus life.

Further investigation into the trustee role and connection to the institution would be interesting. Would board members allow outsiders with the same limited level of connection to govern their companies? How can trustees meaningfully connect to campus life given the time constraints? How do trustees tap the intellectual and emotional energy of campus stakeholders so that they can make important, sometimes difficult, decisions and not conduct business in a vacuum?

A FINAL NOTE

In *The Leadership Imperative*, an excellent report, the task force makes several powerful and important recommendations that have significant implications for presidents in transition. The report calls for "leadership that links the president and governing board closely together in an environment of support, candor and accountability."[3] We could not agree more with this and believe it is essential to a president's long-term success.

The task force further suggests that a "new style of collaborative but decisive leadership—*integral leadership*—is the key to successful presidential leadership."[4] They believe that the president "must exert a presence that is purposeful and consultative, deliberative yet decisive and capable of course corrections as new challenges emerge." Once again, their insight resonates deeply with us.

***

At the end of the day, a president must produce meaningful and important results for the institution, act with integrity, treat people well, and build trust throughout the organization. These are daunting endeavors indeed. We wish them luck. If they succeed, the institution and all of its stakeholders will be enriched.

NOTES

1. Fretwell, E.K. *The Interim Presidency*. Washington: Association of Governing Boards of Colleges and Universities, 1995.

2. Association of Governing Boards of Colleges and Universities. *The Leadership Imperative*. Washington: Association of Governing Boards of Colleges and Universities, 2006.

3. Ibid.

4. Ibid.

APPENDIX A
Transition Map Checklist

I. Exit Strategy

A. Goals

1. Communicate well
2. Celebrate the legacy
3. Exit gracefully

B. Key considerations

1. Provide clear open communication and avoid the campus rumor mill
2. Consider the president's personal situation and needs

C. Steps

1. Determine best timing of the president's announcement
2. Resolve any additional leadership decisions (e.g., interim president, vice presidents, deans, etc.)
3. Communicate resignation

    a) to trustees
    b) to institution community
    c) to alumni and friends
    d) to external constituencies

4. Oversee completion of Strategic Audit Report, Future Challenges Report, and Relationship Map
5. Plan community celebration event(s) for departing president
6. Provide an institutional magazine recap of accomplishments during presidency
7. Utilize print media opportunities to heighten visibility of the institution

II. Search Process

A. Goals

1. Devise a productive process
2. Communicate well to reduce community anxiety
3. Hire the president who is the best fit for the institution and its needs

B. Key considerations

1. Provide opportunities for real input from all constituencies
2. Provide search process information while maintaining candidate confidentiality

C. Steps

1. Name respected trustee who can dedicate time to chair search
2. Identify search committee membership (broad representation)
3. Assess whether to use a search firm and proceed accordingly
4. Create a clear process with input from all constituencies
5. Establish preliminary timetable for each stage of the search
6. Articulate desired presidential leadership qualities
7. Develop a communication plan for regular updates to the board and institutional community
8. Conduct search; announce selection

III. Introduction of New President

A. Goals

1. Introduction of the new president to all constituencies
2. President joins community smoothly and begins to assimilate culture

B. Key considerations

1. Develop a manageable schedule
2. Illustrate collegial bridging from former president to newly-elected president

C. Steps

1. Provide internal communication from board of trustees
2. Make external announcements
3. Host on-campus small group meetings with various stakeholders (e.g., faculty, students, staff)
4. Identify members of a learning network to assist new president
5. Provide external community introductions (local, state, federal)
6. Post Web site information
7. Utilize print media opportunities

IV. Early Activities

A. Goals

1. Initial personal introduction
2. Listen and learn
3. Relationship building

B. Key considerations

1. Continue institutional momentum
2. Lay groundwork for the next strategic plan
3. Identify critical issues
4. Set expectations for communications and good working relationships

C. Steps

1. Welcome the president on the first day—informal event
2. Conduct a retreat with the senior leadership team
3. Participate in new student orientation
4. Host an academic gathering/convocation for faculty
5. Write an in-depth article about the new president for the institution magazine
6. Hold "meet and greets" in departments and with students
7. Host open and informal breakfasts and lunches for faculty and staff
8. Begin to assess progress toward existing strategic plan goals
9. Begin preparations for initial board of trustees meeting
10. Plan an alumni/donor introduction tour
11. Assess fund-raising status and campaign readiness
12. Establish president's first-year goals
13. Begin to develop an outside support network for the president

V. Installation Ceremony

A. Goals

1. Celebrate the institution and the new president
2. Anticipate the future
3. Engage entire community in the events

B. Key considerations

1. President's personal preference for venue and ceremonial style
2. Consider budget impact and message conveyed by events

C. Steps

1. Organize student event(s)

    2. Arrange alumni event(s)

    3. Plan a community-wide installation ceremony

    4. Utilize print media opportunities

VI. First-year Milestones

A. Goals

    1. Productivity

    2. President understanding the culture

    3. Community becomes familiar and comfortable with the new president

B. Key considerations

    1. Organize events to suit the president's leadership style

    2. Provide frequent communications

C. Steps

    1. Board of trustees meetings

    2. Senior leadership team meetings/process

    3. Faculty governance meetings

    4. Convocation

    5. Homecoming

    6. Alumni reunion

    7. Commencement exercises

    8. Presidential performance review and agreement on second-year goals

APPENDIX B
Annotated Bibliography

BOOKS AND MONOGRAPHS

Andringa, Robert C., and Allen P. Splete. *Presidential Transitions in Private Colleges: Six Integrated Phases Essential for Success.* Washington: Council of Independent Colleges, 2005.

This monograph (98 pages) is a helpful resource with some good advice for the entire presidential transition process. Although its target audience is private colleges, the information is useful for any senior leaders who want to understand presidential transitions in higher education.

The six phases that the authors describe include:

- Anticipating a departure

- Departing with style

- Searching successfully

- Preparing for a new presidency

- Launching a new president

- Evaluating presidential and board performance

The authors believe that higher education lacks a well-established habit of succession planning and they offer good advice in the areas of life after the presidency, putting together an ideal search committee, and how to handle big surprises. They also address board relations with the new president and acting versus interim presidents. Their final chapter, "Evaluating Presidential and Board Performance," can assist with the creation of a rigorous performance assessment process for the president. Most importantly, the chapter addresses goal-setting and managing expectations between the board and president.

Ciampa, Dan. *Taking Advice: How Leaders Get Good Counsel and Use It Wisely.* Boston: Harvard Business School Press, 2006.

This excellent book, written by a well-known expert on leadership transitions, is a great resource for both new and experienced presidents. One of Ciampa's major themes is that leaders must learn to be shrewd and discerning *advice takers*. There seems to be no shortage of advice available to leaders. Unfortunately though, much of it is not helpful. How then do leaders obtain the kind of advice they need to be effective?

The author describes four kinds of advisors.

- Expert—individuals who have a deep knowledge of strategy, operations, or political processes. They are able to diagnose situations and recommend solutions.

- Experienced—people who have firsthand experience dealing with the pressures faced by the leader and a grasp of what it takes to succeed.

- Sounding Board—persons who provide objective and trusted counsel and feedback, a safe harbor for leaders.

- Partner—individuals who have a close association with the leader and who can help implement changes by getting to know the organization deeply.

These types of advisors provide very different advice and counsel and the leader must know how to utilize their strengths and understand their limitations.

Also provided are rules for advice taking, much of it common sense, but most of it difficult to actually do.

- Keep an open mind and pay special attention to the advice of more objective people. Understand their perspective because you may have overlooked important information.

- Never make an important decision on the basis of how it might affect your status in others' eyes.

- Put together a balanced advice network. Do not rely only on advice with which you are comfortable.

- When help is available, use it. Never allow pride or shame to get in the way of asking.

- When a goal will take a lot to achieve, pay special attention to the advice of people whose support you will need.

The final chapter, "Listening—the Master Skill and Other Key Success Factors," is excellent. It provides the reader with information on asking good questions, finding the right advisors *before* you need them, and highlights the need for both inside and outsider advisors. It also describes the qualities of good listening, which seems to be a rare capacity.

Downey, Diane, Tom March, and Adena Berkman. *Assimilating New Leaders: The Key to Executive Retention*. New York: AMACOM/American Management Association, 2001.

Although this book does not deal directly with higher education presidential transitions, it is a very helpful resource for senior leaders who are entering a new organization. It also explains how organizations can help new leaders transition and assimilate into organizations. Its biggest contribution is the exploration of the psychological landscape that must be traveled if a new leader is going to be successful in his new situation.

The authors identify four distinct phases of the assimilation journey: anticipating and planning, entering and exploring, building, and contributing. They also provide strategies to effectively manage each phase.

The book identifies several important ideas that will help senior leaders transition into a new system. For example, it is helpful to have an "assimilation coach" who strategizes with the new leader and an internal mentor who can help guide the new leader through the complexities, politics, and shadows of the organization. It stresses the importance of the "enabling agenda," which is relationship-focused, and highlights the importance of small wins instead of home runs.

This is one of the few books about organizations and transitions that discusses the importance of trust and how to create and build it from a leadership perspective. It also describes the emotional "dips" new leaders will experience in the first two years of their assimilation. It is an excellent resource, conceptually strong, full of great advice, and lay-person friendly.

Edwards, Mark R., and Ann J. Ewen. *360° Feedback*. New York: AMACOM/American Management Association, 1996.

This is a very good resource for individuals who want to understand this complex feedback process. Until 20 years ago, 360° feedback had been relatively unknown and little utilized. Famous leaders, including Jack Welch at GE, have recently popularized the notion and it is gradually finding its way into higher education. The book explains the historical evolution of the process and how best to utilize it within an organizational context.

The authors do a good job of describing the process in thoughtful detail and explain how to construct a 360° feedback instrument. They also detail the common pitfalls encountered with the process and, more importantly, how to avoid them. When done well, the 360° feedback process is one of the most effective and powerful personal development experiences available. This book is lay-person friendly and provides solid information.

Fretwell, E. K. *The Interim Presidency*. Washington: Association of Governing Boards of Colleges and Universities, 1995.

This is a very good monograph on the title topic. Recent research indicates that 10 percent of colleges and universities utilize an interim president to help manage the complexities of a presidential transition. This could be between 40 and 60 institutions per year.

Fretwell interviewed 52 interim presidents and 20 college and university systems personnel (e.g., chancellors). He clearly identifies the characteristics of a good interim president and provides excellent advice to interims that can enable them to successfully manage their challenging and fragile role. One of his most important findings was, "An overwhelming majority of the people interviewed emphasized that the interim president *not* be a candidate for the permanent position."

Much of his advice is directed to trustees and governing boards. It is a useful resource for thinking through the issues of selecting an interim, prioritizing the interim's agenda, and defining what the institution will need from their permanent president in the future.

Hackney, Sheldon. *The Politics of Presidential Appointment: A Memoir of the Culture Wars*.
Montgomery, Alabama: NewSouth Books, 2002.

This well-written book by the former president of Tulane University and the
University of Pennsylvania is a wonderful resource for anyone interested in the role
of the presidency. Although the main theme of the book deals with Hackney's nomi-
nation to the chairmanship of the National Endowment for the Humanities, it also
discusses many of the complexities of institutional life.

The author discusses faculty governance, rough campus politics, the role of the
university in society today, dealing with the media, and the management of
perceptions. He was caught in a national debate about political correctness and
had to deal with several complex campus issues. This was in the midst of the "culture
wars" during the early 1990s and he was beaten up regularly in the national media.
He successfully emerged as a wise and thoughtful leader who shares his advice
generously.

Martin, James., James E. Samels, & Associates. *Presidential Transition in Higher Education*.
Baltimore: Johns Hopkins University Press, 2004.

This is a comprehensive and excellent review of presidential transitions. Many of
the chapters were written by former or current presidents. The last chapter, titled
"Knowing the End of the Beginning: A Conceptual Approach to Presidential Transi-
tion," provides a comprehensive flowchart for a presidential transition. It is very good.
The chapter on fund-raising and development, "Weathering the Storm: Institutional
Advancement During a Presidential Transition," is both strategic and informative.

The editors have talked with more than 150 presidents from all over the country
and found that "fewer and fewer candidates apply for the position." They have identified five primary pressures that drive potential candidates away from the presidency.
These pressures have powerful implications for the future of the presidency and the
effective management of higher education institutions. The pressures include:

- To raise extraordinary amounts of money

- To do more with less

- To decide about distance education

- To compete with and outperform for-profit competitors

- To overcome deprofessionalization (caused by the shift from the academic profes-
  sion to administration)

The chapters are organized in three sections—content, action, and key issues. Each
deals with a variety of topics. For instance, content covers a new model for managing
transitions, pressures on presidents, and leadership transitions. The action section
tackles issues such as the board's role during transitions, dealing with sudden departures, and considerations for the community when a president leaves. Key issues
include when to use a search firm, interim presidencies, managing communication,
and fund-raising during times of transition.

McLaughlin, Judith Block, ed. *Leadership Transitions: The New College President*.
San Francisco: Jossey-Bass, 1996.

This interesting and informative monograph includes a series of chapters, written by new presidents, covering a wide range of topics. The editor has been involved with the Harvard Seminar for New Presidents for more than 20 years. The selection of authors and chapters is indicative of her extensive experience. The authors strive to inform and not impress which makes for a very useful resource.

The chapter "Finding a Balance," written by a husband and wife (Milton A. Gordon and Margaret F. Gordon), provides insight and advice about maintaining personal balance with "the very public and all-consuming job of the presidency." It is excellent. McLaughlin's chapter on "Entering the Presidency" also is excellent and gives wise advice on avoiding an "early exit." Among many important topics, other chapters address the importance of relationships, reconciling conflicting values, developing a vision, and the demystification of the presidency.

Moore, John W., and Joanne M. Burrows. *Presidential Succession and Transition: Beginning, Ending and Beginning Again*. Washington: American Association of State Colleges and Universities, 2001.

This is an excellent monograph (89 pages) offering excellent advice. The authors surveyed, interviewed, and conducted focus groups with more than 100 presidents (former, experienced, and new), system administrators, search consultants, and presidents' spouses. This database provides a well-rounded, intelligent, and informative resource. The authors deal with both entering and leaving a presidency as well as the complex relationship between the incoming and outgoing president. The chapter titled, "What Governing Boards Can Do," is excellent. Other chapters address succession and transitions as well as life after a presidency.

Neff, Thomas J., and James M. Citrin. *You're in Charge—Now What? The Eight Point Plan*. New York: Crown Business, 2005.

This popular business book provides excellent advice for any new president as well as more experienced ones. It seeks to create a successful CEO transition by providing a game plan for the first 100 days. The authors realize that just having a good 100 days is not enough but if the first 100 days are not successful, the new CEO will not be successful.

Their advice is easy to explain but difficult to implement. A snapshot of the eight rules for the first 100 days includes:

- Listen: Ask open-ended questions and force yourself to listen.

- Resist the savior syndrome: This is not the time to announce a bold vision.

- Keep it simple: Focus on a handful of concrete priorities wrapped inside a clear and simple theme.

- Hit pause: When posed with a good question, wait a beat. If you do not have the answer, promise to get back to them and do so.

- Look for quick wins: Seek meaningful changes and improvements.

- Spell it out: Use your early management meetings to do more than meet and greet. This is the time to establish what you expect of the team.

- Do not criticize your predecessor: Many people might have loyalty to the previous leader.

- Give feedback: By synthesizing what you learn and communicating it to the organization, you improve your chances for broad-based support.

They offer other useful advice like picking your battles carefully and putting goodwill in the bank whenever possible.

Sessa, Valier I., and Jodi J. Taylor. *Executive Selection*. San Francisco: Jossey-Bass, 2000.

Although the book is written for the corporate world, it has useful advice for presidential transitions because it deals with several complex and difficult issues related to senior leadership and organizational transitions. The authors strongly suggest that the selection process needs to be team-based, disciplined, systematic, and transparent. These all are helpful suggestions for search committees in higher education.

The authors contend that most senior executives and board members would heartily agree that selecting the right people for the top positions is a vital priority. Yet they have found that the decisions around the selection of top leaders tend to be illogical and undisciplined. Concrete steps are offered to improve this process.

CEOs often do not want to face their own mortality and often procrastinate about discussing succession planning. This is especially true of founders and powerful CEOs. The board must insist on discussing a systematic and disciplined succession planning process.

The authors discuss the long-term socialization process that needs to take place for the new leader to deeply understand the complexity of the new organization. There is a great deal to learn and they offer effective advice on how to manage the learning curve the top leader will experience. They also highlight the importance of *how* top executives are introduced to the organization.

Finally, they discuss the need for the board of trustees to deeply understand the core values, beliefs, and goals of the organization to choose the right person at the top. The new leader must meet the real and emerging needs of the organization. There must be a match.

Watkins, Michael. *Taking Charge in Your New Leadership Role: A Workbook*. Boston: Harvard Business School Press, 2001.

This is an excellent resource for any leadership transition and provides both a model and practical suggestions about creating an effective entry plan for a new leader. It is built upon much of the theory and ideas from *Right from the Start*, a popular book the author wrote with Dan Ciampa in 1999.

The book discusses, in relevant detail, the four key challenges of transition: the learning challenge—you need to learn about the new organization as quickly as possible before and during the initial months of the new role; the influence challenge—you need to build effective working relationships both with key internal and external stakeholders while building your own personal credibility; the design challenge—the hard thinking and doing work that aligns the organization's strategy, structure, systems, skills, and culture; and the self-management challenge—dealing with all the pressure, challenges, and stress accompanying a new position, while maintaining personal and emotional balance.

The author provides seven rules for orienting and setting goals for a new leader.

- Leverage the time before entry—learn as much as you can about the new organization before you come on board.

- Organize to learn—learn as rapidly as possible about the organization, *especially* its culture and politics.

- Secure early wins—they build momentum during the transition and get people excited.

- Lay a foundation for major improvements—early wins are helpful but long-term improvement is key.

- Build winning coalitions—you can achieve little by yourself. Therefore, enrolling others in achieving your goals is essential.

- Create a personal vision of the organization's future—have a picture of where you want to take the organization and eventually develop a shared vision with others.

- Manage yourself—self-diagnosis and reflection are essential, as is soliciting advice from the right people.

ARTICLES FROM PERIODICALS

Ancona, Deborah, Thomas W. Malone, Wanda J. Orlikowski, and Peter M. Senge. "In Praise of the Incomplete Leader." *Harvard Business Review* 85,2 (February 2007): 92–100.

This is a particularly important article because it dispels the myth that presidents and other leaders are infallible. It highlights the reality that no one is capable of being all things to all people. The advice to leaders is to acknowledge the weaknesses and gaps in their knowledge so that they can turn to others who possess those abilities and knowledge.

The article highlights four capabilities that comprise a model for distributed leadership.

- Sensemaking—understanding and mapping the context in which an entity and its people operate.

- Relating—building relationships through inquiring (i.e., listening with intention), advocating (i.e., explaining one's own point of view), and connecting (establishing a network of allies who can help with the accomplishment of the leader's goals).

- Visioning—collaboratively developing, with input, a compelling image of the future.

- Inventing—developing new ways to bring the vision to life.

The authors contend that few individuals will be skilled in each of these capabilities. That is why it becomes critical for leaders to recognize their deficiencies and seek to identify those who can complement them. This is the only viable way to function amid today's complexity.

Bullock, Mary Brown. "Presidential Transitions: Planning the Last Year." *The Presidency* 10, 2 (Spring 2007): 32–35.

The author details the process she used to reach the decision to resign from the presidency of a small college and shares insights based on her personal experience transitioning out. Although short, the article is rich with suggestions about the relationship with the board chair, the need to be active during the final year, consideration for those who will remain in place, and other important issues. She closes with a description of things she might have done differently, including her belief that she waited too long to inform the board chair of her decision to resign.

Cotton, Raymond. "Why Colleges Should Avoid Abrupt Terminations." *The Chronicle of Higher Education*. http://chronicle.com/jobs/news/2006/10/2006102701c/careers.html (accessed June 3, 2007).

The author is an attorney who specializes in presidential contracts and compensation matters. In this article he offers excellent advice to boards that find themselves seeking to terminate a president's employment. The article addresses the need for the employment contract to be reviewed by experienced legal advisors, negotiation of the termination, and appointment of a transition committee.

Dowdall, Jean. "Adjusting to a New President." *The Chronicle of Higher Education*. http://chronicle.com/weekly/v49/i34/34c00301.htm (accessed June 3, 2007).

In this article the author, a search consultant and former college president, focuses on the existing leadership team. Although she provides advice for those occupying key leadership positions such as the CFO and vice presidents for academic affairs and student affairs, the insights she shares should be of great interest to presidents—especially those entering their first presidency. She covers the thorny issue of transferring loyalty from the incumbent president to the one entering the scene, along with other important factors that will influence the relationship among the leadership team members.

———. "Going it Alone." *The Chronicle of Higher Education*. http://chronicle.com/weekly/v50/i07/07c00301.htm (accessed June 3, 2007).

The author shares expertise gained during her years as a search consultant facilitating searches for higher education presidencies. She describes the process used by search consultants and explains how an institution can follow the same steps without incurring the expense of outside consultants.

Drucker, Peter. "What Makes an Effective Executive?" *Harvard Business Review* 82,6 (June 2004): 58–63.

The concepts in this article are especially valuable for new presidents because they come from the author's work with executives from both commercial and nonprofit environments. He identifies the eight practices that effective executives in both sectors pursued.

- They asked, "What needs to be done?"
- They asked, "What is right for the enterprise?"
- They developed action plans.
- They took responsibility for decisions.
- They took responsibility for communicating.
- They were focused on opportunities rather than problems.
- They ran productive meetings.
- They thought and said "we" rather than "I."

―――. "Managing Oneself." *Harvard Business Review* 83,1 (January 2005): 100–109.

The primary focus of the article, reprinted as another "best of *Harvard Business Review*," is on career management, but its attention to self-awareness is particularly important to those entering leadership positions—especially presidents. He urges readers to assess their strengths, examine their values, and understand both how they perform best and what they can contribute. He further suggests that individuals not attempt to become someone else. Instead, they should focus on improving their skills and applying them where they can have the greatest impact. Presidents, and those who aspire to a presidency, would be wise to follow the advice—particularly as it relates to the presidencies they pursue.

George, Katherine L., and Karla Hignite. "Prep Your New President." National Association of College and University Business Officers *Business Officer* (March 2007): 41–48.

The article's focus is on the role the chief financial officer can play in presidential transitions. The authors make a compelling case for the importance of the role and discuss the specific issues that naturally fall within the purview of the CFO. These include the obvious issues related to finances and the budget, but others as well such as ensuring that the institution is prepared to respond should a crisis arise. The CFO also is in an ideal position to brief the incoming president on the existing strategic plan and the progress made to date. Also stressed in the article is the need for an open and honest relationship between the CFO and the president.

Read from a broad perspective, the article offers insights that will have significant value for anyone involved in the transition of a new president onto a campus.

Goleman, Daniel. "What Makes a Leader?" *Harvard Business Review* 82,1 (January 2004): 82–91.

The author is noted for introducing the concept of emotional intelligence in the mid 1990s. This article, originally published in 1998 and reprinted as a "best of *Harvard Business Review*" feature in the January 2004 issue, applies emotional intelligence to business. Although the article's focus is the for-profit environment, the principles are equally applicable to the not-for-profit world, including higher education.

There are five elements of emotional intelligence: self-awareness, self-regulation, motivation, empathy, and social skill. Each is of critical importance to the success of a college or university president. What is particularly useful about this article is that the author describes how one can learn to develop and enhance emotional intelligence.

Kramer, Roderick M. "The Harder They Fall." *Harvard Business Review* 81,10 (October 2003): 58–66.

The author examines why those who have reached the pinnacle fall prey to scandals of their own making. He suggests that the process of attaining such lofty positions can change people in profound ways. The climb up the mountain sometimes forces individuals to cut corners and sacrifice behaviors that are necessary to help them succeed once they arrive. For some, there is such a feeling of accomplishment that they begin believing that they are no longer subject to rules.

Those who remain grounded and succeed typically exhibit five behaviors.

- They remain humble.

- They highlight their weaknesses rather than attempting to hide them.

- They float trial balloons to uncover the truth and prepare for the unexpected.

- They sweat the small stuff.

- They reflect more, not less.

There is no guarantee that presidents who practice these behaviors will have successful presidencies. On the other hand, those who do are much less likely to be caught up in scandals or to incur the wrath of the community because of hubris.

Lapovsky, Lucie. "The Best-Laid Succession Plans." Association of Governing Boards of Colleges and Universities *Trusteeship* (January-February 2006): 20–24.

The author, a former college president, describes the importance of grooming internal successors for presidents. This rarely occurs in higher education and the author makes a strong case for it. She also describes the approach taken at institutions that have engaged in succession planning.

Parsons, George D., and Richard T. Pascale. "Crisis as the Summit." *Harvard Business Review* 85,3 (March 2007): 80–89.

This article is particularly relevant for presidents who have held their position for an extended period of time. They are the ones who are susceptible to the problems addressed in this excellent article. The authors define three phases of what they refer to as the "summit syndrome." Summit syndrome is the condition that causes previously successful individuals—those who have mastered the critical elements of their position—to have their performance deteriorate to the point of ineffectiveness.

The authors describe three phases of the syndrome. The approach phase occurs when most challenges have been met and conquered. Individuals in this phase tend to push harder to recapture the special feeling they experienced as they conquered new challenges. The "plateauing" phase is reached when virtually all the challenges have been addressed. Individuals in this phase, who simply cannot slow down and rest a little on their accomplishments, go to even more extreme lengths to produce stellar results. The final phase, descending, is reached when performance slips and is noticed by others. By this time, the downward spiral frequently is irreversible, leading to departures for positions of equal or lesser quality.

The article offers specific advice for actions that can forestall the descending phase. They suggest that it is not easy to reverse the cycle but they contend that prevention/intervention is far better than after-the-fact cures.

Pierce, Susan Resneck. "Toward a Smooth Presidential Transition." Association of Governing Boards of Colleges and Universities *Trusteeship*. (September/October 2003): 13–17.

The author, a former university president, details the efforts taken to effect a smooth transition from her presidency to that of her successor. Excellent advice is offered on numerous topics including attention to the final year goals, ground rules for the president's role with respect to the selection of her successor, and the board's role in the transition.

Porter, Michael E., Jay W. Lorsch, and Nitin Nohria. "Seven Surprises for New CEOs." *Harvard Business Review* 82,10 (October 2004): 62–72.

The focus of the article is the for-profit environment but, for the most part, the information is just as relevant for college and university presidents. The authors contend that nothing fully prepares an individual for what she will experience as a first-time president. Of the seven surprises identified, only six are directly relevant to higher education.

- You cannot run the institution.

- Giving orders hurts in the long run (and usually the short run as well).

- It is hard to know what really is happening and what people are thinking.

- Everything you say and do sends a message.

- You are not the boss.

- You are still only human.

(There are higher education analogs for the seventh surprise—pleasing shareholders is not the goal—but readers are encouraged to develop them on their own based on their particular situation.)

The important lessons provided in the article address the fact that presidents must manage organizational context rather than the day-to-day activities on the campus. Presidents do not have the right to lead, nor should they expect blind loyalty from their community members. They are subject to a wide range of factors that limit their authority, even though some may treat them as if they were all powerful. The authors contend that a president's willingness to accept and deal with the surprises has a lot to do with the likelihood of success in the role.

Sanaghan, Patrick, Larry Goldstein, and Susan Jurow. "A Learning Agenda for Chief Business Officers." National Association of College and University Business Officers *Business Officer* (May 2001): 42–49.

This article is targeted to chief business officers, although the principles apply to anyone in or seeking a leadership position—particularly in higher education.

The article identifies three roles, three skills, and three qualities that are deemed essential for success in a leadership position. It is a given that everyone in a senior leadership position has a high degree of technical knowledge in their area of expertise. It is further assumed that they will not last in the position if they do not produce results. But what differentiates those that perform exceptionally from those who just get by? The authors suggest it is their success in performing the roles, applying the skills, and demonstrating the qualities that makes the difference.

The roles required at this level include the following:

- Capacity building—a continuous focus on enhancing the institution's overall capabilities whether through teaching and learning or through the hiring of individuals who enhance the institution's overall capacity.

- Cultural travel—the ability to move throughout the organization and connect and communicate with people at all levels; to be in demand when critical issues are being discussed and decisions are being made.

- Horizon thinking—focusing both on the near-term and the longer view; looking both internally and externally to assess where the institution is today and how it can respond to issues that will arise in the future.

There are three skills required for success:

- Creativity—seeking alternative and innovative solutions to problem solving as well as communicating and decision making in nontraditional ways to ensure that the best results can be achieved.

- Communication—conveying information in such a way that it can be understood by those who need to receive it. And, just as importantly, listening effectively to ensure that needed information can be received.

- Decision making—recognizing that there are multiple facets of decisions and that it is important to apply the approach that is best in the given situation—whether decision making based on input from others, shared decision making, or delegated decision making.

The qualities related to success can be challenging for some. The authors contend that, as with roles and skills, qualities can be enhanced through practice. Once again, there are three qualities required for success:

- Self-awareness—understanding what my strengths are, what areas of needed improvement I might have, and how I can personally leverage the roles and skills all have an impact on the results of my efforts.

- Trustworthiness—leaders must demonstrate integrity, dependability, and consistency to be worthy of trust on the part of others. Trust is essential to accomplish anything when others are involved.

- Agility—recognizing that there are few "one size fits all" situations in leadership is essential if one is to be able to find creative solutions to the unique problems that arise in day-to-day situations.

Showalter, Shirley H. "When and How to Leave a Presidency." *The Chronicle of Higher Education*. http://chronicle.com/weekly/v51/i35/35c00301.htm (accessed June 3, 2007).

In this candid and very thoughtful article, the author describes the process she used to reach the decision that it was time to move on. She then details the factors she considered and the process she used to ensure that the institution was in the best shape possible to accept her successor.

REPORTS, SURVEYS, AND STUDIES

American Council on Education. *The American College President*. Washington: American Council on Education, 2007.

This report presents information about the backgrounds, career paths, and experiences of college and university chief executives. Using 1986 as a benchmark, it reports on the results of a study conducted during 2006. It compares and contrasts numerous factors related to the chief executives and their institutions. It would be particularly useful to boards seeking to attract presidents to their institutions and to individuals seeking to become presidents.

Association of Governing Boards of Colleges and Universities. *The Leadership Imperative*. Washington: Association of Governing Boards of Colleges and Universities, 2006.

This publication, subtitled "The Report of the AGB Task Force on the State of the Presidency in American Higher Education," is an excellent resource.

This outstanding report (50 pages) focuses on the key relationship between governing boards and presidents and provides powerful and explicit recommendations to boards, presidents, faculty, and state political leaders. The authors want to help preserve and enhance the academic presidency as well as renew the public trust and confidence in higher education.

The report provides important contextual information about low high school graduation rates and the academic proficiency of college and university students. It also provides some interesting statistics on how presidents spend their time. For instance, "53 percent of presidents reported that they work at fundraising at least once a day and 91 percent reported doing so at least once a week."

Boards, presidents, and other institutional leaders are strongly encouraged to embrace "integral leadership," which describes a presidential leadership style that "exerts a presence that is purposeful and consultative, deliberative yet decisive, and capable of course corrections as new challenges emerge."

The report describes five key roles of presidents today: academic leader, chief executive office, fund-raiser, advocate, and public spokesperson. It then calls upon boards to support the president with these complex and important responsibilities. It also discusses the importance of engagement for presidents because, without it, they cannot lead effectively.

Other issues are addressed including the presidential search, evaluation and compensation for the president, board accountability, and presidential renewal and succession. It is an outstanding resource for any institutional leader interested in the presidency.

The Chronicle of Higher Education. "The Chronicle Survey of Presidents of Four-Year Colleges." *The Chronicle of Higher Education*. http://chronicle.com/stats/presidential survey/index.htm (accessed June 3, 2007).

The information available on this Web site provides insights into the challenges faced by presidents of four-year institutions. It addresses a wide range of topics including what worries presidents, how men and women presidents differ on various issues, and the demographic differences among the presidents. It is an excellent resource for presidents who seek to understand how their situation compares with others in similar roles.

The Chronicle of Higher Education. "The Chronicle Survey of Trustees of Four-Year Colleges." *The Chronicle of Higher Education*. http://chronicle.com/weekly/v53/i36/ 36a01901.htm (accessed June 3, 2007).

The information available on this Web site provides insights into the attitudes of trustees of four-year institutions. It addresses a wide range of topics including their preparation for their role as trustees, the relative importance they place on various aspects of institutional mission, how much time they commit to their service as trustees, and a wide range of similar topics. The information in the survey is invaluable for presidents who seek to gain a better understanding of how their trustees compare with trustees generally.

APPENDIX C
Individuals Interviewed

Janice Abraham
President and Chief Executive
Officer
United Educators

Morris Beverage
President
Lakeland Community College

Frank Birckhead
Former member, Board
of Visitors
University of Virginia

Rita Bornstein
President Emerita
Rollins College

Robert J. Bruce
President Emeritus
Widener University

Mickey L. Burnim
President
Bowie State University

Peter Cimbolic
Provost
Marywood University

John Cochran
Former Chair, Board of Trustees
Loyola College in Maryland

Thomas E. Corts
President Emeritus
Samford University

Ronald A. Crutcher
President
Wheaton College

Daniel J. Curran
President
University of Dayton

Gregory Dell'Omo
President
Robert Morris University

Michael DiBerardinis
Ex Officio Member, Board
of Trustees
The Pennsylvania State
University

Stuart Dorsey
President
University of Redlands

James R. Doyle
Vice President for Student
Affairs
DePaul University

Jean Dowdall
Vice President
Witt/Kieffer (search
consultants)

Donald R. Eastman, III
President
Eckerd College

Jerry B. Farley
President
Washburn University

Sister Marylouise Fennell
Former President
Carlow University

Daniel M. Fogel
President
University of Vermont

Rufus Glasper
Chancellor
Maricopa County Community
College District

R. Kirby Godsey
Chancellor and former President
Mercer University

Dennis C. Golden
President
Fontbonne University

Sheldon F. Hackney
Former President
University of Pennsylvania

Leo I. Higdon
President
Connecticut College

Dennis Holtschneider, C.M.
President
DePaul University

Penelope W. Kyle
President
Radford University

Timothy R. Lannon, S.J.
President
Saint Joseph's University

Lucie Lapovsky
Former President
Mercy College

Janice Legoza
Vice President for Finance and
Administration and former Interim
President
Whittier College

Dorothy Leland
President
Georgia State College &
University

Brian F. Linnane, S.J.
President
Loyola College in Maryland

John V. Lombardi
Chancellor
University of Massachusetts, Amherst

Thomas C. Longin
Member, Board of Trustees
Carroll College

William T. Luckey, Jr.
President
Lindsey Wilson College

Sister Karen McNally
Member, Board of Trustees
Loyola College in Maryland

James S. Netherton
Former President
Carson-Newman College

John Palmucci
Vice President for Finance and
Treasurer
Loyola College in Maryland

Leonard T. (Pete) Parker
Vice President for Finance and
Administrative Services and former
Interim President
Paul D. Camp Community College

Richard H. Passon
Former Provost
University of Scranton

Susan Resneck Pierce
President Emerita
University of Puget Sound

Mohammad H. Qayoumi
President
California State
University—East Bay

Matthew J. Quinn
Former President
Carroll College

Sister Francis Raftery
President
College of Saint Elizabeth

Nicholas S. Rashford, S.J.
University Professor and former
President
Saint Joseph's University

Leonard W. Sandridge, Jr.
Executive Vice President and Chief
Operating Officer
University of Virginia

Brian J. Shanley, O.P.
President
Providence College

Michael Shirley
Former President
Elgin Community College

Lawrence H. Summers
  Former President
  Harvard University

Donald C. Swain
  President Emeritus
  University of Louisville

Eugene P. Trani
  President
  Virginia Commonwealth University

Robert Vogel
  Interim President at Bethany College
  (Lindsborg, Kansas) and former
  President
  Wartburg College

INDEX

ABOUT THE AUTHORS

PATRICK H. SANAGHAN is President, The Sanaghan Group, an organizational consulting firm specializing in leadership development, collaborative strategic planning, executive coaching and leadership transitions. He is the co-author/author of several books and numerous articles on leadership, change management, and strategic planning.

LARRY GOLDSTEIN is President, Campus Strategies, LLC (a higher education management consulting firm specializing in financial and organizational services for colleges and universities, governmental entities, and commercial entities serving higher education).

KATHLEEN D. GAVAL is Vice President for Planning, Saint Joseph's University in Philadelphia, Pennsylvania.

30569604R00126

Made in the USA
Middletown, DE
29 March 2016